Mottola's

CYCLOPEDIC

Dictionary of Lutherie Terms

Mottola's

CYCLOPEDIC

Dictionary of Lutherie Terms

"Terminology of the Construction of Stringed Musical Instruments, with Many Illustrations"

by

R.M. Mottola

Credits & Copyrights

This book is original work based on the author's observations and experience. Quantitative data and other specifications are taken from publicly available sources or from the author's observations or from credited sources.

Except as noted all photos and drawings are by the author.

All brand names and model names are properties of their respective rights holders.

Disclaimer of Liability: Although every effort was made to ensure that the information in this book was accurate at the time of publication, the author does not assume and does hereby disclaim any liability for any damage, loss, or disruption caused by errors or omissions. Information in this book is provided as-is, without any express or implied warranty.

Please address all correspondence to the author here:
https://www.liutaiomottola.com/contact.htm

ISBN-13: 978-1-7341256-0-3

First edition, January 2020

Acknowledgements

People

It is my great fortune to be surrounded by lutherie subject matter experts, and my greater fortune that so many of them enthusiastically answered my requests for assistance with this book. The people listed below provided substantial help in one or more of the following: reviewing drafts, suggesting additional entries, providing needed corrections and augmentation, providing additional photographs, copy editing and proofreading. My sincere thanks to them all.

James Buckland is a music professor at Presbyterian College, a guitarist, and a long time luthier, specializing in early Romantic period music and instruments. He has an encyclopedic knowledge of historical and modern musical instruments. He is a frequent author of articles in *American Lutherie*.

Mark French is a professor of mechanical engineering technology at Purdue University and the author of the books *Engineering the Guitar* and *Technology of the Guitar*. He teaches guitar construction and is a frequent author of articles in *American Lutherie* and *Savart Journal*.

Christine King is a member of the production staff of the venerable New England birder publication *Bird Observer*. It is my observation that she has the *Chicago Manual of Style* committed to memory. She took time from her regular gig to copy edit and proofread this book.

Leonardo Lospennato is a highly accomplished luthier specializing in electric guitars and basses. He is the author of the books *Electric Guitar and Bass Design* and *Electric Guitar Making & Marketing* and was the editor of the magazine *Sustain*, the journal of the Fellowship of European Luthiers.

Graham McDonald is a long time luthier specializing in mandolin and ukulele family instruments. He is a frequent *American Lutherie* contributor and is the author of the books *The Bouzouki Book*, *The Mandolin Project: A Workshop Guide to Building Mandolins*, *The Mandolin: A History*, and *The Ukulele: An Illustrated Workshop Manual*.

Tim Olsen is the founder of the Guild of American Luthiers and the editor of *American Lutherie*. At the very center of the modern lutherie movement, Tim knows most everything and everybody.

Frederick (Federico) Sheppard is a long time luthier specializing in Spanish guitars. He is the foremost expert on the life and music of composer and classical guitarist Agustin Barrios and is a frequent *American Lutherie* author. He is currently lutherie artist in residence at Carrion de los Condes, Spain.

My thanks to everyone who helped to make this book possible. With so much expert help the dictionary is a vast improvement over its initial draft. Any remaining errors of fact or omission are my own.

Software

This book was produced using free software. Source notes were maintained using the Apache OpenOffice Calc spreadsheet application. Bulk text editing was performed using the Notepad++ text editor. Bulk photo processing was done using the ImageMagick image editing software suite. Individual photo edits were made using the free version of PhotoFiltre. The book was produced using the Scribus desktop publishing system, and the files it produced were bundled together using the free version of PDFsam.

Fonts used for the book interior and cover include Aboriginal by Christopher Harvey, Gardenia Victorian by Douglas Day, and Clear Sans by Daniel Ratighan at Monotype under the direction of the User Experience team at Intel's Open Source Technology Center. Victorian pen flourishes were provided by http://Vecteezy.com. My thanks to everyone involved in all of these projects for making your work products available.

About the Dictionary

History

Before taking up lutherie in 1994 I had a long career as an engineer. I worked in many different technical areas but the primary task in each one was to computerize and automate tasks that had previously been accomplished by more time-consuming means. Jumping from one technical discipline to another, it didn't take long to realize that getting quickly up to speed in a new discipline would be important to success. The learning curves were steep and in many of these fields I had no previous knowledge whatsoever. After a few such learning experiences it became obvious that the fastest approach to getting up to speed in a new field was to identify the standard textbook for that field and to just plow through it cover to cover. This learning effort was considerably enhanced if there was also available a dictionary or glossary of terminology used in the field. Often the latter was part of the textbook. In some cases such a dictionary was not available, and in those cases I learned to take notes on the vocabulary unique to the field. I would refer to these notes often during my learning experience.

It turns out there is some solid research demonstrating the importance of background information and vocabulary to reading comprehension. My informal observations about the value of having a dictionary or glossary when learning a new subject appear to be supported by experimentation.

So of course when I began my investigations in musical instrument construction I attempted to take the same efficient approach that had worked so well for me in the past. Unfortunately a single reference textbook was not available for lutherie but a small library of books served that purpose well. Equally unfortunately there existed no comprehensive dictionary of terminology, and in lutherie I found there was a lot of terminology. So I began taking notes on the terminology. The notes grew to where they became difficult to search and modify and at that point they were put into a spreadsheet. This format worked well enough for a long time for my personal use. After a while the rate of new entries settled down considerably but I found I was continuing to access this information for myself and for other people as well. It was then that it became apparent that publishing these notes in book form would be most generally useful. Considerable effort was made to add photos and drawings and to fill in classes of information that were only sparsely covered in the original notes.

Overview

The dictionary intends to provide conventional spelling and short descriptions of the most common terms used in modern lutherie as well as historical terminology that a modern luthier may come across in plans and other media. Luthiers, musicians, and others that read or write about stringed musical instrument construction should find it useful. Lutherie beginners who are attempting to navigate a mass of unfamiliar terminology will find the dictionary particularly useful. Use of the dictionary will increase the rate of understanding for the new luthier. As with any such work appearing in book form there is a trade off between completeness and accessibility. Although it certainly is possible to include a lot more terms than currently appear, doing so would make for a larger and more expensive book and it would make looking up terms more time consuming. I feel the number of terms presented offer a good balance.

Descriptions are short and are not intended to be exhaustive. Enough information is provided to enable the reader to further research a topic if so desired. I've found in my own work that having access to the basic terminology is key to conducting efficient information searches in academic databases and on the Internet. The dictionary is not intended to be prescriptive in terms of spelling and definitions. It is often the case that more than one spelling of a word is common and it is often that more than one definition is in use. The dictionary attempts to point out such ambiguities. To avoid duplicate definitions for each synonym of a word, synonym entries refer to a common definition. The entry associated with the common definition is the most commonly used word or term, in my observation. In a few cases I could not identify a single most commonly used word, and in these cases I simply picked one arbitrarily to anchor the definition.

Terms included in the dictionary most often fall into one of a number of classes. These are identified in a section following, along with a description of how entries of that class are generally treated in the dictionary.

Formatting Conventions

Each entry begins with the word or phrase in boldface. Proper names (people, places, product names) are capitalized. Product names are assumed to be covered by trademark. Names of people appear last name followed by first name. Please note that Spanish naming conventions often use more than one last name and that for ordering purposes these can be considered as the same as English hyphenated last names.

Following the term is its abbreviated part of speech. This does not appear for people or places.

The next field is optional and contains pronunciation. These generally appear only for non-English words or phrases but occasionally appear for terms where mispronunciation is common.

If the term is a synonym the next field will be a reference to the term to see for the definition. The dictionary uses a broad definition of synonym, which also includes abbreviations. Note also that all popular names for wood species will always refer to the entry for the Latin binomial for that species. If there is no reference to another entry then the definition will appear in this field.

Following the definition are optional fields specifying synonyms and abbreviations, and references to related entries. Related entries are often antonyms or other members of the same class as this entry. If terms are used in the description that also appear in the dictionary these are usually referenced here as well. Note that when people are named here the format is first name then last name.

Pictures are truly worth a thousand words and it is often the case that a photo or drawing will accompany an entry. These usually follow the entry but may end up in a subsequent column or on a subsequent page.

Italicization is conventionally used to denote a foreign word or phrase but in the dictionary its use is limited to denoting Latin. It is not used more widely simply because so many of the terms used in lutherie in English are from other languages.

Physical dimensions are generally presented in USCS fractional inches and in equivalent SI units. In cases where it is conventional in lutherie to use USCS decimal fractions (such as for scale lengths, string diameters) then decimal fractions are used.

Relative locations on an instrument generally assume the instrument is positioned head up and viewed from the front. The left side of the instrument is the left side when viewed from this perspective.

Classes of Entries

Although there are lots of entries which do not fall into any particular class there are quite a few that can be grouped that way. The following paragraphs list some of the major classes of entries appearing in the dictionary and explains how each class is covered.

English Translations. For the benefit of those attempting to read non-English plans and manuscripts a number of common lutherie terms are translated from French, Italian, Spanish and, to some extent, German. Note that translations and pronunciation of non-English terms was done by a non-native speaker of the source languages. For the benefit of North American speakers of English a number of British English terms are also translated to American English.

Adhesives. The glues that are typically used in lutherie are described.

Component Parts. This class is reasonably well filled out in the dictionary. Also included are non-English names for a lot of the component parts of stringed instruments.

Electronics. A number of common electronic components and circuits are covered. Although the list is not comprehensive it includes most parts and circuits that luthiers would encounter.

Finishing Materials and Techniques. The subclass of finishes that are typically used in lutherie is covered comprehensively in the dictionary. This includes hand finishes and production spray finishes. Components of shop-made violin varnishes are comprehensively covered.

Flattop Guitar and Ukulele Sizes. The conventional sizes for these instruments are included with basic dimensions. Guitar sizes use the now conventional designations as originally used by the C.F. Martin Co. for most of the range with the exception of the smallest ("parlor") and largest ("jumbo").

Guitar Top Bracing styles. Some typical bracing patterns used for guitar tops are listed and described.

Hand Tools. Particular attention is paid to those tools used for specific lutherie operations. There are also entries for some of the more arcane tools that some builders find useful.

Instruments. No attempt was made to be comprehensive in this category. Instruments included in this class tend to be antiques that are in the lineage of modern instruments, and also common instruments that are not in the European/Western tradition that may be encountered in articles and other texts.

Lumber and Sawing Terminology. Luthiers invariably come in contact with wood suppliers and the part of the latter's terminology most likely to be of use to luthiers is included. This includes sawing and grain orientation terminology and a few other subclasses as well.

Luthiers. Deceased makers of iconic instruments are fairly well covered here, although there are far too many influential deceased violin makers to list. Attempting to list living luthiers is an insurmountable task. Although I know (and know of) a lot of contemporary luthiers, it is clear to me that I am familiar with only a fraction of those currently working. Attempting a comprehensive list of living luthiers would be a massive project in its own right. To keep the dictionary to a manageable size and cost, and to prevent it from becoming primarily a Who's Who of lutherie, I have limited entries in this subclass severely. Inclusions are heavily weighted to luthiers who are also authors or teachers. As a result of this limitation readers should consider this subclass to be exemplary but by no means comprehensive. This subclass doesn't even include most of the great living luthiers I know. Although I am satisfied with the included entries I am not nearly satisfied with the great number that has not been included. Readers should not assume exclusion here to be significant in any way.

Planes. A small number of common woodworking planes are included. These are listed using the common Stanley model numbering system.

Science and Engineering. Formal terminology used to describe the vibration of physical parts, the mechanics of materials and structures, and human perception of sound as relate to lutherie and stringed musical instruments are included in the dictionary.

Solvents. Solvents in general use in instrument finishing are listed. Entries generally include evaporation rate and Permissible Exposure Limits.

Wood Species. Some of the most common wood species used in lutherie are included, along with a few lesser used species. Although in some cases a species is known universally by a single common name, there are many cases of multiple common names referring to the same species. Often these common names are used regionally. For this reason wood species are listed by Latin binomial, with common name entries referring to the main entry. Information generally includes stiffness and specific gravity in addition to general appearance and application. Shrinkage data are also included for some species. Material properties were collected from a number of sources. It is often the case that a property value differs depending on the source. In some of these cases I have published averages from multiple sources. Some property data have been provided by wood suppliers. My primary source for property data is the USDA Forest Products Laboratory, which has a searchable online database at https://www.fpl.fs.fed.us/research/centers/woodanatomy/. I also retrieved material property values from Eric Meier's *Wood Database*. This excellent resource is online at http://www.wood-database.com/.

Feedback

As noted the dictionary is the result of one person's observations over a period of many years. There are doubtless items that should appear here that do not and there are doubtless items that are not as well described as they should be. Please feel free to contact me with any suggestions for enhancement and improvement. I will strive to include such proposals in future revisions of the dictionary. Please send all feedback here: https://www.liutaiomottola.com/contact.htm

R.M. Mottola
January 2020

About the Author

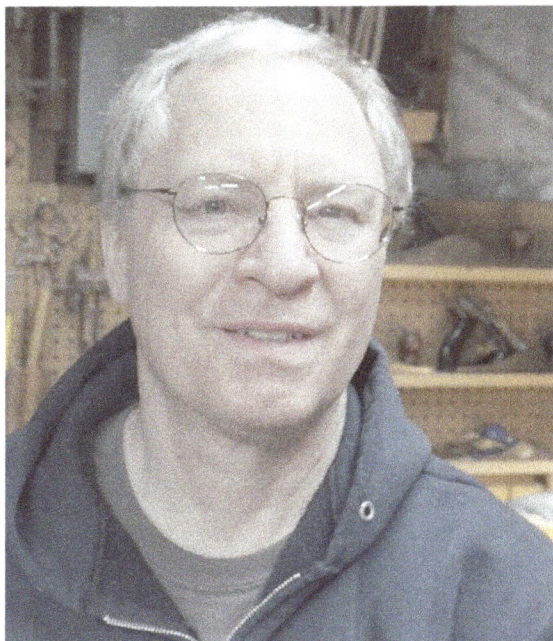

A former engineer, R.M. Mottola has been building electric and acoustic guitars and bass guitars since 1994. He maintains the popular Liutaio Mottola Lutherie Information website (http://LiutaioMottola.com). He is a contributing editor and the technology editor for *American Lutherie*, the journal of the Guild of American Luthiers, and has written over sixty articles on guitar construction and related topics. R.M. is the editor of the *Savart Journal*, the online research journal of science and technology of stringed musical instruments, and has written a number of research articles on topics of geometry, acoustics, and psychoacoustics of stringed musical instruments. He has provided editorial input to many popular books on lutherie and stringed musical instruments. R.M. is a member of New England Luthiers and lives in the Boston area.

123

$^1/_4$ **size** *adj*. A qualitative size descriptor of an instrument of the violin family. Although considerably larger than a fourth the size of a full size instrument, this size is generally suitable for beginner children.

$^1/_2$ **size** *adj*. A qualitative size descriptor of an instrument of the violin family. Although considerably larger than a half the size of a full size instrument, this size is generally suitable for mid aged children.

$^3/_4$ **size** *adj*. A qualitative size descriptor of an instrument of the violin family. Although considerably larger than three quarter the size of a full size instrument, this size is suitable for older children. The exception is for the three quarter size double bass, which is actually the size played by most adult players.

1-D wave equation *n*. Equation which describes the motion of ideal vibrating strings. It is the basis for various formulae used in lutherie to calculate the relationship among vibrating frequency, string tension, mass per unit of length, and vibrating length.

#4 plane *n*. The Stanley #4 smooth plane is generally considered to be the standard smoothing plane. It is approximately 9″ long.

$^4/_4$ *adj*. (four quarter) North American lumber thickness. Rough sawn $^4/_4$ boards are approximately 1″ in thickness and can be planed to a maximum thickness of approximately $^3/_4$″.

#5 plane *n*. The Stanley #5 jack plane is generally considered to be the standard jack plane, and the one plane to have if you only have one plane. It is approximately 14″ (35.5cm) long.

Stanley #4 plane.

$^6/_4$ *adj*. (six quarter) North American lumber thickness. Rough sawn $^6/_4$ boards are approximately 1 $^1/_2$″ in thickness and can be planed to a maximum thickness of 1 $^1/_4$″.

6L6 *n*. Component number of a vacuum tube used in tube amplifiers. This is a power output tube. See also: tube amplifier, vacuum tube.

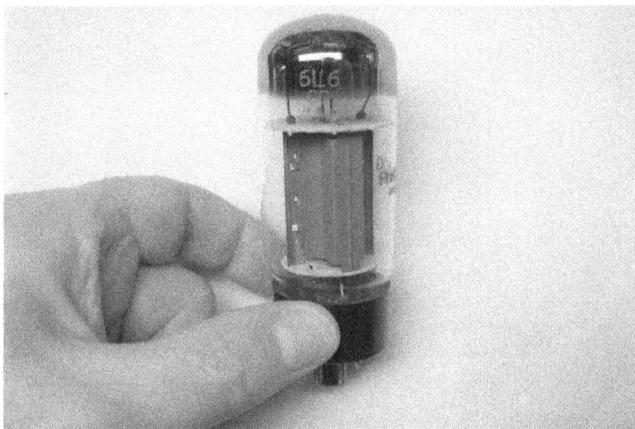

6L6 power tube for a guitar amplifier.

#7 plane *n*. The Stanley #7 jointer plane is generally considered to be the standard jointer plane. At approximately 22″ (56cm) long, it is mostly used in lutherie with a shooting board to joint the two halves of instrument plates.

8 hour time weighted average *n*. Method of expressing a permissible exposure limit (PEL) to a chemical. The average exposure to the chemical over an 8 hour period. Syn.: TWA. See also: permissible exposure limit.

8/4 *adj*. (eight quarter) North American lumber thickness. Rough sawn 8/4 boards are approximately 2″ in thickness and can be planed to a maximum thickness of 1 3/4″.

#9 1/2 plane *n*. The Stanley #9 1/2 block plane is generally considered to be a standard block plane. It is a low angle plane, with the blade angled at 20 degrees. The plane is used one-handed. This is a common lutherie tool, and is often found in the tool collection of luthiers that use power tools for most of their work.

12 fret neck *n*. A guitar neck in which the neck-to-body join is at the 12th fret.

Steel string guitar with a 12 fret neck.

12 hole bridge *n*. 12 hole variation on the 18 hole bridge. See also: 18 hole bridge.

12AX7 *n*. Component number of a vacuum tube used in tube amplifiers and in preamplifier circuits. This is a preamplifier tube. Syn.: . See also: preamplifier, tube amplifier, vacuum tube.

12th root of 2 *n*. The number which, when raised to the power of 12, equals 2. Its value is approximately 1.059463. The 12th root of 2 is used in lutherie to describe the fret spacing relationship of fretted instruments in equal temperament. A simple way to make use of this constant in locating frets is to use a fret position constant derived from it, 17.817. The scale length is divided by this, the result of which is the distance from nut to first fret. That distance is subtracted from the scale length and the resulting value is divided by the fret position constant to yield the distance from the first fret to the second fret. The process is repeated for all frets. While the technique yields mathematically correct results, resulting pitches are not quite accurate. With added compensation the results may be within the range of human pitch differentiation for stringed musical instruments. See also: compensation, fret position constant, rule of 18.

14 fret neck *n*. A guitar neck in which the neck-to-body join is at the 14th fret.

15th fret crosspiece *n*. Trim piece on Gibson style mandolins. The piece is set between the end of the neck shaft and the start of the neck extension, just under the 15th fret of the fretboard. See also: neck extension.

18 hole bridge *n*. Classical guitar bridge with 18 holes drilled in the tie block, three for each string. The holes provide an alternative method for terminating the strings at the bridge end. These are generally tied to the tie block with a conventional six hole bridge. With an 18 hole bridge, each string end is passed back and forth through the three holes provided for it. This provides enough friction to terminate the string without a knot. See also: tie block.

#60 plane *n.* The Stanley #60 block plane is generally considered to be a standard low angle block plane. The blade is angled at 12 degrees. The plane is used one-handed. It is intended for shaving the end grain.

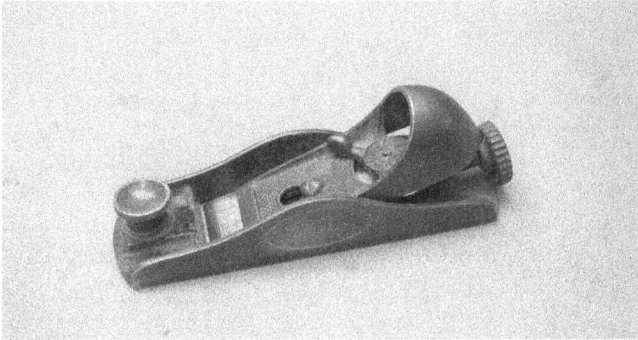

Stanley #60 low angle block plane.

#90 plane *n.* The Stanley bull-nosed rabbet plane is a small plane (about 4″ long) intended for precision rabbeting and mortise work. It is used primarily in lutherie as a brace shaving plane.

Stanley #90 rabbet plane.

#100 plane *n.* The Stanley #100 block plane is a small (3 ¹/₂″ long) general purpose block plane with a "squirrel tail" handle.

Modern interpretation of a Stanley #100 plane.

"1704" varnish *n.* A spirit (alcohol) based varnish used in violin finish repair, but also used by some for new instrument finishing. Contains alcohol, seedlac, lavender spike oil, and gum elemi. Recipes vary with source. There is no definitive explanation of the origin of the name of the varnish. See also: gum elemi, lavender spike oil, seedlac, spirit varnish, varnish.

6111 *n.* Component number of a vacuum tube used in tube preamplifiers. This is a small tube with low power consumption and so is often used in applications with limited space and where heat generation may be an issue, such as in microphones and stomp boxes. See also: preamplifier, stomp box, vacuum tube.

A

A bracing *n*. Bracing style used in some flattop guitar tops with offset soundholes. Two longitudinal braces diverge from near the neck block to near the tail block. These braces are crossed by a transverse brace near the bridge. This style was popularized by instruments made by Tacoma. Note that the closeness of the longitudinal braces would position them under the soundhole of a guitar with conventionally located soundhole. Guitars with offset soundholes made by Ovation use a similar but more complicated bracing scheme which is called Adamas bracing and sometimes referred to as A bracing. See also: fan bracing, ladder bracing, V bracing, X bracing.

Acoustic bass guitar top with offset soundhole and A bracing.

A style mandolin *n*. A mandolin with physical features similar to those of the Gibson A series of instruments. These include a symmetrical pear-shaped body and arched top and back plates.

GRAHAM MCDONALD

1923 Gibson A2-Z mandolin.

Abalam *n*. Brand name of an inlay material made of thin sheets of abalone laminated with an epoxy binder. Abalam sheets are bigger than typical abalone shell slices. See also: abalone.

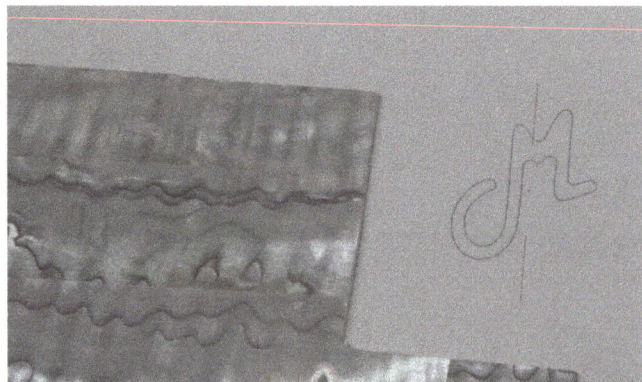

Abalam sheet cut for use in a headstock inlay.

abalone *n*. (ah-ba-LOW-nee) Abalone are sea snails (genus *Haliotis*), the shells of which are used in lutherie inlay work. Shell material is typically available cut into thin slices of approx. 1″ (3.25cm) square. Abalone is preferentially used as a purfling shell material for guitars as small breaks between pieces are less visible in this material than in other shell materials.

ABG *abbr*. see acoustic bass guitar

ABS *abbr*. see acrylonitrile butadiene styrene

Acacia koa *n*. Koa. Hardwood found in the Hawaiian islands. The wood is medium hard, medium heavy and medium dense. The color is reddish brown. It is used primarily for backs and sides of guitars and ukuleles, but is sometimes used for tops of those instruments as well. Specific gravity of typical dry wood is 0.55. Modulus of elasticity is 10.37 GPa. Syn.: koa.

access panel *n*. A panel, usually located in the ribs of a guitar at the tail block, that can be removed to gain access to the insides of the guitar for repair work. Syn.: access door, access port.

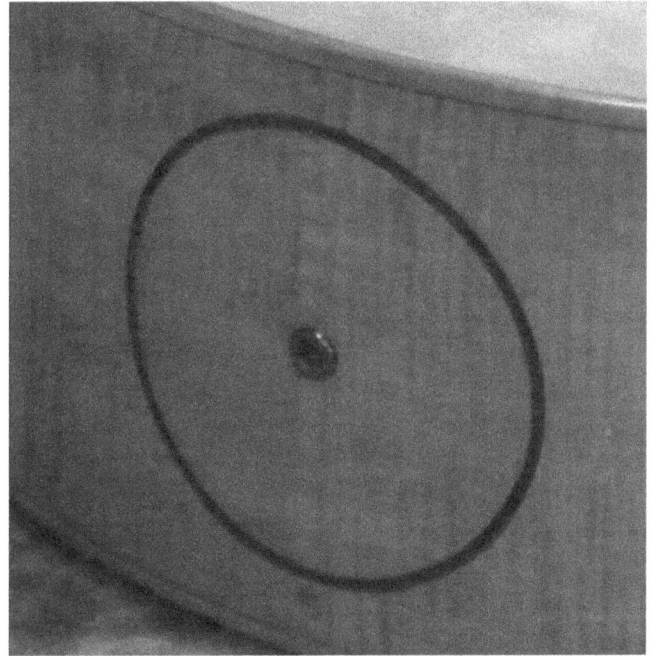

Access panel in tail end of an acoustic bass guitar.

Acer macrophyllum *n*. Bigleaf maple, broadleaf maple, Oregon maple. Found in the western part of the US and Canada. The wood of the tree is moderately hard, moderately heavy, and moderately dense, and light in color. It is somewhat stringy and does not carve as well as other maples. Specific gravity of dry wood is approximately 0.55. Modulus of elasticity is 10 GPa. Figured wood can display a flamed or quilted pattern. It is commonly used for drop tops for electric guitars and is often used for mandolin backs and sides.

Acer platanoides *n*. Norway maple, European maple. European hardwood is used for backs and sides of violin family and similar instruments. Can exhibit a tiger or flame pattern. The wood of the tree is moderately hard, moderately heavy and moderately dense, and light in color. Specific gravity of typical dry wood is 0.65. Modulus of elasticity is 10.6 GPa.

Acer pseudoplatanus *n*. European sycamore, sycamore, European maple. Not a true sycamore but a maple, this European hardwood is used for backs and sides of violin family and similar instruments. Note that this is not the wood generally referred to as sycamore in the USA (*Platanus occidentalis*). Can exhibit a tiger or flame pattern. The wood of the tree is moderately hard, moderately heavy and moderately dense, and light in color. Specific gravity of typical dry wood is 0.61. Modulus of elasticity is 9.92 GPa.

Acer rubrum *n*. Red maple, swamp maple, Eastern soft maple. Found in the eastern part of the US and Canada. The wood of the tree is moderately hard, moderately heavy and moderately dense, and light in color. Specific gravity of typical dry wood is 0.54. Modulus of elasticity is 11.3 GPa. Figured soft maple can display a tiger or flame pattern. It is used for the backs, sides and necks of archtop guitars and mandolins, and for drop tops for solid body electric guitars.

Acer saccharum *n.* Sugar maple, rock maple, eastern hard maple. Found in the northeastern part of the US and in eastern Canada. The wood of the tree is hard, heavy and dense, and light in color. It is used primarily in lutherie for Fender style electric guitar necks. Specific gravity of typical dry wood is 0.63, and modulus of elasticity averages 12.62 GPa. Figured hard maple can display a tiger or flame pattern. This species also sometimes shows a birdseye figure.

acetone *n.* Organic solvent used primarily in lutherie as a fast drying solvent in varnish and other finishing materials, and as a solvent for celluloid binding material. It is also sometimes used as a denaturant in denatured alcohol. Evaporation rate is 6.3 (n-butyl acetate = 1). OSHA PEL TWA is 1000 ppm. See also: celluloid, denatured alcohol, evaporation rate, OSHA, PEL, ppm, TWA.

Acker, Alton "Bear" Editor of *Guitarmaker* magazine.

acoustic *adj.* An instrument that produces sound by directly moving air, without the aid of electronic devices. One way that stringed instruments can be classified is as either acoustic or electric, i.e. acoustic guitar, electric guitar. See also: electric.

acoustic bass guitar *n.* An acoustic version of the electric bass guitar. Basic versions have four strings tuned EADG. The most common body style is similar to that of the steel string acoustic guitar, but archtop versions also exist. Syn.: ABG.

acoustic coupling *v.* see coupling

acoustics *n.* Science of the study of sound, that is, of waves in matter. In lutherie we are generally interested in both room acoustics and musical instrument acoustics. The latter may better be described as musical instrument

The author's Tinozza acoustic bass guitar is a fretless flattop instrument that uses orchestral strings.

physics, which includes not only the study of audible sound waves but the generation of those waves by musical instruments. See also: musical instrument physics, room acoustics.

acrylonitrile butadiene styrene *n.* Thermoplastic used to make plastic bindings, pickguards and other plastic parts for stringed instruments. The plastic is strong and tough and easy to injection mold. Syn.: ABS.

action *n.* The height of the strings of an instrument above its fingerboard or above the tops of its frets if the instrument has frets. What is considered low, normal, or high action varies with instrument type. If action is too low the vibrating strings can touch the fingerboard, and if action is too high the instrument will be difficult to play. For fretted stringed instruments action is usually measured as the space between the apex of the 12th fret crown and the underside of the string.

active back *n.* A back plate of a guitar that is flexible and light enough to contribute in a non-trivial manner to the frequency response of the instrument. See also: frequency response function.

active electronics *n*. Guitar electronic circuitry that uses power, either from an onboard battery or from phantom power. Active electronics provides tone control and other effects and can be used to lower noise levels and for impedance matching. See also: passive electronics, phantom power.

active pickup *n*. Magnetic pickup which includes a preamplifier in the pickup case. Power output of a passive pickup is a function of the number of turns of wire of the pickup coil. But more turns of wire also increases induced noise and attenuates high frequencies. The preamp of an active pickup can provide a high level output from a pickup coil with fewer turns of wire. See also: passive pickup, preamplifier.

actual bridge location *n*. In the context of the scale length of an instrument, the actual location of the bridge. This is the nominal bridge location plus any compensation offset added. See also: compensation, nominal bridge location.

Adi spruce *n*. see *Picea rubens* (Adirondack spruce)

Adirondack spruce *n*. see *Picea rubens*

adjustable bridge *n*. Most electric guitars and some acoustic guitars and other instruments feature bridges that are adjustable. Adjustments include action (string height) and intonation. Some adjustable bridges provide for adjustment on a per string basis. Adjustable bridges are less common on acoustic instruments as the added mass of the adjustable components is thought to be detrimental to the sound of the instrument. See also: action, adjustable saddle, intonation.

adjustable neck joint *n*. An adjustable neck joint provides a means to easily change the angle at which the neck meets the body of the instrument. This type of neck joint can be found on some acoustic and electric guitars and on some other instruments as well. An adjustable neck joint provides a means of adjusting action (string height) on instruments that do not have an adjustable bridge. It also provides adjustment to compensate for permanent deformation of the instrument as a result of string tension. Without such an adjustment capability an instrument would require a neck reset to compensate for this deformation. See also: action, neck reset.

adjustable saddle *n*. A bridge saddle which provides adjustment of action (string height) and/or intonation. See also: action, adjustable bridge, intonation.

admittance *n*. The measure of the ease of the flow of energy, the inverse of impedance. In musical instrument acoustics the term is used to describe the ease with which vibrational energy flows from one component of the instrument to another, e.g., from the string to the bridge. See also: impedance.

afinadores mecánicos n. (ah-feen-ah-DOE-res meh-CAN-ee-cohs) Tuning machines (Spanish).

African blackwood *n*. see *Dalbergia melanoxylon*

African rosewood *n*. see *Guibourtia demeusei*

after length *n*. The length of string between the bridge (saddle) and the string anchor point.

Agathis australis *n*. Large hardwood tree native to New Zealand. Growing trees are protected from logging but wood from ancient trees (called ancient kauri wood) finds limited use for lutherie purposes. Specific gravity is 0.54. Modulus of elasticity is 11.87 GPa. Syn.: ancient kauri.

air cap *n*. The part of a spray gun which directs air on the fluid stream, atomizing the finishing material.

air dried wood *n*. Wood that has been dried at naturally occurring temperatures, without additional heat. Air dried wood is often considered to be more stable than kiln dried wood. See also: kiln dried wood.

air resonance *n*. The air inside a stringed instrument is subject to resonance at varying frequencies. Air between reflective surfaces such as the top and back of the instrument will resonate with a frequency which is a

A

The after length is the portion of the string between the bridge and the tailpiece.

function of the distance between those surfaces. It is unknown if these internal standing waves affect the tone of the instrument either directly or indirectly. The entire mass of air inside an instrument and the air in and around the soundhole(s) comprise a different kind of air resonance, called a Helmholtz resonance. This resonance does affect the sound of the instrument and is a primary source of sound of an instrument, particularly of its lowest notes. Air and body resonances are usually coupled to some extent with other resonances. See also: coupling, Helmholtz resonance, standing wave.

aliphatic resin glue *n.* Generally referred to as carpenter's glue, wood glue or yellow glue, this is the most common glue used in lutherie for all instruments except violin family instruments. It has a relatively fast tack time and it hardens quickly. It is moderately water resistant, but there are versions of this glue that have very good water resistance as well. Syn.: yellow glue.

alkyd resin *n.* Resin used in some oil varnishes. The resin is made from linseed, soy, or other vegetable oils.

Alkyd resin varnishes are commonly available. Short oil alkyd resin varnishes are used in lutherie applications because they can be rubbed up to a high gloss. See also: oil varnish, short oil varnish.

alox *abbr.* see aluminum oxide

alto ukulele *n.* see concert uke

aluminum hydroxide *n.* A binder used in some lake pigments. See also: lake pigment.

aluminum oxide *n.* Sanding abrasive. It is red brown in color and is found on sandpaper products generally suited for sanding wood.

amalgamator *n.* see ethylene glycol monobutyl ether

Amati, Antonio (1550-1638) Italian violin luthier from Cremona. With his brother Girolamo he established Cremona as the center of fine violinmaking. See also: Girolamo Amati.

Amati, Nicolò (1596-1684) Italian violin luthier from Cremona, considered to be one of the three greatest makers of the instrument. Son of Girolamo Amati. See also: Girolamo Amati.

Amati, Girolamo (1556-1630) Italian violin luthier from Cremona. With his brother Antonio he established Cremona as the center of fine violinmaking. Father of Nicolò Amati. See also: Antonio Amati, Nicolò Amati.

âme n. (ahm) Soundpost (French).

American Lutherie n. The quarterly journal of the Guild of American Luthiers. It features articles on lutherie and other topics of interest to luthiers. See also: Guild of American Luthiers.

amplitude *n.* The displacement of a vibrating object such as a string or a wave. For sound waves, amplitude is directly related to loudness.

ancho inferior n. (ON-cho een-fer-ee-OR) Lower bout (Spanish).

ancho superior *n.* (ON-cho soo-per-ee-OR) Upper bout (Spanish).

ancient kauri *n.* see *Agathis australis*

anima *n.* Soundpost (Italian). See also: soundpost.

animal glue *n.* Glue composed of animal protein. This term generally refers to hide glue but may also refer to fish glue. See also: hide glue, fish glue.

aniline dye *n.* Chemical dye based on aniline (phenylamine) compounds. Aniline dyes are the most popular modern wood staining dyes. They provide strong colors and are fairly resistant to fading over time. See also: metalized dye.

anisotropic *adj.* Not uniform in all directions. As applies to materials this means the material properties are not uniform in all directions through the material. Wood is an anisotropic material. It is stiffer along the grain than it is across the grain, for example. Much of the specificity of grain orientation in lutherie is due to the fact that wood is an anisotropic material. See also: isotropic.

antinode *n.* An area of high displacement (movement) on a vibrating string, plate or air mass. See also: node.

aperture *n.* Describes the length of the section of string that a magnetic pickup is sensitive to. The aperture of most magnetic pickups is about as long as the dimension of the pickup parallel to the strings. Syn.: window.

Apex grit grade *n.* see structured abrasives

apex *n.* Highest point. In lutherie this is generally used to describe the highest point of an arch or dome. See also: nadir.

apoyando *n.* (ah-poy-ON-doe) see rest stroke (Spanish).

Appalachian mountain dulcimer *n.* see mountain dulcimer

Aram, Kevin North Devon, England, classical guitar luthier and educator. Known for the use of oil finished classical guitars.

arbor press *n.* A bench tool used to install any component that is pressed in. In lutherie the most common uses of the arbor press is to press frets into fret slots and to press tuning machine bushings into their holes. The arbor press has a toothed rack that can accept a tool on one end. The rack is driven by a pinion gear to which is attached a handle. Pressing the handle down turns the pinion which moves the rack and attached tool downward.

archaic construction *n.* Traditional construction technique for guitars or similar flat instruments. The top

A

An arbor press is used to press in frets on this guitar fingerboard. A fret pressing caul has been installed in the arbor.

is positioned face down on a solera, the neck attached to it, and then the ribs fitted into slots on the neck. This is still used for classical guitar construction. Syn.: in the air construction. See also: solera.

Archaic construction.

archetier *n.* Bow maker. Maker of bows for violin family instruments.

arching profile *n.* A curved line indicating the arching of an arched plate, as if the plate was sectioned (cut through). Syn.: arching contour.

archlute *n.* Any member of the lute family that features two peg boxes. The general configuration is to have one peg box for the fretted strings and a separate one for harp-like bass strings. See also: theorbo.

archtop *adj.* Stringed instruments can be classified by the type of top plate they have. Those with carved and arched top plates are called archtops, while those with "flat" top plates are called flattops. These terms are generally used to differentiate guitar family instruments. See also: flattop.

archtop guitar *n.* Guitar with an arched, usually carved, top. The top plates of such instruments are approx. $1/4''$ (6.35mm) thick at the edge and the apex of arch is about $3/4''$ (19.05mm) higher than the edge. The inside surface is also carved, resulting in a violin style arched plate of roughly $1/4''$ (6.35mm) in thickness. Archtop guitars generally have floating bridges, f holes and arched back plates as well. See also: apex, f hole, floating bridge.

area moment of inertia *n.* see second moment of area

area tuning *v.* The tuning of different parts of the top and possibly back plate of an instrument. The process involves carving the inside of the plate and/or the braces so that each specified area vibrates to a particular pitch when struck. Details of division of the plate into areas and of the target pitches vary among proponents of this technique.

armrest bevel *n.* A bevel or roundover of the edge between the top plate and ribs of a guitar or similar instrument in the area that is normally contacted by the arm of the player's picking hand. Armrest bevels are implemented to improve player comfort. They are often found on Fender style solid body electric guitars and also on some acoustic guitars.

aro *n.* Rib (Spanish).

arpa llanera *n.* (AR-pah yan-AIR-ah) Venezuelan folk harp from the plains region.

Araucaria bidwillii *n.* Bunya pine. An Australian softwood used for guitar tops in some models made by Australian guitar factories Maton and Cole-Clarke. Specific gravity is 0.52.

Ashbory bass *n.* Product name of a small fretless electric bass guitar featuring very short scale (18″) silicone rubber strings and a piezo pickup.

ASIA *abbr.* see Association of Stringed Instrument Artisans

Association of Stringed Instrument Artisans *n.* Luthier member organization. Produces the magazine *Guitarmaker.* Syn.: ASIA.

Athrotaxis selaginoides n. King William pine. An Australian softwood with a specific gravity of 0.25, sometimes used in Australia as a top wood. This species is not available in commercial quantities and so has limited use. Syn.: King Billy Pine

atmospheric pressure clamping n. Any method of clamping that relies on atmospheric pressure (approximately 15 pounds per square inch). All these methods involve removing the effect of atmospheric pressure on the glue joint itself, so that atmospheric pressure opposite the glue joint can exert clamping pressure. See also: rubbed joint, vacuum clamping, veneer hammering.

audition n. Hearing.

audio spectroscopy n. Analytical technique for audio signals. Audio spectroscopy involves the use of dedicated instruments or general purpose computers with specialized software to analyze audio signals to produce spectrograms. These are 3D plots of amplitude of frequency over time. Computations are performed by Fourier analysis. Spectroscopy is useful in research in the physics of stringed musical instruments. See also: Fourier analysis, spectrogram.

auditorium size guitar n. One of the general size classifications for steel string guitars, adopted from C.F. Martin size designations. The body of an auditorium size

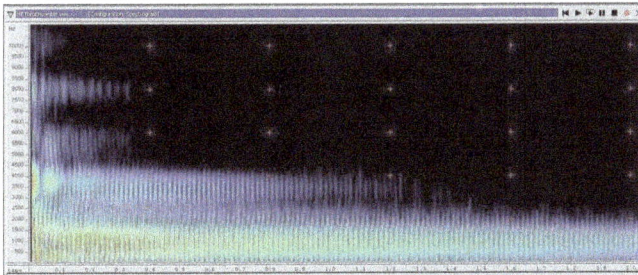

Audio spectroscopy. A spectrogram of a single string pluck over a few seconds.

guitar is approximately 20″ long and 15″ wide at the lower bout. Syn.: OOO.

Autoharp n. Zither family instrument used for accompaniment featuring keys that can be pressed to mute most strings, allowing only those of a chord to vibrate. See also: zither.

automotive polishing compounds n. Liquid polishes used to buff automotive finishes. These are often used in lutherie to buff instrument finishes by hand. The compounds come in a variety of grades, specified by their manufacturer. The grade of a compound indicates how fine the abrasive grit of the compound is.

Automotive polishing compounds.

A

B

back *n*. The bodies of stringed musical instruments have two large plates. The one that supports the bridge and has the soundhole(s) in it is called the top or belly or front, and the other large plate is called the back.

back bow *n*. A bend in the fingerboard and neck of a stringed instrument in which the fingerboard playing surface is rendered convex. Back bow is generally undesirable because it allows the fretted string to hit the fingerboard or frets while vibrating, causing buzzing. See also: front bow, neck relief.

back brace *n*. A brace on the back plate of an instrument.

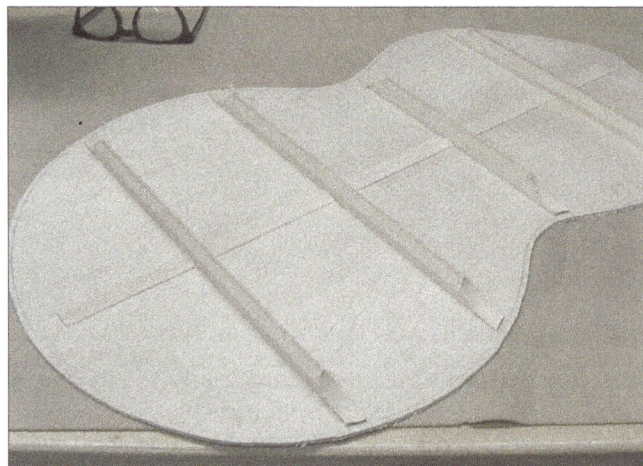

Back braces on the back of an acoustic bass guitar under construction.

back buzz *n*. Buzzing against the frets of that portion of a fretted string between the nut and the fret.

back pin *n*. Small pin located on the back of some 19th century guitars. Guitars with such pins generally have two: one on the centerline near the heel and the other near the tail end. The pins were used to attach the guitar to the player for playing standing up. Small lengths of string or gut were tied to the pins and then to some point on the players clothing, such as a button or button hole. Syn.: back button.

back plate *n*. see back

back reinforcing strip *n*. Thin strip of cross grain wood used to reinforce the center seam or other seams of the back of flattop guitars.

back sawn *n*. see flat sawn

The back of an archtop acoustic guitar.

Back pin.

back strip *n*. Decorative strip on the centerline of the back plate of a flattop guitar. Syn.: back stripe.

back stripe *n*. see back strip

back tilt *n*. The amount the bridge of a violin family instrument tilts backward (toward the tailpiece) from perpendicular to the surface of the belly, when viewed from the side. Some amount of back tilt is considered desirable to keep the top edge of the bridge from bending forward.

A maple-rosewood-maple back strip on a mahogany guitar.

backer board *n*. The sturdy and usually thicker piece of wood that veneer is applied to. Also any construction board used to back up a thin piece of wood during work on that piece.

bağlama *n*. Turkish long neck lute-style instrument family. The instruments generally have seven strings in courses of two, two, and three strings and have tied frets and tuning pegs. Tunings vary and scales are generally microtonal and approximate quarter-tone equal temperament scales. Size/pitch variants are common. Syn.: saz.

balalaika *n*. Russian three steel string instrument with a triangular body. Various sizes/pitches of the instrument are common, including the prima, tuned E4 E4 A4; the secunda, tuned A3 A3 D4; the alto, tuned E3 E3 A3; the bass, tuned E2 A2 D3; and the contrabass, tuned, E1 A1 D2. The contrabass features a pin at one corner of the body that rests on the ground when in playing position. Other variations of the instrument are common as well.

balanced tension *adj*. Describes a string set in which all strings will be at nearly the same tension when tuned to pitch.

ball *n*. The terminating part of ball end strings. See also: ball end.

ball end *adj*. Strings can be classified by the termination features at the string anchor end. Ball end strings terminate in a ball-shaped part. The term is also used as a

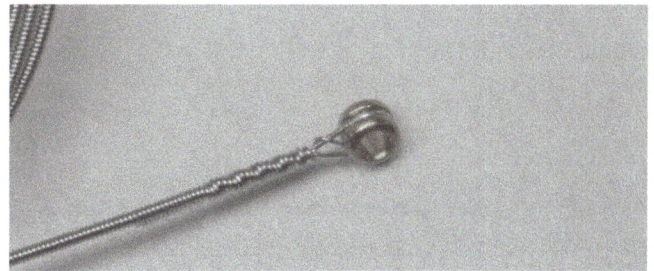

Ball end of steel guitar string.

noun to identify the string anchor end of the string. See also: loop end.

balsa *n.* see *Ochroma pyramidale*

bandola *n.* (ban-DOE-la) An instrument from various regions of South America. The bandola is a mandolin-like instrument with a "flat" top. Those from the Andean region of Colombia have twelve metal strings in six courses.

bandola llanera *n.* (ban-DOE-la yan-ERE-ah) Venezuelan bandola from the plains region with four nylon strings. The instrument has a guitar-like body with a narrow upper bout.

bandora *n.* Renaissance cittern family instrument with wire strings in six or seven courses of two strings each. Similar to the orpharion. See also: cittern, orpharion.

bandpass filter *n.* An electrical circuit or an acoustic system which passes frequencies in a defined range (band) relatively intact but attenuates lower and higher frequencies. See also: highpass filter, lowpass filter.

bandurria *n.* Mandolin like instrument from Spain. It features flat plates and five courses of steel strings tuned in fourths. Variants of this instrument appear in Bolivia and Peru. These instruments generally have four courses.

bandwidth *n.* Width of a frequency band, measured from some low frequency to some high frequency. In lutherie the term is often used to describe the width of some mode of vibration of the instrument.

banjo *n.* Four or five string American instrument with African origins. The body of the instrument is like a tambourine, consisting of a wood ring over which is stretched a skin or plastic head to form the instrument's top. The back is open or features a cover called a resonator. The two most common configurations of the instrument are the tenor banjo, a four string instrument played with a pick, and the five string banjo, which adds a short string to the bass side of the neck. The five string

banjo is generally finger-picked using metal finger picks. See also: banjo head.

banjo head *n.* The top "plate" of a banjo is really a plastic or skin membrane called the head, stretched over the ring (ribs).

banjo pot *n.* Rib assembly of a banjo.

bar *n.* see brace

bar clamp *n.* A screw type clamp based on a long metal bar. The clamp can be quickly adjusted for clamping length by moving the screw retainer along the bar. Once in position, tightening the screw fixes the effective length of the clamp and applies clamping pressure.

bar fret *n.* The frets in older instruments were made of thin rectangular bars of metal. Unlike the modern T fret with a thin tang that inserts into a thin slot on the fingerboard, the bar fret is a plain rectangular bar that inserts into a wide slot on the fingerboard. See also: T fret, tied fret.

barber pole binding *n.* see rope binding

Barbero, Marcelo (ca. 1904-1956) Madrid guitar luthier, noted for his flamenco guitars. Worked in the shops of José Ramirez and José Ramirez II, and also in the shop of Santos Hernandez after the death of Hernandez. His own guitars include one made for Carlos Montoya.

baritone ukulele *n.* The largest "standard" instrument of the ukulele family. It is generally tuned DGBE, the same as the highest four strings of the guitar. Overall length is approx. 30″ (762mm). Typical scale length is 19″ (483mm). Typical body dimensions include a length of 14″ (356mm) and a width of 10″ (254mm) at the lower bout.

baroque *adj.* Pertaining to the European Baroque musical period, spanning approximately the years 1600-1750.

baroque guitar *n.* A baroque era guitar or a guitar built in that style. These instruments feature small, narrow bodies, somewhat in the style of the modern parlor guitar and are generally strung with five double courses of gut strings. Frets are usually tied on and also made of gut, and there may be solid frets inlaid into the top to effectively extend the fingerboard. Baroque guitars often feature a high level of decoration. Striped backs and sides and fancy carving of the bridge are common. The soundhole often contains an elaborate rosette. See also: course, gut, parlor guitar, tied fret.

barra *n.* (BAHR-ah) Brace, bar (Spanish).

barra de abanico *n.* (BAHR-ah dey ah-bahn-EE-co) Fan brace (Spanish). Syn.: refuerzo de abanico.

WIKIPEDIA COMMONS, IMAGE IS IN THE PUBLIC DOMAIN

The Guitar Player (c. 1672) *by Johannes Vermeer features a baroque guitar.*

barre *n.* (bahr) Brace, bar (French).

barre d'harmonie *n.* (bahr dar-mo-nee) Bass bar (French).

barrel nut *n.* Machine screw nut used in some bolt-on necks. The nut is a short length of metal rod with a threaded hole through its diameter. The nut is inserted in a hole drilled through a straight tenon at the neck end. A machine screw inserted through the neck block from inside the instrument engages the threads of the barrel nut.

barrier coat *n.* Coat of finishing material used to separate two other coats. Barrier coats are used when the application of a coat of finish would dissolve or otherwise damage a previous coat. For example, an oil varnish barrier coat may be applied over alcohol based stain before the application of subsequent coats of French polish (shellac). The varnish is not dissolved by the alcohol in the shellac, but application of the shellac directly over the stain could dissolve and smear the stain.

baryton *n.* Eighteenth century viola with sympathetic strings. See also: sympathetic string, viol.

bass bar *n.* Violin family instruments feature a single brace on the top plate called the bass bar. This brace runs more or less parallel to the grain of the top and extends from near the neck block, under the bass string side bridge foot, and ends near the tail block.

bass viol *n.* see double bass

bassoguitar *n.* Upright double bass produced by the Regal Musical Instrument Company in the late 1930s. The bodies of these instruments were constructed in the same manner as the flattop guitar, with the exception of a floating bridge, string anchor tailpiece and an end pin so the instrument could be played upright. See also: Regal Musical Instrument Co.

basswood *n.* see *Tilia americana*

B

bastard grain *adj.* Describing wood with grain angle that varies across the width of the board when viewing the end grain. The term is sometimes also used to describe any board that cannot be classified as quarter sawn or flat sawn. See also: flat sawn, quarter sawn.

bead *n.* The part of a fret that, when the fret is installed in the fretboard, remains above the playing surface of the fretboard. See also: fret.

bearclaw *n.* A figure pattern of spruce that usually includes a number of thin figure lines that look like they were formed by a bear scratching the tree.

bearing end string roller *n.* A feature found on high end classical guitar tuning machines. String rollers of classical guitar tuning machines fit into blind holes drilled into the side of the headstock. The end of the

Bastard grain.

roller turns inside the hole. Repeated use can cause the hole on that end to wear. Bearing end rollers have a small bearing on that end which does not turn inside the hole, thus reducing wear and tuning friction. See also: string roller, tuning machine.

beats *n.* Two notes sounded simultaneously that are close in frequency will produce audible pulsations called beats. The most common example are the beats generated during tuning of an instrument when two notes approach the same frequency. The frequency of the beats approaches zero as the two notes approach the same pitch. Beats are the result of destructive interference. Syn.: primary beats. See also: second order beats.

Beller, Kevin Vice president of engineering and new product development for guitar pickup manufacturer Seymour Duncan.

belly *n.* The bodies of stringed musical instruments have two large plates. The one that supports the bridge and has the soundhole(s) in it is called the top or belly or front. Of these three terms, the one most used to describe this plate for violin family instruments is belly.

belly bridge *n.* A style of bridge used in flat top steel string guitars. The tops of the bridge wings of this style of bridge are flat, and they transition to the central portion of the bridge with rounded curves. See also: bridge wing, pyramid bridge.

belly cut n. Beveled area of the back of a solid body electric guitar at the edge in the area of the waist. This body feature is typical of Fender style electric guitars and is intended to allow the guitar body to better fit the body of the player. Syn.: belly cavity, belly contour, belly cut, belly recess, waist cut.

bench copy *n.* A close copy of an instrument, usually one that is well known and valuable. The term implies that the copier had the original instrument in front of him or her when making the copy, which may not always be true. Syn.: close copy.

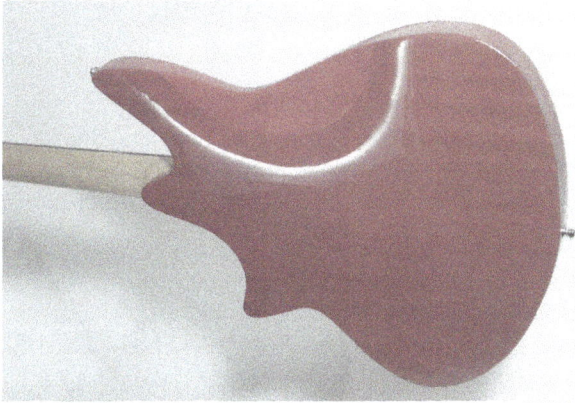

LEONARDO LOSPENNATO

Belly cut on a solid body electric guitar by Leonardo Lospennato.

bending form *n.* A mold used to bend the ribs of a stringed instrument. The bending form usually contains a heater and possibly some peripheral clamping devices to aid in bending the side(s). Some are simple inside molds, over which are bent one or more side slats and a flexible silicone heating blanket. See also: inside mold, silicone heating blanket.

bending iron *n.* A heated tube over which the ribs of an instrument are bent. Commercial electric bending irons are available, and shop built irons heated by electric heating elements or torches are used by many builders.

bending stiffness *n.* A measure of a component's rigidity to bending.

Benedetto, Robert USA luthier and author, best known for archtop guitars.

Bertolotti, Gasparo di see Salò, Gasparo da

bevel *n.* A ramped area at the end of a part. Syn.: ramp.

Bézier curve n. Type of mathematical curve used in CAD drawing and other drawing software to model smooth curves. Named after French engineer Pierre Bézier who

used them in the design of cars at Renault. See also: non-uniform rational b-spline, spline curve.

Bieber, Alain Contemporary French classical guitar luthier and author on lutherie topics, Bieber has written about the history of the adjustable neck joint and is a proponent of the reconsideration of this type of neck attachment in modern instruments. See also: adjustable neck joint.

bigleaf maple *n.* see *Acer macrophyllum*

billet *n.* A rough hunk of wood. For example, processing guitar tops involves splitting a section of a spruce log into billets, which in turn are resawn into top blanks.

A commercial electric bending iron.

binder *n*. Basic component of finishing materials. The binder provides structural integrity in the cured finish. Paint and stain contain a vehicle, a pigment, and a binder. The vehicle evaporates away during curing. The binder provides the structure of the remaining film and fixes the pigment. See also: pigment, vehicle.

binding *n*. Edging on instrument bodies, also found on fingerboards and headstocks. The binding is decorative but also serves to protect the edge and to seal the end grain. Bindings are typically made of wood or plastic, and may be combined with purflings, which decorate and contrast the inside edges of the bindings.

Mahogany guitar featuring rosewood binding and maple purfling.

binding channel *n*. The channel (rabbet) into which binding is glued. After the top and back are attached to the ribs, the binding channels are cut into the top and back edges. Binding and possibly purfling are glued into these channels. Syn.: binding ledge. See also: binding, purfling, rabbet.

Binding channels routed on the back of a guitar.

binding cutter *n*. Tool used to cut the binding channel. The two major classes of such tools are hand tools like the gramil, and power tools. The most common power tool is the router with a rabbeting bit. For archtop instruments and flattop instruments with domed plates, the router is usually held by a special binding router jig. See also: binding, binding channel, binding router jig, gramil.

binding frame *n*. An infrequently used jig used to hold an instrument for installation of the body binding. It consists of a rigid frame around the perimeter of the body. Glue is applied to the binding and purfling ledges, and then the binding is held in place while the glue dries with wedges placed between the frame and the binding. See also: binding, binding ledge, purfling.

The binding frame in use.

binding jig *n*. see binding router jig

binding ledge *n*. see binding channel

binding router jig *n*. A jig used to hold a router while cutting the binding channel. For an instrument with truly flat plates and not much back taper, a router with a rabbeting bit can be used to cut the binding channel, with the router base sitting right on the top or back plate of the instrument. But for archtop instruments or flattop instruments with domed plates, the arching or doming makes it impractical to use the router with it sitting right on the plate. A binding router jig holds the router so that it is always perpendicular to the ribs. There are two basic types. In the first the router is free to move up and down but is otherwise fixed in position. The instrument, held in a special cradle, is moved to route the channel. In the other type of jig, the router is attached to an articulated or sliding arm and is free to move around.

binomial *n.* see binomial name

binomial name *n.* Scientific name, Latin name for a species. Binomial names have two parts, genus and species. A number of sources including this dictionary use binomial names as the primary identification for wood species, to eliminate ambiguity associated with the use of less formal names.

birdseye maple *n.* A figure pattern of domestic maple, usually of eastern hard maple (rock, or sugar maple), *Acer saccharum*. The pattern consists of tiny dot shaped imperfections that have the characteristic look of the eye of a bird. See also: *Acer saccharum*.

Bissinger, George Musical instrument acoustician and researcher. Bissinger was involved in the Catgut Acoustical Society at its inception. He is involved in a long term research project (Strad 3D VIOCADEAS Project) to document vibrational properties of well known violins and to correlate this data with acoustical and subjective evaluations.

biwa *n.* Japanese lute-like instrument.

black locust *n.* see *Robinia pseudoacacia*

blackface *adj.* Describes Fender tube guitar amplifiers built in the 1960s. These have a distinctive black painted control panel. See also: silverface.

Guitar headplate made of birdseye maple.

blackface *v.* To modify the circuitry of a Fender silverface tube guitar amp to be similar in characteristics to that of a Fender blackface amp. See also: silverface

bleached bone *n.* see bone

blend pot *n.* see pan pot

Blilie, James Shoreville MN, USA, luthier specializing in classical and steel string guitars. He is also a mechanical engineer specializing in materials testing and has done much work on quantifying mechanical properties of wood species and glue used in lutherie.

block *n.* Any large solid component of a stringed musical instrument. Common blocks include the neck block and tail block. Classical guitar bridges have a tie block, the place where the strings are tied. Violin family instruments have corner blocks at the body corners.

block marker *n.* A fretboard position marker in the shape of a rectangle, or roughly in the shape of a rectangle. See also: dot marker.

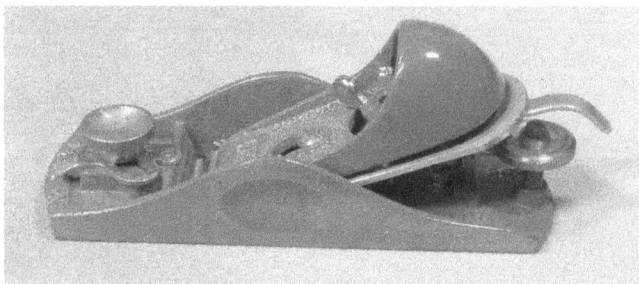

Block plane.

block plane *n.* A small hand plane, often with the blade mounted at a low angle. The block plane is generally used one-handed for small planing operations. It is probably the most generally used plane for lutherie applications, and can be found in the tool set of both hand tool users and those that rely primarily on power tools. The term also refers to any plane in which the blade is mounted bevel side up. See also: #9^1/$_2$ plane, #60 plane.

bloque de extremo *n.* (BLOW-kay dey ex-TREM-oh) Tail block (Spanish).

blush *n.* A rose colored pigmentation in sprayed clear lacquer, caused by moisture trapped in the lacquer. Lacquer can blush when it is applied at times of high humidity. Blush can generally be removed by the application of lacquer blush remover. See also: blush remover.

blush remover *n.* A solvent that softens lacquer enough to let any water trapped in the lacquer evaporate. Syn.: blush eraser. See also: blush.

board foot *n.* The standard U.S. customary unit of lumber volume. Lumber is generally sold by the board foot. One board foot measures 1' x 1' x 1". The measurement applies to the rough sawn board, even if the board is sold surfaced, so a surfaced board that is 11 ^{1}/$_2$" wide x ^{3}/$_4$" thick x 1' long is sold as 1 board foot, since that was its volume before surfacing.

boat neck *adj.* Typical cross section profile of the neck or a guitar or other plucked instrument. The boat neck profile has the shape of the hull of a sailboat, coming to a hard edge at the centerline of the back of the neck. Syn.: V neck. See also: D neck, flattened oval.

bobbin *n.* Plastic or fiber spool onto which the coils of a magnetic guitar pickup are wound.

boca *n.* (BOW-kah) Soundhole (Spanish).

body *n.* The major part of a stringed instrument which supports the bridge. The body of an acoustic instrument generally is composed of a top and back plate attached to a bent side framework. The term is also used as part of a description of electric guitars to differentiate them on the basis of body construction, i.e. solid body, hollow body, semi-hollow body. See also: hollow body, semi-hollow body, solid body.

bodying *v.* In French polishing, to apply shellac to build up the finish. See also: French polish.

bodying session *n.* One unit of application during bodying French polish. Each application applies a thin layer of shellac, so thin that it doesn't really make sense to refer to it as a coat. A typical bodying session consists of the application of shellac to the surface about three times.

Bogdanovich, John North Carolina USA guitar luthier, educator and author.

boiled linseed oil *n.* Oil of linseed (also called flax seed) to which metallic driers have been added. It is used as a finishing material. It is not boiled. See also: linseed oil, metallic drier.

bois de rose *n.* (bwah de rows) see *Dalbergia maritima*

Bolivian rosewood *n.* see *Machaerium* spp.

bolt *n.* A section of a tree trunk.

bolt-on neck *n*. An instrument neck that attaches to the instrument body with either bolts or screws. Acoustic instruments with bolt-on necks usually use bolts that go through the neck block and screw into either barrel nuts or threaded inserts in the neck heel. Electric instruments with bolt-on necks usually use screws that go through the heel area of the body and screw into the neck. See also: neck through construction, set neck.

bolt-on neck joint *n*. The neck to body joint of a bolt-on neck. See also: bolt-on neck.

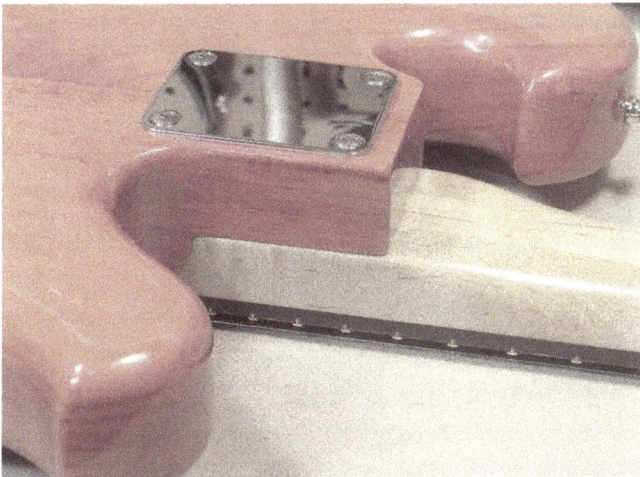

A Fender style electric guitar with a bolt-on neck. Four screws go through a metal neck plate, through holes drilled into the heel part of the body, and screw directly into the neck.

bone *n*. Material used for bridge saddles and nuts (guitars) and for other functional and decorative purposes. Bleached cow or water buffalo is the bone usually used in lutherie.

bone black *n*. Black pigment made from charred bone, used in inlay mastic, paints and varnishes. See also: carbon black.

bookmatched *adj*. The plates of most stringed instruments are made of two pieces of wood. These pieces are generally cut as successive slices from the same billet. If the two slices are opened up like a book, each side will be a mirror image of the other, more or less. This orientation of two successive slices of wood is called bookmatched. Bookmatched tops and backs are standard for most musical instruments, even inexpensive modern instruments. But there are a number of examples of historical instruments, some extremely well regarded, that do not have bookmatched plates.

borescope *n*. see inspection camera

Borreguero, Modesto (1910?-1960?) Madrid guitar luthier. Worked in the shop of Manuel Ramírez and continued there following Ramírez' death. Eventually started his own shop.

boss *n*. In machining and other materials-forming operations, a boss is a raised portion of material that remains when material is cut away around it. See also: pocket.

bottom dumper case *n*. Slang name for a case for a stringed instrument that opens from the bottom. Baroque period instrument cases often were built this way. There were also inexpensive soft cases built up to the 1950s that opened from the bottom.

bottone *n*. (boh-TONE-ee) Button, end pin (Italian).

Bouchet, Robert (1898-1986) Parisian self-taught classical guitar luthier. Bouchet learned guitarmaking by observing in the shop of Julian Gomez Ramirez.

bound fretboard *n*. Fretboard with decorative binding strips attached to the sides and the end. There are two basic styles of bound fretboards. The most common style has the ends of the frets overlaying the binding and ending flush with the outside surface of the binding. Another style, common to Gibson instruments, has the fret ends flush with the sides of the fretboard and the binding applied so as to cover the ends of the frets. The binding is then scraped down, leaving a small hump at each fret end.

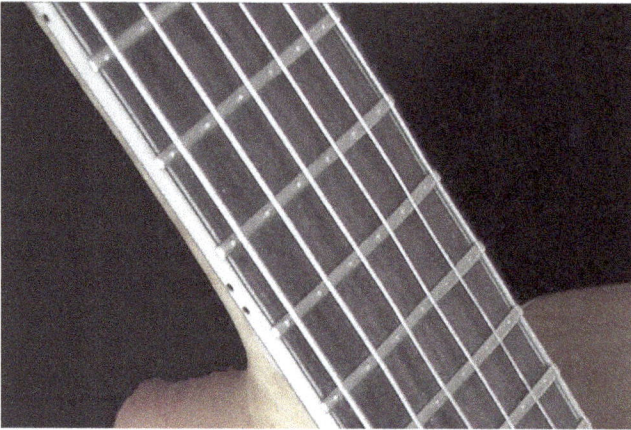

Detail of neck of a guitar with a bound fretboard.

bourdon *n.* Low pitched drone string, as found in the hurdy-gurdy. See also: hurdy-gurdy.

Bourgeois, Dana *n.* Guitarmaker, author and educator, Dana Bourgeois builds Bourgeois and Pantheon guitars. He has written extensively for *American Lutherie* on lutherie topics including the use of CAD, CAM and CNC, and on the voicing of guitars for optimal tone. He is probably best known for his production techniques which combine highly automated manufacturing with individual instrument voicing.

bout *n.* An area of widening or indentation in the outline of a stringed instrument body. The bouts of a guitar are typically labeled upper bouts, waist, and lower bouts. The bouts of violin family instruments are typically labeled upper bouts, c bouts, and lower bouts. See also: c bout, lower bout, upper bout, waist.

bouton *n.* (boo-tone) Button, end pin (French).

bouzouki *n.* Greek long necked fretted lute-like instrument with three or four double courses of steel strings. The body is typical of lute-like instruments with a bowl back and flat top. It is played with a pick.

bow *n.* Sound actuation device for violin family instruments. The bow is composed of a stick of wood (traditionally Pernambuco, *Caesalpinia echinata*) or other material with fittings at both ends to mount a bundle of horse hair. The fitting at one end is called the tip or head; the fitting at the end held in the hand while playing is called the frog or nut. A screw at the latter end provides for tensioning the hair for playing or loosening it for storage of the bow. See also: bow tip, *Caesalpinia echinata*, frog, screw.

bow drill *n.* A hand powered drill that uses a bow with its string making one turn around a spindle. When the bow is pushed and pulled the string turns the spindle.

bow hair *n.* Horse hair used in the manufacture of bows for bowed stringed instruments.

bow hair jig *n.* Jig used to hold the bow and hair while attaching hair to the bow of a bowed stringed musical instrument.

bow tip *n.* The fitting on the end of a bow that is opposite to the end that is held in the hand while playing. Syn.: head.

bowl back mandolin *n.* see Neapolitan mandolin

box *n.* The body of an acoustic instrument is often referred to as a box when discussing construction, e.g. "close up the box."

braccio da fabbrica *n.* Antique Cremona, Italy, unit of measurement, possibly used in the design of guitars by Stradivari. It is 483mm-484mm in length.

brace *n.* Any structural member attached to the underside of a plate to add stiffness to the plate. Braces are features of the plates of all flattop instruments. The bass bar of the violin top plate is also a brace. Syn.: bar, strut.

brace arching jig *n*. The top plate of most modern flattop guitars are actually slightly domed. The doming is effected by arching the gluing surfaces of all the top braces so that once the glue dries the top maintains the domed shape. The gluing surfaces of the braces can be planed or sanded to the required arch after the arch is transferred onto each brace. But in production environments it is quicker to use a brace arching jig. The jig bends the brace into the desired arch and holds it like that. Then the gluing surface is planed, sanded, or sawn flat. When the brace is released from the jig, the gluing surface will then have the desired arch. See also: brace.

brace end bracket *n*. Wood bracket glued to the inside of the rib to support the end of a transverse brace. Brackets are often used in Spanish guitar construction. It is possible that this feature was introduced to help keep braces glued down under hot and humid conditions of the tropics. Syn.: bracket, rest. See also: transverse brace.

brace jack *n*. Repair tool used when re-gluing braces. Glue is applied between the brace and the plate, then the jack is placed between the back of the instrument and the brace, and jacked up to provide pressure. See also: jack.

brace wood *n*. Softwood, usually spruce, used to make braces for the plates of stringed instruments. Wood that is not cosmetically suitable or is too narrow for use in tops is often used for brace wood.

bracing *n*. The word here is used to describe the bracing of the plate of an instrument. Instruments with relatively thick plates such as those of the violin family, archtop guitars, and mandolins tend to have simple bracing, while flattop guitars and similar instruments use bracing that is more complex. In all cases, thin strips of softwood, usually spruce, are glued to the underside of

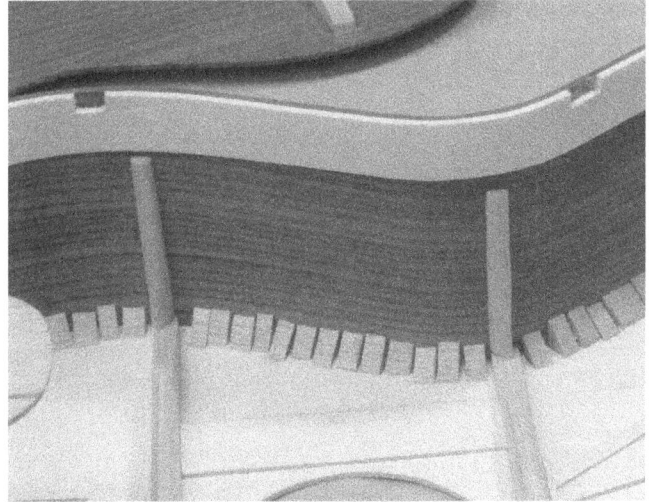

In this top down image, the brace end brackets are shown supporting the ends of the transverse braces.

the plate to help support the loads in the plate resulting directly or indirectly from string tension.

bracing pattern *n*. The layout of the braces on the underside of an instrument plate. There are some standard bracing patterns as well as a large number of patterns that are used less frequently. Standard patterns include: for mandolins and archtop guitar tops - "parallel" and X bracing; for steel string guitar tops - X bracing; for classical guitar tops - fan bracing, lattice bracing; for most flattop guitar backs and for the tops of most antique instruments - ladder bracing. See also: fan bracing, ladder bracing, lattice bracing, parallel bracing, X bracing.

bracket *n*. see brace end bracket

brad point bit *n*. A drill bit with a sharp center point. Brad point bits are used extensively in woodworking because they are easy to center in awl pricked center points and because they do not tend to wander as much as bits with other types of points.

The business end of a brad point drill bit.

Brazilian ironwood *n*. see *Machaerium* spp.

Brazilian rosewood *n*. see *Dalbergia nigra*

Brazilian walnut *n*. see *Handroanthus* spp.

break angle *n*. see breakover angle

breakover angle *n*. The strings pass over the bridge (saddle) of a stringed instrument at an angle. The breakover angle is the angle between the projection of the straight path of the string past the bridge, and the actual path of the after length of the string. See also: after length.

bridge *n*. The structure that terminates the speaking length of the strings at the body end of a stringed musical instrument. There are two basic types of instrument bridges. The type used in violin family instruments and also in mandolins and archtop guitars is called a floating bridge as it is not glued down to the top. The strings contact the bridge but termination of the strings is in a separate tailpiece. This type of bridge is held in place by the downward force exerted by the strings. The other type of bridge is the fixed bridge, used in flattop guitars

and similar instruments. It is glued in place, and contains the string anchors right in the bridge. See also: fixed bridge, floating bridge, speaking length, string anchor, tailpiece.

bridge beads *n*. Small beads used to terminate the strings on the bridge end of classical guitars and gut strung guitars with bridge pins. Classical guitar bridge end string termination is conventionally done by tying the string to the tie block. When bridge beads are used the string end is run through the hole in the tie block then tied or looped through a bead instead. When bridge beads are used with pin bridges the beads are tied to the ends of the strings and serve the same function as the balls on ball end strings. See also: ball end, pin bridge, tie block.

bridge blocking *v*. Inserting a block, usually made of wood, into a vibrato tailpiece to prevent it from moving. Players that never use tailpiece vibrato will often do this to maintain more reliable tuning.

bridge clamp *n*. A special purpose clamp used to clamp the bridge of an acoustic guitar to the top during glue up.

The bridge of an acoustic guitar is being glued on with the aid of two wooden cam clamps and two special purpose bridge clamps.

This is a deep C clamp that is inserted through the soundhole. Syn.: soundhole clamp.

bridge eye *n*. Round shaped holes through the bridge of violin style instruments.

bridge feet *n*. Floating bridges (including violin style bridges) generally have two feet which sit on the top of the instrument when the bridge is in position. These are (not surprisingly) called bridge feet. See also: floating bridge.

bridge hill *n*. That part of the frequency response curve of a violin family instrument which includes resonances of the instrument bridge and the area of the top on which it stands. The bridge hill is a cluster of strongly radiating

A bridge for an archtop acoustic bass guitar. The bridge feet are the two points of contact with the top of the instrument, here, the two parts of the bridge under the black height adjusting wheels.

resonances in the 2,000 to 5,000 Hz range for the violin. See also: frequency response curve.

bridge mask *n*. A mask, usually made of adhesive backed paper, to mark and mask the position of the bridge on a guitar top prior to finishing. After the instrument is finished the mask is removed to reveal bare wood in the shape of the bottom of the bridge. The bridge is glued to the bare wood.

bridge patch *n*. see bridge plate

bridge pickup *n*. Indication of placement of a pickup on an electric guitar. Electric guitars with two pickups identified by location include the bridge pickup (the pickup located near the instrument bridge) and the neck pickup (the pickup located near the instrument neck). See also: neck pickup.

bridge pin *n*. A pin used to secure the end of a string to the bridge of a steel string guitar. The pin goes into the string hole of the bridge and keeps the ball at the end of the string under the bridge plate. Bridge pins are usually made of wood, bone, or plastic. See also: pin bridge.

bridge plate *n*. Flat patch, usually made of hardwood, located on the underside of the top directly under the bridge. The bridge plate distributes the load imposed by the bridge and also serves as a stop for the ball ends of

Bridge mask applied to guitar top prior to application of finish.

B

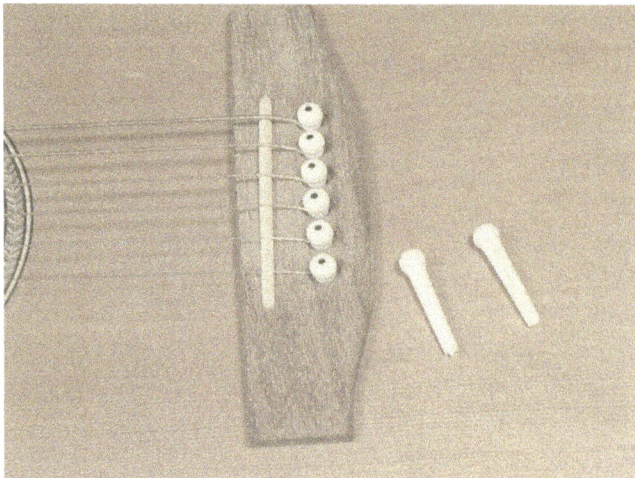

Pin bridge and two extra bridge pins.

steel strings on steel string guitars, which are anchored using bridge pins. See also: patch, bridge pin.

bridge rotation analysis *n*. Analyzing rotation of the bridge of a flattop guitar or similar instrument as a means of achieving good and consistent tone and structural integrity. The basic method involves measuring amount of rotation of the bridge under string loading (i.e. when strings are tuned to pitch). Proponents of this technique generally use measurements taken from instruments recognized to possess good tone and long term structural stability as target measurements in the building of subsequent instruments. In a simplified approach, a pointer is clamped to the bridge of the guitar and a card with deflection scale is placed on the bench behind the end of the pointer. The difference in rotation of the bridge between when the strings are under tension and when they are slack is measured in this manner. A more sophisticated approach uses pointers on both sides of the bridge, thus reducing measurement of other movement of the instrument top.

bridge slot *n*. The slot (channel) in the bridge of an acoustic guitar for the saddle.

bridge slot cutting jig *n*. a jig used to route the slot in the bridge of an acoustic guitar for the saddle. Since the bridge is so small relative to the size of a router, a bridge must be held in some kind of fixture for the routing of the slot. A bridge slot cutting jig holds the bridge and provides either a template or a guide for the router when cutting the slot.

bridge wing *n*. On violin style bridges the wings are the sides of the bridge. On flattop guitar bridges, the wings are the thin, flat ends of the bridge, the parts that do not contain either the saddle or the string anchor holes.

Bruand Montreal, Canada, guitar lutherie college, offering a three year guitar lutherie program taught in

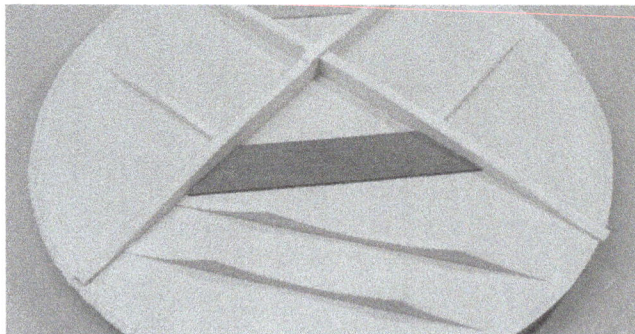

This steel string guitar top plate under construction features a rosewood bridge plate.

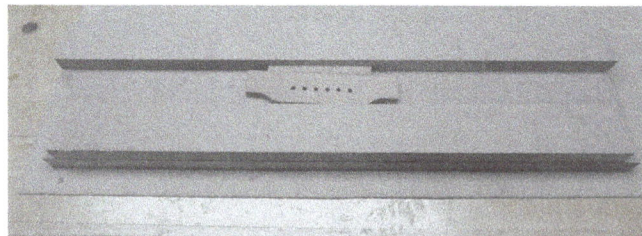

A simple bridge slot cutting jig for use with a router with and edge guide.

French. The full name is École-atelier Lutherie-Guitare Bruand.

Brune, R. E. Chicago Spanish guitar luthier, instrument dealer and author.

Brunet, André Founder and director of École-atelier Lutherie-Guitare Bruand, a Montreal based lutherie school.

brushing lacquer *n*. Lacquer with added retarders to keep it from drying too quickly so that it can be applied by brush. See also: lacquer.

bubinga *n*. see *Guibourtia demeusei*

Buckland, James Clinton SC, USA, left handed classical guitarist, teacher, guitar historian and luthier specializing in 19th century guitars.

Bucknall, Roger Cumbria, UK, builder of steel string guitars and other instruments, and musical instruments acoustics researcher.

build n. A single instrument construction project is often referred to as a build.

build variation *n*. Variability among instances of a manufactured item. Applied to musical instruments, the term indicates the extent to which individual instruments from a manufacturer differ. Build variation is generally considered to be inversely related to quality. A high degree of build variation makes it difficult to assess the effects of small changes intended to improve quality.

Bunya pine *n*. see *Araucaria bidwillii*

burn-in *n*. The quality of finishes applied in multiple coats which describes how well those coats fuse with one another. A coat of a finish with good burn-in will fuse completely with the previously applied coats. Evaporative finishes like shellac and lacquer offer good burn-in. Waterborne finishes have good burn-in if subsequent coats are applied soon after previous coats. Reactive finishes like varnish don't burn in at all.

Burns, James Ormston (1925-1999) London UK electric guitar and bass builder.

Burton, Cyndy Portland OR, USA, classical guitar luthier, author and teacher best known for her oil-free French polishing method. Burton is also a contributing editor for *American Lutherie*, the journal of the Guild of American Luthiers.

butt block *n*. see tail block

butt graft *n*. see end graft

butt joint *n*. A wood-to-wood joint where the joined pieces butt up against each other. Generally the surfaces in contact are perpendicular to the joined pieces.

butt neck joint *n*. A neck-to-body butt joint. In instruments that use this joint the inside surface of the heel of the neck is simply butted up against the body at the neck block area and either glued or bolted in place. See also: bolt-on neck joint

button *n*. An extension of the back plate to cover the bottom of the neck heel. This construction is used in most violin family instruments and is sometimes used in guitar construction as well. See also: heel cap.

Butyl CELLOSOLVE *n*. see ethylene glycol monobutyl ether.

Byers, Greg Willits CA, USA, classical guitar luthier and author. Byers is well known for writing what is generally considered to be the reference article on the subject of guitar intonation "Classical Guitar Intonation" which appeared in *American Lutherie* #47. His guitars feature shortened fan braces.

B

C

c bout *n*. The area of narrowing near the middle of the outline of violin family instrument bodies. The bouts of violin family instruments are typically labeled upper bouts, c bouts, and lower bouts. See also: bout, upper bout, lower bout.

C clamp *n*. A screw type clamp with a body, usually made of metal, in the shape of the letter 'C'.

C section trussrod *n*. Single acting trussrod that is constructed with a solid adjustable round section rod surrounded by a metal C section. This style of rod can be inserted into a straight routed slot. It is used extensively on Martin guitars. See also: single acting trussrod.

CA glue *n*. see cyanoacrylate glue

cabeza *n*. Headstock (Spanish).

cabinet scraper *n*. Two handled tool used to scrape a flat surface. It looks a lot like a spokeshave, but it is bigger and holds a high angled scraper blade. See also: card scraper, scraper plane.

Stanley #80 cabinet scraper.

Cab-O-Sil *n*. Brand name of a fused silica powder used to thicken epoxy or other grain filling materials. In lutherie thickened epoxy is often used as a grain filler. See also: epoxy, grain filler.

CAD *abbr*. (cad) see computer aided design

Caesalpinia echinata *n*. Pernambuco wood. This tropical hardwood is traditionally used in the manufacture of bows for violin family instruments. Other species of this genus are often called pernambuco in the wood trade, but in the context of violin bows only wood of this species bears that name. The species is CITES listed. Syn.: Brazilwood. See also: Convention on International Trade in Endangered Species.

caisse de résonance n. (kes de rez-own-OWNS) Body (French).

calamander *n*. see *Diospyros celebica*

calcite *n*. A polymorph of calcium carbonate, calcite has been identified in the finishes of old violins.

calcium sulfate *n*. A mineral identified in the finishes of old violins. The hemihydrate form is known as plaster of Paris, the dihydrate is known as gypsum.

Caldersmith, Graham Australian physicist, author, and guitar and violin luthier. Caldersmith is probably best known for experiments in musical acoustics and the design and construction of a family of scaled guitars.

caliper *n*. Calipers are measuring tools, used to measure the distance between two parallel surfaces. There are several types that are used in combination with a ruler. The types most often used in lutherie are the dial caliper or the digital caliper, which can be used to take inside, outside, or depth measurements of small distances with high resolution. A special purpose caliper used in lutherie is the thickness gauge, used to measure thickness of plates during construction.

Calkin, John USA luthier and author. Calkin builds guitars and other stringed instruments and is a contributing editor for *American Lutherie*, the quarterly journal of the Guild of American Luthiers. He is a proponent of what he calls "outlaw lutherie", simple design and construction techniques that enable beginner luthiers to build usable instruments with confidence. See also: *American Lutherie*, Guild of American Luthiers

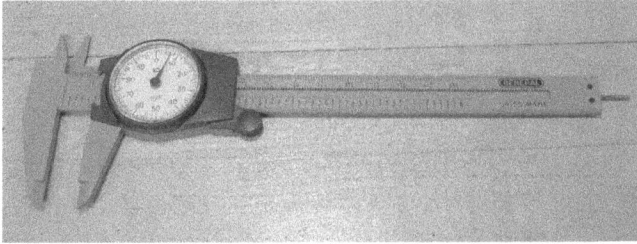

Dial caliper.

CAM *abbr.* (cam) see computer aided manufacturing

cam clamp *n.* A type of bar clamp, usually made of wood, with a cam that is moved to exert clamping pressure. Cam clamps can be used one handed and do not tend to twist the clamped pieces. They do tend to pull one of the clamped pieces in one direction, but this can sometimes be used to advantage. Also called luthiers' cam clamps. See also: bar clamp.

camber *n.* The curvature of the playing surface of the fingerboard of some stringed instruments. With the exception of most classical guitars and early instruments, the fingerboards of stringed instruments are shaped so that the playing surface exhibits an arch. This is considered by some to make barring easier as it follows the natural curve of the insides of the fingers. In lutherie the term radius is also used as a synonym for camber. Syn.: radius.

CAMI *abbr.* (cam-ee) see Coated Abrasive Manufacturers Institute

candle *v.* To shine a bright light through an object to check for defects. In lutherie the planed joints of the plates are often candled before gluing to be sure there are no gaps.

cant *n.* 1. A section of a log that has been sawed flat on two or more sides. 2. a fold or crease, typically in a soundboard behind the bridge, as in the Neapolitan mandolin.

canted top *n.* see cranked top

cap iron *n.* Part of a hand plane (bench plane) that clamps to the blade and directs shavings out of the mouth. Syn.: chip breaker.

cap *abbr.* see capacitor

capacitance *n.* A fundamental electrical quantity, capacitance is the ratio of change in electric charge to

C

Cam clamp.

Cap iron.

change in electric potential. The unit of capacitance is the farad (F). Capacitance is exhibited by a primary passive electrical component, the capacitor. Those typically used in musical instrument circuitry are measured in microfarads (μF or uF) or picofarads (pF). Capacitance is also present in magnetic pickups and affects the resonant peak and thus the overall tone. Instrument cables used to connect instrument to amplifier also exhibit capacitance. The amount is dependent on the construction and length of the cable. Cable capacitance can result in some high frequency roll off particularly with electric guitars with passive electronics. See also: capacitor, magnetic pickup, passive electronics, resonant peak.

capacitor *n*. Passive electrical component found in all electronic circuits such as amplifiers, preamplifiers, stomp boxes and tone control circuitry. Electric guitars with passive electronics generally make use of a simple tone control circuit composed of a single capacitor and a potentiometer, called a treble bleed circuit, which rolls off high frequencies in relation to the position of the potentiometer.

capotasto *n*. (cap-oh-TAS-toe) Nut (Italian).

Cappelle, Jan van Dutch guitar luthier and author, specializing in historical lutes and guitars and also Danelectro style instruments. He is the author of the book *Making Masonite Guitars*.

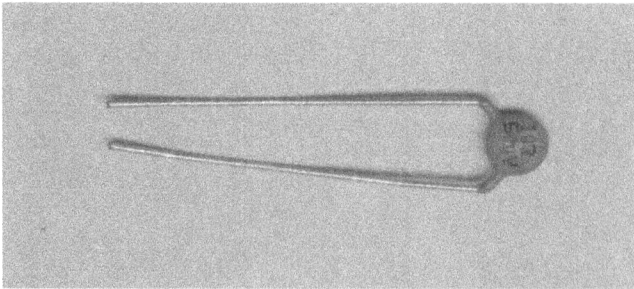

Ceramic disc capacitor of the type typically used in the passive tone control circuitry of electric guitars.

carbon black *n*. Black pigment used in paints, varnishes and lacquers. See also: bone black.

carbon fiber *n*. Thin fibers of crystals of some form of carbon. These fibers are twisted into yarns which are woven into cloth, which is combined with plastic resins to make a moldable composite. Carbon fiber composites have very high strength and stiffness to weight ratios. The fibers are extremely strong and stiff in tension. Carbon fiber and carbon fiber composites find many uses in lutherie. Bars are used for stiffening and bracing members. Thin sheets are used to make stiff braces by covering a lightweight material such as balsa. In addition to sheets and bars of composite material, carbon fiber cloth and rovings (bundles of fibers) are available for those who want to form their own composite shapes. Complete instruments, both electric and acoustic, have been made of this material.

carbon fiber composite *n*. see carbon fiber

carbon fiber guitar strings *n*. see fluorocarbon guitar strings. Syn.: carbon guitar strings

card scraper *n*. A thin sheet of steel that can be sharpened and used to scrape wood. The thin edges are generally honed square, and then a scraper burnisher is used first to draw out an edge and then to turn it into a hook. The scraper is held in both hands with the thumbs pressing on the center, slightly bowing the scraper. The scraper is held against the workpiece at a slight angle away from the user and pushed. A well sharpened scraper leaves behind fine wood shavings, and behaves much like a plane with a very finely set blade. Scrapers are generally used instead of sandpaper, or in preparation for very fine grit sanding. Syn.: scraper See also: cabinet scraper, scraper plane.

Carlson, Fred *n*. Santa Cruz CA, USA, luthier, author and artist, best known for drone string instruments and fanciful body shapes.

Commercial card scraper.

Carcagno, Samuel Italian psychoacoustics researcher specializing in human perception of sound of acoustic guitars. See also: psychoacoustics.

Carter, Walter Stringed musical instrument historian, dealer, and author based in Nashville TN, USA.

carving machine *n*. A machine for carving duplicates of arched plates. A model plate is "read" by the carving machine's probe and a router that is mechanically connected to the probe carves a duplicate of the plate. Carving machines are manual - the operator must move the probe and router around to cover the entire area of the plate. Machines of this sort are used by violin, mandolin, and archtop guitar makers in small and medium sized shops. When higher production is needed CNC machines are used to carve plates, as they work unattended. Syn.: plate copier, plate duplicator See also: CNC machine.

CAS *abbr*. see Catgut Acoustical Society See also: *Catgut Acoustical Society Journal*.

CASJ *abbr*. see *Catgut Acoustical Society Journal*

catalyzed finish *n*. Any finishing material that requires a catalyst to be added just prior to application. Catalyzed finishes are also called two-part or two-pack finishes.

Catalyzed finishes generally cure hard and fast and go on thick so that multiple coats are not necessary. Drawbacks include toxicity and the fact that they are often dissoluble once they cure. The latter property means they can be difficult to repair, and letting them cure in the spray gun can mean the end for the gun.

catenary curve *n*. The curve described by a hanging cable or chain supported on both ends. This curve is used by some as a model for arching profiles of archtop instruments.

catena *n*. (cat-YEN-a) Bassbar, bar, brace (Italian).

catgut *n*. see gut

Catgut Acoustical Society *n*. A now essentially defunct organization of researchers of musical instrument acoustics and related subjects. The CAS was founded in 1963 and published a newsletter which was named the *Catgut Acoustical Society Journal* in 1984. The society effectively disbanded when it joined the Violin Society of America in 2004, under the name CAS Forum, and publication of the journal ceased.

Catgut Acoustical Society Journal *n*. The journal of the Catgut Acoustical Society was a juried research journal containing articles on the subject of stringed musical instrument acoustics and related topics. It was published from 1984 until 2004.

cathedral arch *n*. An arching profile with a pointed apex. The tops of braces are sometimes arched to this profile. See also: Roman arch.

caviglieri *n*. (cav-ee-LAIR-ee) Pegbox (Italian).

caviuna *n*. see *Machaerium* spp.

cavo *n*. (CAH-vo) Tailgut (Italian).

***Cedrela* spp.** *n*. Spanish cedar, cedro. The tree is not a true cedar. Growing in central and south America, the wood is red-brown and is moderately light and stiff. It is used in lutherie primarily for the necks of Spanish

C

guitars. Dry wood has a specific gravity of approximately 0.47 and a modulus of elasticity of 9.12 GPa.

cedro *n.* see *Cedrela* spp.

cejilla *n.* (say-HE-yah) Nut (Spanish).

cello *n.* Bass instrument of the violin family. Syn.: cello, violincello.

cello guitar *n.* Archtop jazz guitar (British).

celluloid *n.* A moldable plastic made from nitrocellulose and camphor. Celluloid has largely been replaced by new plastics with superior properties, but it is still used widely in lutherie for decorative bindings, pickguards, tuning machine knobs and other parts. It is used in lutherie as a matter of tradition - early 20th century instruments made use of this plastic and modern instruments that want the same vintage look use it for the same parts.

Celtic harp *n.* A small harp, also called a folk harp, Irish harp or a lever harp. Changes in key are effected by the use of sharping levers, which press on the string and shorten it. Syn.: folk harp, Irish harp, lever harp.

cent *n.* One hundredth of an equal temperament semitone, on a logarithmic scale. There are 1200 cents to the octave.

center of gravity *n.* see centroid

center seam *n.* The plates of most stringed musical instruments are made of two bookmatched pieces of wood glued together. On the instrument, the pieces are oriented so that the seam between the two halves of the plate is in line with the vertical center line of the instrument. So this seam is called the center seam. See also: bookmatched.

centroid *n.* The center of mass of a body or cross section, the point at which the body or cross section could be balanced.

chalk fit *v.* A method for fitting two irregular surfaces together so they have continuous contact. Chalk is applied to one surface and then the other piece is held in contact with it. Some chalk will be transferred to the second piece at the places they contact. The wood at the chalked locations on the second piece is scraped down, and the fitting process is repeated. Each iteration of the fitting process results in a larger area of contact and so more chalk is left on the second piece. The process is done when a test fitting shows the surface of the second piece to be completely covered in chalk. This indicates continuous contact between the two surfaces.

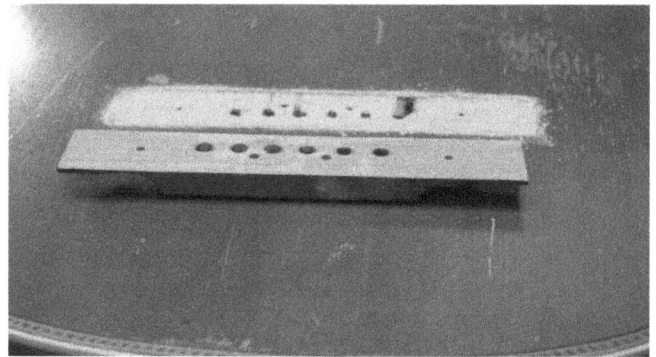

Chalk fitting the bridge of a guitar under restoration.

chanterelle *n.* (French) The highest pitched strings. The term is usually used to describe these strings on Renaissance instruments. Syn.: cantino (Italian).

Char, Kerry Portland OR, USA, luthier and repairman specializing in guitars and ukuleles. He builds replicas of and restores old harp guitars as well.

Charlie Christian pickup *n.* Jazz guitarist Charlie Christian is considered to be the musician that popularized the electric jazz guitar. He played a Gibson ES-150 archtop guitar with a magnetic pickup installed. This pickup was one of the first to have the configuration of components common to most modern magnetic pickups - a coil of wire around a metal core, to which is attached two bar magnets. The entire assembly is attached to a heavy baseplate. The mass of the baseplate helped to reduce feedback.

chatoyancy *n.* (sha-TOY-an-see) A quality of the appearance of shell and figured wood, chatoyancy describes a 3D effect to the appearance of the underlying wood. The term is also used to describe the quality of old violin finishes where color and depth appear different when viewed from different angles.

checking *n.* Small cracks in wood or finish.

chemical stain *n.* A wood coloring agent that reacts with substances in the wood to make a change in surface color. Chemical stains were some of the earliest wood coloring agents. Their use today is generally limited to restoration or replication projects. Examples of chemical stains include potassium dichromate, which will impart a reddish hue to some light colored woods, and sulfuric acid, which will turn woods like locust a reddish brown. Most chemical stains are hazardous enough that much care should be taken in their use.

chevalet *n.* (shuv-val-lay) Bridge (French).

cheville *n.* (SHEV-ee) Tuning pegs (French).

chin rest *n.* A fitting of violins and violas that provides a place for the player to rest his or her chin.

Chinery, Scott (1960 - 2000) USA guitar collector, most famous for his collection of commissioned blue archtop guitars.

chip breaker *n.* see cap iron

chip brush n. Paintbrush used to remove chips and other debris during machining of metal. Also describes any cheap paint brush.

chitarra *n.* (key-TAR-rah) Guitar (Italian); also name for early guitar.

chitarra batente *n.* Four string southern Italian wire strung folk guitar.

chitarrone *n.* (key-tar-ROWN-eh) 16th century Italian archlute. See also: archlute, theorbo.

chiterna *n.* (key-TERN-ah) see cittern

Chladni pattern *n.* (KLAD-nee PAT-tern) Instrument plates have a number of resonant frequencies of vibration. If a plate is induced to vibrate at one of those frequencies it will vibrate in a particular pattern with some parts of the pattern not vibrating at all. These areas of no (or low) vibration are called nodes. It is usually difficult to see these nodes with the eye, but if the plate is sprinkled with sand or glitter or some other fine powder, that material will tend to collect along the nodes, because it is bounced off those areas that are strongly vibrating. These patterns of plate vibrations are called Chladni patterns, after the person that first demonstrated the technique, German physicist Ernst Chladni (1756-1827). Chladni patterns are used by some as the primary mechanism of free plate tuning. See also: free plate tuning, mode, node.

chordophone *n.* Stringed musical instrument.

chromium oxide buffing compound *n.* Fast cutting green buffing compound used as a metal polish, often the final step in the sharpening and honing of edge tools. Syn.: green rouge.

cimbalom *n.* An eastern European hammered dulcimer. Also called the santouri or sandouri in middle Eastern countries.

cinnabar *n.* Mercury sulfate. A red pigment used in violin varnishes.

cintura *n.* Waist (Spanish).

circle cutter *n.* A tool for cutting circles in thin wood. Also called a fly cutter. The device consists of a center drill bit and a horizontal arm on which is mounted a

Chromium oxide buffing compound.

chisel-like blade. The tool is mounted in the drill press and turned at low speed. When pressed into the workpiece, the drill bit drills a center hole while the cutter cuts a circular channel. These are used in lutherie to cut the soundhole in guitar tops and also sometimes to cut the channels for the soundhole rosette. Syn.: fly cutter. See also: compass gramil.

CITES *abbr*. (SIGH-tees) see Convention on International Trade in Endangered Species

citole *n*. (SEE-toll) Medieval flat back guitar-like instrument, often with a body featuring pointed upper bouts or pointed upper and lower bouts. Syn.: citola, citula, cetula, cythera, citera, chytara, cithara, cetola, cythole, sitole, sytholle, cytolys, cetera, cetola, citola, cistola, cedra, cuitole, zitol, cistole.

cittern *n*. Renaissance wire strung instrument with a teardrop shaped body and flat back, similar to a modern flat backed mandolin. Syn.: cetra.

clamp *n*. Device used to temporarily exert compressive pressure, usually to hold pieces in close contact while glue sets. Luthiers use a variety of clamps since the instruments are primarily held together with glue. In addition to common woodworking clamps such as C clamps, bar clamps and pipe clamps, luthiers also use types of clamps less commonly used in general woodworking. These include spring clamps, cam clamps and spool clamps. Luthiers also use a number of special purpose clamps such as guitar bridge clamps. See also: bridge clamp, cam clamp, spool clamp, spring clamp.

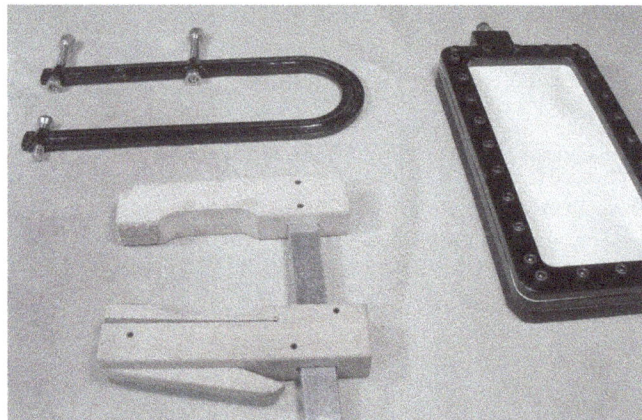

Some clamps used in lutherie. The wooden clamp is a luthiers' cam clamp, the black, deep C clamp is a special purpose bridge clamp for acoustic guitars, and the rectangular black frame with tan rubber internal diaphragm is a vacuum bridge clamp.

clamping caul *n*. A piece of wood or plastic that is placed between a clamp and the object clamped. Cauls are used to spread clamping pressure over a wider area than that of the clamp itself, or to clamp a piece that can not be reached by the clamp itself, or to keep the clamp from damaging a delicate piece.

clang tone *n*. A tone audible in some bass strings of some instruments caused by longitudinal vibration of the string. The tone is higher pitched than the fundamental frequency of the string. The clang tone pitch is a function of the cross sectional area of the core wire, the modulus of elasticity of the core wire material, the total mass per

Clamping cauls are used both above and below when gluing this scarf joint to spread clamping pressure evenly over the entire joint area.

unit length of the string, and the string length. See also: mass per unit length.

Clark, Eugene (1932-2016) Tacoma WA, USA, luthier and lecturer, specializing in Spanish guitars. His treatises on the construction of Spanish rosettes and on French polishing are considered by many to be the reference works on these subjects.

class A amplifier *n*. Class of audio amplifier circuit in which the active component conducts throughout the phase change of the input signal. Class A amplifiers offer low distortion of the input signal but are very inefficient, dissipating most of their power as heat. This circuit is used in preamplifiers but due to its inefficiency is rarely used in power amplifiers for musical instruments.

class AB amplifier *n*. Class of audio amplifier circuit which includes two active components, one to amplify the portion of the signal above zero level and one to amplify the portion below. Class AB amplifiers offer good efficiency but distort the input signal a bit around the zero level. This circuit is commonly found in power amplifiers for musical instruments. Syn.: push-pull amplifier.

class D amplifier *n*. Class of audio amplifier circuit which digitally encodes the input signal and uses it to drive a fast switching power supply. Class D amplifier circuits offer high efficiency and are often used for power amplifiers for musical instruments.

classic guitar *n*. see classical guitar

classical guitar *n*. The modern classical guitar is a six string acoustic flattop roundhole instrument of moderate body size with nylon strings. It is played with the fingers. It generally has a scale length of either 650 or 660 mm. The classical guitar has a slotted peghead and uses geared tuners. Size, shape, materials and style of decoration have been fairly stable since the time of Torres. The back and sides of modern classical guitars are generally made of rosewood and the top of either spruce or red cedar. The neck is generally made of mahogany or Spanish cedar and the fingerboard of ebony. The playing surface of the fingerboard is generally flat. The neck joins the body at the 12th fret. Syn.: classic guitar. See also: Torres.

clavijero *n*. (clahv-ee-HAIR-oh) Peg head, peg box (Spanish).

clay dot *n*. Early Fender guitars and basses used fingerboard dot markers that have a light clay color. It is unknown what these markers were actually made of. See also: dot marker.

cleat *n*. Small thin patch of wood used to prevent a crack from opening up or to prevent a repaired crack from re-opening. After the crack is repaired one or more cleats are glued cross grain over the crack on the inside of the instrument. Cleats for the top plate are usually made from thin pieces of softwood.

climb cut *n*. In routing, a climb cut is a cut where the direction of rotation of the bit tends to move the router in the same direction that you are pushing it. It is a potentially dangerous cut since it is possible for the tool

C

to "run away" from the operator. It is used to prevent tearout that would occur if a conventional cut is used.

climbing cut *n*. see climb cut

close copy *n*. see bench copy

closed jawari *n*. Relatively flat shape of the top of the bridge of a sitar. Syn.: band.

closing bar *n*. see cutoff bar

CNC *abbr*. (see-en-see) see computer numerical control

CNC machine *n*. A computer controlled machine. Machining actions are controlled by a program on the controlling computer, so the operations of the machine are also programmable. See also: computer numerical control.

CNC router *n*. A general purpose CNC machine, the CNC router can move a wood router under programmed control to any location in its machinable area. It is a general purpose woodworking production machine. Nearly all large instrument manufacturers use CNC routers as do a number of smaller builders. See also: CNC machine, laser cutting machine.

coalescing finish *n*. Any finishing material in which the liquid form is an emulsion containing solids that coalesce to form a homogeneous mass in the cured finish. All waterborne finishes are coalescing finishes. See also: waterborne finish.

Coated Abrasive Manufacturers Institute *n*. Standards organization which provides the most commonly used system for grading sandpaper grits in the USA. Syn.: CAMI. See also: sandpaper grit.

coated fingerboard *n*. Fretless electric basses that use round wound strings often have the fingerboard playing surface coated with a hard clear finish, such as polyester or epoxy. This prevents the wood of the fingerboard from being gouged up by the strings.

coaxial cable *n*. Electrical cable consisting of an inner conducting wire surrounded by an insulating material, which is in turn surrounded by braided wire shielding and an outer insulating material. Coaxial cable provides excellent shielding against electrical noise because the inner signal wire is completely surrounded by the shielding. This cable is used for guitar and microphone cables and for wiring inside acoustic guitars.

cobalt dryer *n*. see metallic dryer

cochineal *n*. Red pigment from the insect *Dactylopius coccus*, used in traditional varnishes.

cocobolo *n*. see *Dalbergia retusa*

coffin case *n*. Musical instrument case featuring an outline composed of only straight lines. The side walls of these cases are made of straight pieces of board. Musical instrument cases built before the 20th century were usually of this style. They were usually made of painted wood and had sparse padding inside.

Coffin case.

Cohen, Dave Fort Bragg CA, USA, mandolin luthier, musical instrument acoustics researcher, and author.

coin *n*. (kwon) Corner, corner block (French).

cold creep *n*. Movement or permanent dimensional change (also called plastic deformation) over time, at moderate temperatures. Wood used in musical instruments is subject to cold creep. Some glues are subject to cold creep.

cold molded *adj*. Referring to laminated parts that are formed (molded) without heat. Instrument ribs are often laminated from veneers forced into a mold. Syn.: cold laminated.

Colombian tiple *n*. (TEE-play) An instrument from the Andean region of Colombia, the tiple looks a lot like a small classical guitar, but with a solid headstock and four courses of three steel strings each. The instrument is played solo and in various ensembles including the Colombian Andean quartet, consisting of two bandolas, one tiple and one classical guitar. See also: bandola.

Colombian tiple.

colophon *n*. see rosin

colophony *n*. see rosin

common mode rejection *n*. Principle of operation of humbucking guitar pickups. Noise induced into the two coils of such a pickup cancels out due to the noise signal being inverted in one of the coils. See also: humbucking pickup.

compass *n*. The pitch range of an instrument - the range between the lowest and highest note the instrument is capable of making.

compass gramil *n*. Hand tool used to make a circular knife cut. The tool consists of a body which holds the

knife blade and a pivot pin. The distance from blade to pin is adjustable as is the depth of cut of the knife blade. In use the pin is placed in a drilled hole at the center of the circle and the tool is rotated around the pivot pin. Each pass is made a bit deeper than the previous one until the desired depth of cut is achieved. In lutherie this tool is used to cut out round sound holes and to cut the walls of soundhole rosette pockets. See also: circle cutter, gramil.

compensated bridge *n*. An instrument bridge which provides compensation. See also: compensation.

compensated nut *n*. An instrument nut which provides compensation. See also: compensation.

compensated saddle *n*. A saddle of an instrument bridge which provides compensation. See also: compensation.

compensation *n*. Change in saddle and/or nut position from calculated locations to compensate for the sharping affect of fretting strings and the bending stiffness of strings. Instruments which use less elastic strings such as those made of steel generally need more compensation than do instruments with more elastic strings. Bridge

The "business end" of a compass gramil, showing the center pin and the cutting blade. The distance between these two parts is adjustable for different size circles.

saddle compensation is generally found on all fretted instruments with steel strings and on most nylon strung instruments as well. Nut compensation is found on some steel and nylon strung instruments. In general, compensation values are not included in descriptions of the scale length of instruments, but are given as separate values. For all practical purposes compensation values are not precisely calculable, as the inputs to such calculations require the longitudinal stiffness of the core of the string, values for which are not readily available and vary from string set to string set and are affected by action and relief. In addition, same-note pitch variability is quite high for steel string instruments. Instruments with fixed bridges such as flattop guitars generally use some conventional value for compensation that has worked well in the past.

composite *n.* A material made of more than one component materials. An example is graphite epoxy composite, a material made of woven graphite cloth and epoxy resin.

compound radius fretboard *n.* see conical section fretboard

compression trussrod *n.* see single acting trussrod

computer aided design Computer Aided Design/Drafting/Drawing. CAD software provides facilities for drawing manufacturing designs using a computer. CAD drawings can be printed out on paper or can be used directly by other manufacturing software to build parts. All large lutherie shops use CAD software and a large number of small shops and hand builders also use it. Syn.: CAD.

computer aided manufacturing *n.* Computer Aided Manufacturing. Software that converts CAD drawn components into instructions that can be fed into CNC machinery to produce parts. Some CAM software also has facilities for running a CNC machine. Syn.: CAM.

computer numerical control *adj.* CNC. Using computers to control machines via a signal connection and a program running on the computer. CNC machines can run unattended and can be reprogrammed to manufacture different parts or configurations. Syn.: CNC.

concert guitar *n.* An ill-defined marketing term, used to denote a high-priced instrument or an instrument of superior tone or projection.

concert size guitar *n.* One of the general size classifications for steel string guitars, adopted from C.F. Martin size designations. The body of a concert size guitar is approximately 18.5″ long and 14″ wide at the lower bout. Syn.: O.

concert ukulele *n.* Slightly larger than the soprano ukulele. It is generally tuned GCEA and has an overall length of approx. 23″ (584mm). Typical scale length is 15″ (380mm). Typical body dimensions include length of 11″ (279mm) and width of 7.625″ (194mm) at the lower bout. Syn.: alto ukulele.

Condino, James Ashville NC, USA, guitar, mandolin and double bass luthier and repairman. James Condino is also an author and lutherie teacher.

cone heel *n.* The heel of an instrument that is shaped like a section of a cone. The neck shaft is usually built as a separate part, then the heel and shaft are joined together. Syn.: ice cream cone heel.

conical section fretboard *n.* A fretboard the playing surface of which describes a conical section, that is, a piece of the surface of a cone. Conical fretboards are considered to provide optimally low action since they better reflect the curvature described by the strings of an instrument than do cylindrical radius fretboards. But research indicates that the difference between the two is smaller than the tolerances of fretboard manufacture and fret leveling. Syn.: compound radius fretboard.

Cone heel.

Control cavity of a solid body electric guitar.

contact thermometer *n*. A thermometer that measures the temperature of a surface when the thermometer is in contact with it. These are used in lutherie to measure the temperature of wood in side bending machines during bending.

contralto violin *n*. Violin family instrument similar to the viola but with an oversized body. The instrument is attributed to Jean Baptiste Vuillaume. See also: Jean Baptiste Vuillaume.

contre éclisse n. (cone-TREY-clees) Lining (French).

controfasce *n*. (cone-tro-FA-shuh) Lining (Italian).

control cavity *n*. Pocket routed into the body of a solid body electric guitar to provide space for the electronics hardware. Syn.: electronics pocket.

Convention on International Trade in Endangered Species *n*. An international agreement to preserve endangered species of plants and animals. Species listed can not be traded among member countries except under special circumstances and in specified quantities. The materials most commonly used by luthiers that are CITES listed are ivory and Brazilian rosewood

(*Dalbergia nigra*) but other species are listed as well. Syn.: CITES.

copal *n*. Resin used as a component of violin varnishes. Copal is from trees found in central and south America, the Caribbean, and east Africa.

corda *n*. (CORD-a) String (Italian).

cordal block *n*. see tie block

cordiera *n*. (cord-ee-ER-ah) Tailpiece (Italian).

core *n*. The central part of an assembly. For wound strings, the core is the central part of the string. For solid body electric guitars with neck-through construction, the core is the part of the neck structure that continues through the body.

corner *n*. The acute transition between the upper bout and center bout, or lower bout and center bout of a violin family instrument. See also: bout.

cornerless *adj*. see soft corner

corner block *n*. Block used as a gluing surface between the rib material of the center bout and the rib material of either the upper or lower bout of a violin family instrument. See also: rib, bout.

corning *n*. Spotty buildup of sanding dust on the surface of sandpaper, usually when dry sanding. Corning is

Sandpaper used to sand epoxy exhibits corning on the surface.

caused by either the melting and reforming of the sanded material when sanding finish, or the polymerization of finish or wood dust due to the heat of sanding when sanding some woods and some finishes. Corning can be reduced by the use of stearated sandpaper or by wet sanding in cases where it is feasible to use these materials and methods. See also: dry sanding, polymerization, stearated sandpaper, wet sanding.

coromandel *n.* see *Diospyros celebica*

cotton waste *n.* Cotton fiber mass commonly used as the padding inside the tampon used in French polishing. Cotton waste is available from craft suppliers and from specialty woodworking suppliers. See also: French polishing, tampon.

coupling *v.* A stringed musical instrument can be modeled as a collection of oscillators for purposes of electronic synthesis of tones or for purposes of controlling the tone of a real instrument. Each of these oscillators is realized by a mode of vibration of some part of the instrument structure or of the air inside it. Such simple modeling is not perfect, and one reason is that all of these oscillators are coupled to each other in various ways, and so the behavior of each oscillator is dependent on other oscillators and the nature of the coupling.

course *n.* A group of strings that are all fretted at the same time. For example a 12 string guitar has six courses of two strings each, and a mandolin has four courses of two strings each. If an instrument has a combination of single strings and multi-string courses, the single strings are also each referred to as a course.

Courtnall, Roy British luthier and author, specializing in Spanish guitars. The author of the book *Making Master Guitars*.

crack repair *n.* Fine cracks in the plates or ribs of stringed instruments are often repaired by simple gluing and clamping. Wider cracks are repaired by gluing thin wedges of matching wood into the crack. The crack is generally opened up with a knife to give it a V shaped profile. A sliver of wood is prepared that will fill the crack when it is wedged into it. The sliver is glued in, and excess wood is shaved off after the glue dries. Repaired cracks are often backed up with cross grain cleats to provide additional support to prevent the crack from opening up again. See also: cleat.

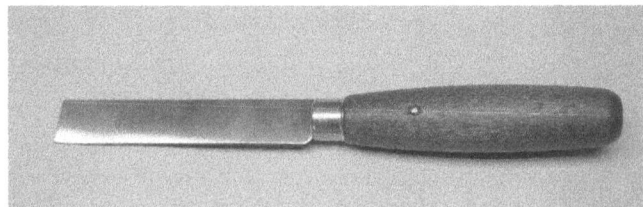

Crack repair knife.

crack repair knife *n.* A specialty knife used for crack repair. The blade of the crack repair knife is ground to a wedged profile.

cramp *n.* Clamp (British).

cranked top *n.* An instrument top plate that has a relatively sharp bend in it, perpendicular to the grain.

Almost all bowl backed mandolins have cranked tops. Sharp bends in wood are generally implemented by excavating a thin channel part way through the wood and then bending the wood at that channel using heat and moisture. Syn.: canted top.

crazing *v*. Development of small cracks in a finish as it hardens. Crazing is usually the result of too much finish applied too quickly, or drying too quickly.

creep *n*. see cold creep

cross brace *n*. see X brace

cross grain *adj*. Referring to the direction perpendicular to the wood grain.

cross grain stiffness *n*. Stiffness to bending across the grain. This property is generally not important for beams (braces, neck shaft, etc.) which support loads which induce bending along the grain. But it is an important property of plates and is considered to be particularly important for instrument top plates. Stiffness across the grain is generally much less than along the grain. Although longitudinal stiffness is not generally affected by the orientation of the grain lines, cross grain stiffness is. Quartersawn wood generally has higher cross grain stiffness than flatsawn wood does. See also: cross grain, flat sawn, quarter sawn, stiffness.

cross linked *adj*. Describes a state of cured finishing material in which molecules of the un-cured finish link to each other to form larger molecules in the cured finish.

crwth *n*. Ancient bowed stringed instrument.

cuatro *n*. (QUAT-roh) Small Latin American guitar-like instrument. The cuatro of Venezuela is a four nylon stringed instrument. The cuatro of Puerto Rico has ten steel strings in five courses.

cuerda *n*. (QUWHERE-da) String (Spanish).

cümbüş *n*. Turkish banjo-style instrument family, originally conceived as an inexpensive alternative to the

Venezuelan cuatro.

oud. There are a number of different instruments of this construction including mandolin and ukulele versions. See also: oud.

Cumpiano, William Amherst MA, USA, guitar luthier, author and teacher. Cumpiano is coauthor of the book *Guitarmaking Tradition and Technology*.

Cupressus macrocarpa *n*. Softwood sometimes used for backs and sides of guitars. It is generally referred to as Monterey cypress. It grows on the central coast of California.

curly maple *n*. Any species of maple (*Acer* spp.) exhibiting a curly figure due to compression of the wood. Syn.: fiddleback maple, flamed maple, tiger maple.

curtate cycloid arching *n*. Arching profiles for violin family instruments and other archtop instruments that follow a curtate cycloid curve. The curtate cycloid curve is made by a point on a rolling circle that is somewhere between the center and the outside edge. The length of the curve depends on the radius of the circle and the height of the arch depends on how far from the center the drawing point is located. Interest in curtate cycloid arching is a result of a *CASJ* paper by Quentin Playfair that compared portions of curtate cycloid curves with

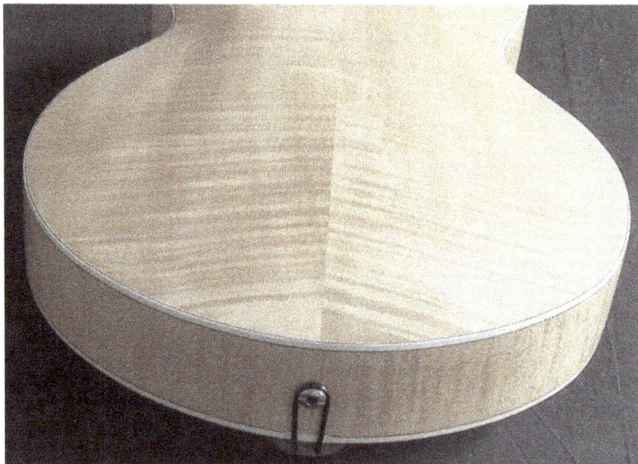

Archtop jazz guitar featuring curly maple back, sides and neck.

portions of selected arching profiles of selected golden age Cremonese violin family instruments.

Curtin, Joseph USA violin maker, researcher, author and educator. Based in Ann Arbor MI, Curtin builds violin family instruments. His research into the physics and psychoacoustics of the violin and experimentation in design and materials is well regarded. He won a MacArthur fellowship in 2005. He is a member of the Violin Society of America and is a director of that organization's annual Oberlin Acoustics Workshop.

cut *n.* Specifies the dilution of shellac in alcohol. A one pound cut is one pound of shellac flakes mixed with one gallon of alcohol. Probably the most common cut is the two pound cut (two pounds of shellac flakes to one gallon of alcohol), which is used for general application of shellac by spraying, brushing or French polishing. A two pound cut can be approximated by pouring some shellac flakes into a container and then adding alcohol to twice the level of the shellac flakes. See also: French polish.

cutaway *n.* An indentation in the body of an instrument near the neck which provides better access to the upper frets (those frets over the body of the instrument). A single cutaway body provides such an indentation on one side of the neck only. For instruments designed to be played by right handed players, the single cutaway is on the right side of the body when facing the body. A double cutaway body is cut away on both sides of the neck. Stylistically, the two major classes of cutaway are the Florentine (pointy) cutaway and the Venetian (rounded) cutaway. See also: Florentine cutaway, Venetian cutaway.

cutoff bar *n.* A brace of a typical fan braced top plate. The cutoff bars run diagonally across the bottom of the plate from a point near the tail end of the center fan brace to a point near the side at the width of the lower bout. An instrument with cutoff bars usually has two, one on each side. Syn.: closing bar. See also: fan bracing.

cut through *v.* During rubbing out or any other abrasive leveling of a finish, abrading so much that you remove all the finish in spots and expose the wood underneath. (Don't you hate when this happens?) The general fix is to reapply finish to the whole surface and then rub out again.

cyanoacrylate glue *n.* A clear, fast drying glue, also known by one of its brand names, Crazy Glue. Cyanoacrylate glue is used for many lutherie applications including the gluing of bindings and inlay, and the repair of catalyzed finishes. The glue is available in different viscosities. Thick CA glue is used for filling gaps; medium viscosity is used as a general adhesive. Thin CA glue is useful in crack repair as it will wick into very fine gaps. Syn.: CA glue, Crazy Glue, super glue.

D

D2S *adj.* see S2S

D4S *adj.* see S4S

D neck *adj.* Typical cross section profile of the neck of a guitar or other plucked instrument. The D neck profile has the shape of the letter 'D' rolled onto its side, with rather square sides and a rounded bottom. See also: boat neck, flattened oval.

D neck *n.* Describes the length of the neck of the double bass. When the thumb is against the heel of a bass with a D neck, the first finger will be in position to play a D on the G string.

Dalbergia baronii *n.* The species most generally known as Madagascar rosewood although there are a number of other species known by that name including *Dalbergia maritima*. The wood is hard and heavy and is often figured or at least striped in appearance. Specific gravity of dry wood is 0.93 and modulus of elasticity is 12 GPa. It is used for guitar backs and sides and also for fingerboards and bridges. It is CITES listed. See also: *Dalbergia maritima*.

Dalbergia latifolia *n.* An Indian rosewood commonly used in lutherie. The wood is hard, heavy, stiff and strong. Colors range from dark brown to lighter shades of brown with black, brown and purple streaking. It is used for guitar backs and sides and also for fingerboards and bridges. The trees are grown for shade in Indian tea plantations and production of the wood is managed by the Indian government. Specific gravity of dry wood is 0.83 and modulus of elasticity is 11.5 GPa. Syn.: East Indian Rosewood, EIR, Indian rosewood.

Dalbergia maritima *n.* The species most generally known as bois de rose, this is a rosewood from Madagascar. The wood is hard and heavy with beautiful colors of reds, browns and purples when fresh cut that oxidize to dark brown and near black with age and exposure. It is used in guitar backs and sides and also in fingerboards and bridges. Specific gravity of dry wood is 0.93. This species is CITES listed.

Dalbergia melanoxylon *n.* African blackwood, mpingo. A member of the rosewood family, this wood is hard and dark in color and is sometimes used for flattop guitar backs and sides and also as a substitute for ebony in fingerboards and headplates. Specific gravity of dry wood is 1.27 and modulus of elasticity is 18 GPa.

Dalbergia nigra *n.* Brazilian rosewood. This rosewood is hard, dense and red/brown in color. It was the traditional wood for top of the line steel string guitars and classical guitars for some time, but it is now essentially unavailable except at extremely high prices. It grows in Brazil, but it is endangered by loss of habitat as forests have been converted to farmland. It is CITES listed. The dry wood has a typical specific gravity of 0.84 and a modulus of elasticity of 13.9 GPa.

Dalbergia retusa *n.* This and a few other related species supply the wood commonly known as cocobolo. It is a member of the rosewood family. It is a South American wood that is hard, stiff and strong. It is used for guitar backs and sides and also for fingerboards. Oil and dust from this wood can cause an allergic reaction in some people. Specific gravity of dry wood is 1.1, and modulus of elasticity is 18.7 GPa.

Dalbergia sissoo *n.* An Indian rosewood, not often used in lutherie. It is hard, stiff, dense and strong. Heart wood is golden in color with brown, black and purple streaks. Although not native to the USA it does grow in Florida where it is considered to be an invasive species. Specific gravity of dry wood is 0.77 and modulus of elasticity is 10.4 GPa. Syn.: sissoo.

damping *n.* The reduction of vibrating motion by dissipation of energy. Damping is a fundamental property of vibrating systems. In lutherie we are primarily concerned with material damping of the materials used to construct the instrument and of the whole instrument as well.

D'Angelico, John (1905-1964) USA luthier, noted for his archtop jazz guitars. D'Angelico's instruments were often heavily decorated and in the art deco style. He also made mandolins.

D'Aquisto, James (1935-1995) USA archtop guitar luthier and educator. D'Aquisto worked for John D'Angelico before building under his own name. He is best known for innovations to the archtop guitar, including reshaped sound holes, simplified bindings and other decorations, and an all-wood bridge with adjustable action.

Davis, Rick Seattle WA, USA, guitar luthier and former editor of *Guitarmaker* magazine.

dead flat *adj.* Describes the surface of the finish during/after level sanding. A dead flat surface shows no shiny spots, which indicate places where sanding has not yet reached. See also: level sanding.

dB *abbr.* see decibel

decibel *n.* Ten times the logarithm to base 10 of the ratio of two power quantities. A measure of relative sound level. Syn.: dB.

de-damping *v.* Controversial mechanical treatment of an instrument intended to improve its tone by vibrating it with an external device. Efficacy of the process has not been definitively established. It is based on research demonstrating a decrease in damping of wood samples vigorously vibrated for a period of time.

deflection analysis *n.* Analyzing the deflection of the plate of an instrument as a means of achieving good and consistent tone and structural integrity. The basic method involves placing a weight on the plate at one or more points and measuring the deflection using a dial indicator. Proponents of this technique generally use measurements taken from an instrument recognized to possess good tone as target measurements in the building of subsequent instruments. See also: bridge rotation analysis.

deflection testing *n.* see deflection analysis

degrees of freedom *n.* The number of independent parameters which define the behavior of a mechanical system. The term appears in lutherie literature usually to describe simple mechanical models for the vibration of an instrument. Common models include those with two and three degrees of freedom. Syn.: DOF.

denaturant *n.* Any substance added to ethanol (ethyl alcohol) to render it undrinkable. See also: denatured alcohol.

denatured alcohol *n.* Alcohol that is made non-drinkable by the addition of other chemicals. Denatured alcohol is typically composed of ethanol (grain alcohol) with 5% to 15% methanol (wood alcohol) added. Other denaturants are often used, usually in small quantities. Some brands of denatured alcohol contain up to 50% methyl alcohol. Denatured alcohol is used as a solvent for shellac and is a component of lacquer thinner. See also: ethanol, methanol.

dendrochronological analysis *n.* Analysis of the growth rings of trees. In general, a tree will produce one growth ring per year. From an analysis of the rings of a living or just felled tree it is possible to determine how old the tree is and the calendar year at which each ring was formed. Syn.: dendrochronology.

dent steaming *v.* Dents in wood are generally best dealt with by steaming, which tends to push the dent out, often to the extent that it is no longer visible. A wet rag is place over the dent and then the back of the rag is rubbed with a hot iron. For small dents of the size normally seem in lutherie, a soldering iron makes a good dent steaming tool.

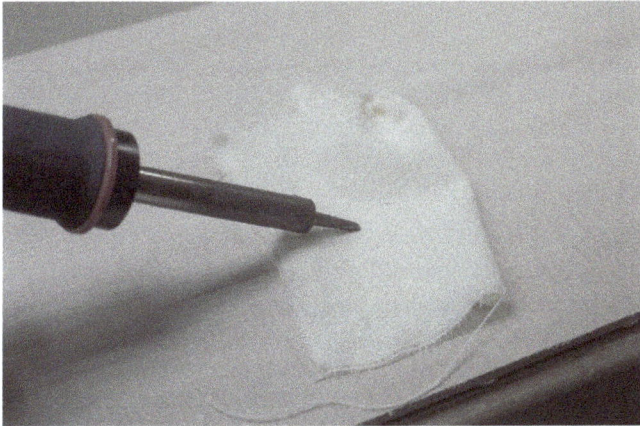

Steaming a dent out of the surface of a spruce guitar top using a soldering iron and wet rag.

dental bur *n*. A bit used to excavate pockets for inlay work and for other small grinding jobs. The bit is originally intended for use in dentistry.

dentellone *n*. see tentellón

descant *adj*. Describing the highest pitched instrument of an instrument family, such as the descant viol.

desktop CNC machine *n*. A small CNC machine, usually a CNC router or CNC milling machine, which is small enough and light enough to be used on a desk. Desktop CNC machines are used by small lutherie shops that can't afford or don't have the room for larger machines. They are used for inlay and the production of small parts like bridges and tailpieces. See also: CNC machine.

DET *abbr*. Double end trim. Term used to describe lumber that has both ends trimmed perpendicular to the board sides.

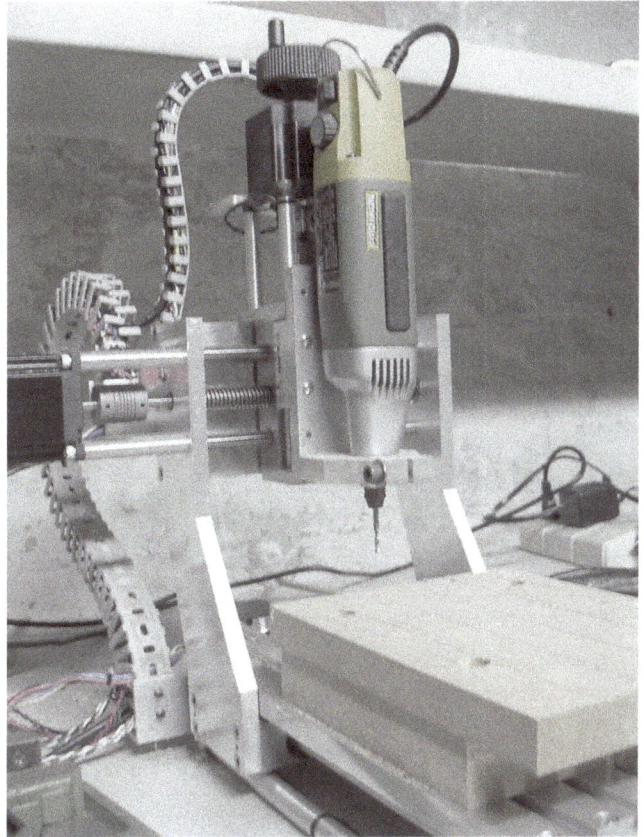

Desktop CNC machine.

dewaxed shellac *n*. Shellac from which wax has been removed. Some dry shellac is available dewaxed. Shellac can be dewaxed by dissolving it in alcohol, letting it stand until the wax precipitates out, and then decanting it, leaving the wax behind. See also: shellac

dial gauge *n*. A tool used to measure small changes in length or distance. The maximum displacement of typical dial gauges is 0.5 to 2 inches (13 to 51 mm), and resolution is typically 0.001 to 0.0001 inches (0.0254 - 0.00254 mm).

D

A dial gauge is used to measure the deflection of an electric guitar neck when the weight of a small plane is placed on the fretboard.

dial indicator *n.* see dial gauge

diamond peghead *n.* Guitar peghead which has a raised diamond shaped feature on the underside of the peghead where it meets the shaft of the neck. This feature is a signature of Martin guitars and is also seen on instruments that are derived from Martin guitar designs. The modern implementation of this feature is purely decorative, but in early instruments this was part of the peghead joint. See also: diamond peghead joint.

diamond peghead joint *n.* A joint used to join peghead to neck shaft on early Martin guitars.

diapasón n. (dee-ah-pa-SOWN) Fretboard (Spanish).

dichroic *adj.* Describing a varnish that appears to change color with viewing angle. The varnish of the violins of Stradivari are said to display a dichroic effect.

Dickens, Frederick (1935-2000) USA classical guitar maker, engineer, and instrument acoustics researcher. Dickens is most known for work on the tuning of free plate modes of violins and guitars using Chladni patterns. See also: Chladni patterns, free plate tuning.

Didelotia africana *n.* see *Guibourtia demeusei*

Diospyros celebica *n.* Macassar ebony, also called coromandel or calamander. It is hard and dense, with brown and black stripes. The wood is used for guitar backs and sides and fretboards. It has a specific gravity of 1.12, and modulus of elasticity of 17.35 GPa.

Diospyros spp. *n.* Ebony wood. Ebony is from a number of species of the genus *Diospyros*, and there are a number of other black or nearly black woods that are called ebony as well. *Diospyros ebenum* is more generally called Ceylon, Sri Lanka, or Indian ebony. It is hard, dense, brittle and black or nearly black in color. World supplies are being decimated and the wood is expensive and sometimes difficult to obtain. It is used in lutherie for fingerboards and headstock veneers, also for the fittings of violin family instruments and archtop guitars. Ebony shrinks a lot when drying and takes a long time to air dry.

dipole *n.* Vibrating element which contains two areas of movement. In lutherie this is usually used to describe a mode of vibration of a plate, where one half of the plate moves in while the other half moves out, and then reverses. Dipoles are considered to be inefficient radiators of sound because positive pressure caused by the outward movement of one pole is canceled out by negative pressure of the other pole moving in. See also: monopole.

dish sander *n.* The plates of modern flattop instruments are not really flat but are instead slightly domed. To glue a domed plate onto the garland (rib, linings and blocks subassembly) the gluing surface must first be sanded with a dished sanding board with the same radius as the doming of the plate. This can be done by hand, but production shops often have a dish sander, which has a spinning sandpaper covered dish. The garland is clamped inside a mold and then lowered onto the spinning sanding dish to profile the gluing surface.

dished form *n.* see dished workboard

dished workboard *n.* The plates of modern flattop instruments are not really flat but are instead slightly domed. The plates are domed by being assembled on a dished workboard. Braces and patches are glued onto the plate while it is sitting face down on a dished workboard. The clamps used to glue the braces down also bend the plate into the workboard so it takes on the dish shape. When the glue dries and the plate is removed it retains its dished shape. Turning the plate face up shows the plate domed on the outside surface.

dital harp *n.* see harp lute

divergence *n.* see string divergence

division viol *n.* Small size bass viol. See also: viol.

Dobro *n.* A Dobro is a brand name of a resonator guitar, but the term is sometimes used to denote any resonator guitar. The Dobro was built by the Dobro Manufacturing Company which was started by the Dopyera Brothers in 1928. The brand name is now owned by Gibson. See also: resonator guitar.

DOF *abbr.* see degrees of freedom

domed plate *n.* The plates of modern flattop instruments are not really flat but are instead slightly domed. Top plate radii typically range from 20' to 30' (6.1 - 9.1 m), and back plate radii range from 12' to 20' (3.7 - 6.1 m).

Doolin, Mike Portland OR, USA, luthier, author and musician best known for innovative double cutaway acoustic guitars and fully adjustable neck joints.

Dopyera, John (1893–1988) Inventor of the resonator guitar. See also: resonator guitar.

dot marker *n.* A small round marker on the playing surface of an instrument fingerboard. Dot markers are probably the most common type of position marker as they fit into a drilled hole and are thus easy to install. Dot markers are typically made of plastic or shell. See also: side dot.

Abalone dot markers at the 12th and 15th frets of a guitar.

double acting truss rod *n.* Truss rod that can be adjusted to provide more back bow or more front bow. See also: back bow, front bow, truss rod.

double bass *n.* Variously called the double bass, bass viol, upright bass, bass fiddle, dog house or sometimes just plain bass, this is the lowest pitched orchestral bowed instrument. It is also the traditional bass instrument of bluegrass and jazz and is played (mostly) pizzicato in these styles. The name double bass comes from the fact that the instrument is tuned an octave below its written notation on the bass staff.

double bass viol *n.* Six string predecessor to the modern double bass. See also: viol.

double cutaway *adj.* see cutaway

double neck guitar *n.* A guitar with two necks. Double neck instruments are most often solid body electric guitars with one six string and one twelve string neck, but other configurations are found as well.

double top *n*. Top construction for flattop instruments which uses three layers. The inside and outside layer are usually thin veneers of wood species generally used in lutherie like spruce or cedar. The inside layer is often a honeycomb of Kevlar, but some builders use other lightweight materials such as balsa. The layers are glued together.

doubling *v*. Restoring a plate of a considerably worn or damaged instrument by removing wood from the back of the plate, fitting new wood to the back surface to replace the old wood, and gluing the new wood in. The result is a laminated plate with the same or similar thickness to the original, and retaining the original finish. This type of repair is generally reserved for instruments that would lose considerable value if the plate was simply replaced.

dovetail *n*. see dovetail joint

dovetail joint *n*. A mortise and tenon joint in which the sides of both mortise and tenon are not parallel to each other but instead diverge.

dovetail neck joint *n*. Neck joint using a dovetail. The tenon is at the end of the neck and the mortise is in the body at the neck block. There are three types of dovetail neck joints commonly seen. In the violin, the end of the tenon and the end of the mortise are in the triangular shape of a dove's tail, but the sides of both mortise and tenon are straight. In this type of joint it is the shear strength of the glue that holds the joint together. The other type is the compound dovetail joint used in the steel string guitar. In this joint the side walls of the mortise and tenon also exhibit the dovetail shape. This is a mechanical joint that, if well fitted, will hold together without glue. These joints are however always glued in practice. The third type of dovetail joint is found in some electric guitars with set (glued in) necks. Here a dovetail shaped tenon is cut into the bottom of the end of the neck. The top surface of the body has a matching mortise.

doweled joint *n*. Wood joint in which both parts have aligned holes drilled into their mating surfaces. Sections of dowel are glued into the holes to both strengthen and align the joint. Doweled joints are often found on lutes and ouds.

down spiral router bit *n*. Router bit used to excavate shallow pockets and groves with clean upper edges. In operation the groves of the bit spiral down, which does not work well for chip removal but also does not tend to tear up the grain on the upper edge of the pocket being excavated, particularly in soft wood. Syn.: spiral down router bit, downcut router bit. See also: up spiral router bit.

downdraft sanding table *n*. Workbench designed specifically for power sanding. The top of the bench features a series of small holes connected to a vacuum or other dust collection machinery. Sanding dust is sucked down into the table, away from the operator and the work.

dozuki *n*. Japanese pull saw. This is a backsaw used for cutting tenons, dovetails and other fine work. See also: Japanese pull saw.

Japanese dozuki backsaw.

dragon's blood *n.* Red resin used as a coloring agent in varnish. The resin is from plants of the species *Calamus rotang* and species of the genera *Croton*, *Dracaena*, *Daemonorops*, and *Pterocarpus*.

drawknife *n.* A knife with a handle on both ends used to carve objects of basically cylindrical form, such as the shafts of instruments necks. The drawknife can be used by pulling it toward the user (thus the name) or pushing it away from the user.

dread *abbr.* see dreadnought

dreadnought *adj, n.* One of the "standard" acoustic steel string guitar body shapes. The dreadnought shape is characterized by relatively square shoulders and a relatively flat tail end. It also features a rather wide waist with a large radius curve, which results in a more trapezoidal look. The Martin D-28 is an iconic dreadnought. The term is also used to denote a standard steel string guitar size. The bodies of instruments of this size are approximately 20″ (508mm) long and are 15 ⅝″ (397mm) wide at the lower bout. A common variation is the slope shouldered dreadnought, which features more rounded shoulders. Syn.: dread. See also: slope shouldered.

Dremel *n.* Brand name of a small hand held grinder. The term is also used generically to mean any small electric hand held grinder.

driving point frequency response function *n.* Frequency response function of an instrument taken by placing a sensor on the instrument top, usually on or near the bridge, tapping the top at or near the sensor, and recording and processing the results. See also: frequency response function.

driving the bus *v.* The plates of modern guitars are domed using a dished workboard. Before gluing plates to garland, the ribs, blocks and linings must be sanded to the contours of the dish. This is done with the dished workboard, covered in sandpaper. In production

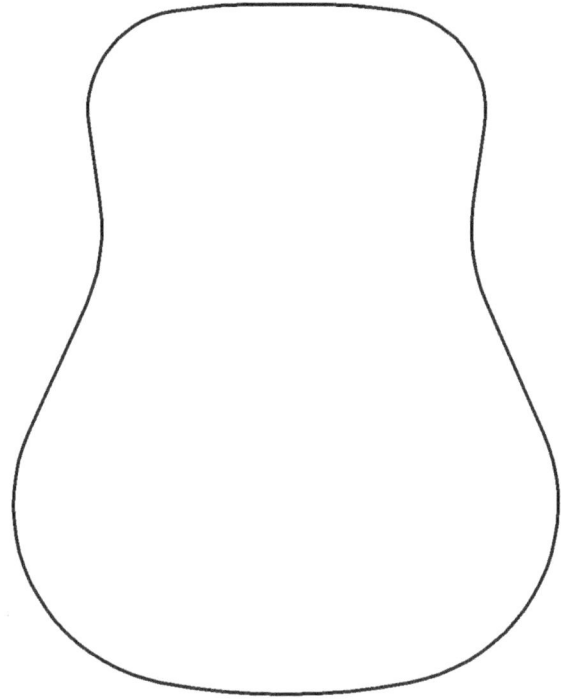

Outline of a dreadnought guitar body.

D

environments this dish is usually motor-driven, but hand builders usually just invert the dish over the garland and sand using a back and forth rotation of the dish. This sanding process is often referred to as "driving the bus." See also: dished workboard, garland.

drop fill *v.* Process of filling small imperfections in a finish with some finishing material. Typical drop filling materials include thickened lacquer and cyanoacrylate. Drops of the filler are applied to the imperfection using a small brush or toothpick. After they are dry the drops are leveled with the surface of the finish. The technique is used while finishing between application of finish coats, and also as a repair technique. See also: cyanoacrylate, lacquer.

Driving the bus. The luthier is sanding the garland of a guitar (inside the mold) using a sandpaper lined dished workboard.

drop top *n*. Bodies of solid body electric guitars are often constructed of a plain looking base wood with a laminated top of figured or otherwise visually appealing wood. The laminated top piece is called a drop top.

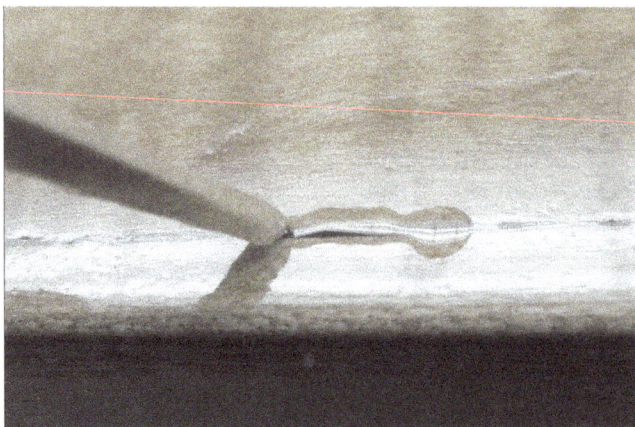

Lacquer drop filling of a small hollow in the finish over the purfling of a guitar.

drum sander *n*. see thickness sander

dry pigment *n*. Powdered dry colorant. These come in various colors and are used to make paint (opaque coating) and to color varnish. Pigments are traditional colorants and will always impart some opacity to a coating depending on how much pigment is used. Completely transparent color can be had using dyes instead of pigments. Syn.: fresco powder, furniture powder. See also: dye, pigment.

dry sanding *v*. Sanding without the use of a lubricating liquid. Wood is almost always dry sanded. Although finishes are often wet sanded to level them, some instructions for finishing specify that the finish should be dry sanded, usually to avoid any negative affect of the lubricating liquid on the underlying wood. Dry sanding on finish makes use of stearated sandpaper. See also: stearated sandpaper, wet sanding.

dry wood *n*. Wood which has been either kiln or air dried to a moisture content suitable for use. For lutherie purposes this is between 12% and 15%. See also: air dried wood, green wood, kiln dried wood.

dryer *n*. see metallic dryer

drying oil *n*. An oil that hardens with exposure to air. Drying oils can be used as finishes by themselves or as components of varnishes. Common drying oils include linseed oil and walnut oil. See also: linseed oil, non-drying oil, walnut oil.

dulcimer *n*. Two stringed instruments share this name. The mountain dulcimer is an hourglass shaped instrument that is played on the lap. It is a simple instrument to make and often serves as an introductory lutherie project. The hammered dulcimer is a large trapezoidal instrument that is played on a stand or table. The strings are hit with special spoon shaped hammers. See also: hammered dulcimer, mountain dulcimer.

duplicating carver *n*. see carving machine

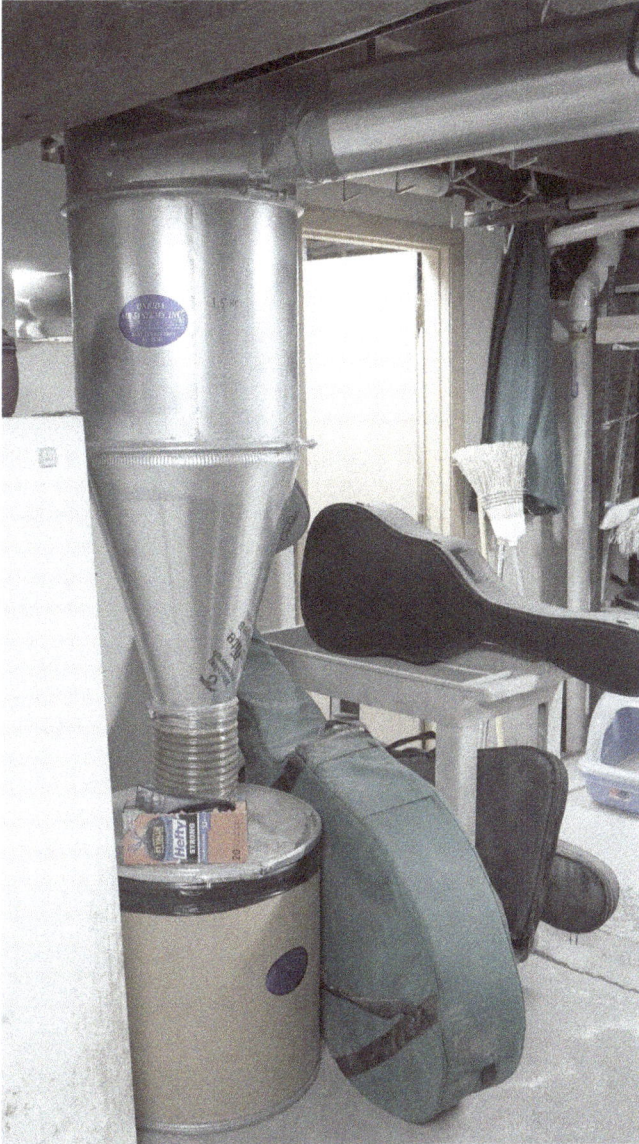

Small cyclone type dust collector.

dust collector *n.* A machine for removing wood dust as it is created by a power tool. Portable dust collectors are usually configured with a centrifugal blower and either a cartridge filter or a filter bag. Stationary dust collector systems usually include a cyclone separator to remove large particles before they reach the filter.

dye *n.* A coloring agent that completely dissolves in the finishing material to which it is added. Technically a dye is a coloring agent the particles of which are smaller than the wavelengths of visible light. Dyes do not affect the transparency of a finishing material. Dye colors tend to be more vibrant than those of pigments, but dyes are generally less colorfast. A distinction can be made between the dye substance and prepared dye or dye solution, which is the dye mixed with a vehicle. See also: dye solution, ink, pigment, vehicle.

dye solution *n.* Ready to use mixture of dye and vehicle solvent. Syn.: prepared dye. See also: dye, ink, vehicle.

Dyer, William J. Late 19th and early 20th century musical instrument retailer in Minneapolis and St. Paul MN, USA. The Dyer stores featured a number of house branded stringed instruments including guitars and mandolins. See also: house brand.

dyestuff *n.* Substance used as a dye. Various chemical, mineral, plant, and animal substances are used as dyes.

D

E

early wood *n*. The softer, lighter, more porous and faster growing part of the annular ring or grain of wood. See also: late wood.

earthing *v*. Electrical grounding (British).

East Indian rosewood *n*. see *Dalbergia latifolia*

eastern hard maple *n*. see *Acer saccharum*

eastern soft maple *n*. see *Acer rubrum*

Eban, Gila Connecticut, USA, luthier specializing in Spanish guitars and using Kasha style bracing. See also: Michael Kasha.

ebonize *v*. To blacken a light color wood so that is resembles ebony. Light wood can be blackened by the application of dye, pigment, or by chemical means.

ebony *n*. see *Diospyros* spp.

éclisse n. (ey-clees-eh) Rib (French).

École-atelier Lutherie-Guitare Bruand see Bruand

ecological validity *n*. In scientific research this term is used to indicate that the conditions of an experiment closely resemble real world conditions. A high degree of ecological validity is generally preferred because experimental results are then more likely to be of practical value. This is of particular value in formal listening experiments of musical instruments. For example, a listening experiment that closely matches conditions under which an instrument would normally be played and heard would have high ecological validity. As a counter example, a listening experiment in which ambient noise level exceeded sound output level of the played instrument would have low ecological validity, because instruments are not usefully played under those conditions.

effe *n*. (EH-fey) F-hole (Italian).

EGB *abbr*. see European Guitar Builders association

egg white *n*. The whites of eggs are used as a sealer in some instrument finishing schedules, and are also used as a binder for mineral coatings.

EIR *abbr*. see *Dalbergia latifolia* (East Indian rosewood)

elastic axis *n*. see neutral axis

elastic modulus *n*. see modulus of elasticity

electric *adj*. An instrument that produces sound primarily with the aid of electronic devices. One way that stringed instruments can be classified is as either acoustic or electric, i.e. acoustic guitar, electric guitar. See also: acoustic.

electric bass guitar *n*. A bass guitar that produces sound primarily with the aid of electronic devices. A typical electric bass guitar is a solid body instrument with magnetic pickups and a 30″ - 35″ (762mm - 889mm) scale length. A 34″ (863.6mm) scale length is standard. The bass guitar is tuned like the double bass. See also: solid body, magnetic pickup, double bass.

electromagnetic noise *n*. Any unwanted electrical noise induced into a magnetic pickup. Typical sources of such noise are electrical power lines, light dimmers, computers, and radio transmission.

electromagnetic shielding *n*. see shielding

electronics pocket *n*. see control cavity

elevated fretboard *n*. see raised fretboard

Elliott, Jeffrey Portland OR, USA, classical guitar luthier, educator and author. His classical guitars make

Solid body electric bass guitar.

use of open harmonic bar construction. Elliott originally worked in the shop of Richard Schneider before building under his own name. See also: open harmonic bar, Richard Schneider.

ellipse cutter *n*. Tool used to mark or cut oval holes.

EMC *abbr*. see equilibrium moisture content

end block *n*. see tail block

end clasp *n*. Body component of bowl back mandolins and similar instruments. The end clasp wraps around the

End clasp of an oud under construction in the shop of Peter Kyvelos.

tail end of the body and covers the point at which the body stave ends meet. It provides additional gluing surface for the top and more mechanical support for the tail piece.

end graft *n*. A decorative feature of flattop guitars and other instruments. The end graft is an inlaid strip of wood at the end seam of the ribs. It often contrasts with the ribs and is often of the same material as the bindings and/or back strip. There are two basic configurations for the end graft, tapered or straight. Syn.: butt graft, tail graft, tail strip.

end grain surface *n*. The surface of a cut piece of wood that displays the end grain. For lumber these are always the ends of the boards. See also: radial surface, tangential surface.

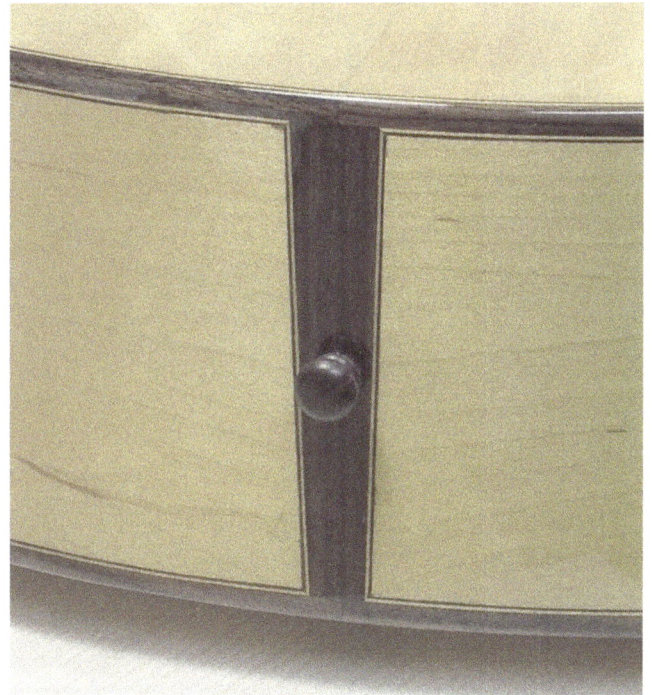

This guitar end graft matches the bindings.

E

End grain surface of an oak block.

end mill *n.* A milling cutter for use in a milling machine. The end mill can make side cuts and usually can also make axial (plunge) cuts as well. End mills are used for various routing and shaping operations in lutherie. They are used in routers and CNC routers and milling machines.

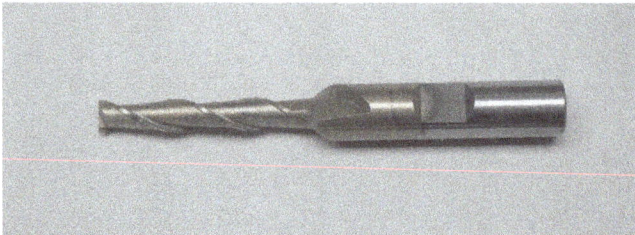

End mill.

end pin *n.* Pin or button on/in the end of the instrument. For violin family instruments and some archtop guitars, the end pin secures the tailgut, which attaches the tailpiece to the body. For other instruments the end pin is used as a strap button, to secure the end of a strap. See also: strap button.

The end pin of this archtop guitar secures the tailgut.

end pin jack *n.* An electrical jack that replaces the end pin of an acoustic guitar. The end pin jack provides a connection with onboard electronics without making an additional hole in the instrument for a jack. See also: end pin.

Engelmann spruce *n.* see *Picea engelmannii*

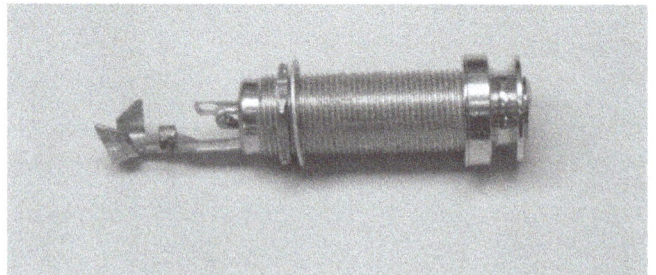

End pin jack.

English guittar *n*. Steel strung cittern type instrument, generally tuned to an open chord and used as accompaniment. The instrument was popular in England during the late 18th and early 19th centuries.

envelope *n*. Describes the change in loudness of a musical tone (played note) over time. The general epochs of the envelope are the attack, sustain, decay, and release, although not all of these epochs will appear in typical envelopes for all stringed instruments. For example, plucked instruments, with the possible exception of electric instruments, do not have a sustain section of the envelope, proceeding directly from attack to decay.

epoxy *n*. A two part glue consisting of a resin and a hardener. Epoxy is used in lutherie as a gap filling glue. With pigment added it is used as a filler for shell inlay. It is also used as a grain filler. Epoxy is a thermosetting polymer that does not shrink when cured.

equal temperament *n*. The most common system of tuning in western music. The octave is divided into twelve semitone parts. Equal temperament is used to tune all common western stringed instruments and is

Epoxy.

used to locate the frets for all common western fretted instruments.

equilibrium moisture content *n*. Moisture content of wood at which it will no longer lose or absorb water from the air. Higher temperatures will lower EMC, higher humidity will raise it. Syn.: EMC. See also: moisture content.

espalda *n*. (es-PAL-dah) Back plate (Spanish).

Erlewine, Dan USA guitar repairman, author and educator. Dan Erlewine has written books and articles on various aspects of guitar repair, setup and finishing and has presented at Guild of American Luthiers conventions. He is on the staff of Stewart MacDonald, a large guitar shop supply house.

Esteso, Domingo (1882–1937) Spanish flamenco guitar luthier. A student of Manuel Ramírez.

ethanol *n*. Also called grain alcohol, ethyl alcohol, or neutral grain spirits, ethanol is a simple alcohol made from the fermentation of grain, usually corn. It is the alcohol found in alcoholic beverages. It is used in lutherie as a solvent and thinner for shellac.

ethyl alcohol *n*. see ethanol

ethylene glycol monobutyl ether *n*. Solvent used to soften cured lacquer finish for repair. It is often used to weld cracked lacquer back together. Syn.: amalgamator, Butyl CELLOSOLVE.

Euphonon see Carl and August Larson

European Guitar Builders association Membership organization of European guitar builders. The organization has two classes of membership. Full membership is available to professional guitarmakers that build their instruments in Europe. Associate membership is available to hobbyist builders, musicians, collectors, and guitar aficionados. Syn.: EGB.

E

European maple *n.* see *Acer platanoides, Acer pseudoplatanus*

European spruce *n.* see *Picea abies*

evaporation rate *n.* Rate at which a solvent evaporates. This is generally expressed on a numerical scale relative to the evaporation rate of n-butyl acetate (BuAc), i.e. the evaporation rate of n-butyl acetate = 1. The evaporation rate of solvents is important to the drying speed of finishing materials, which can be sped up with the use of fast evaporating solvents or slowed down with the use of slow evaporating solvents. Fast evaporating solvents have evaporation rates of greater than 3. Acetone is a fast evaporating solvent with an evaporation rate of 5.6. Medium evaporating solvents have evaporation rates between 0.8 and 3. Ethyl alcohol is a medium evaporating solvent with an evaporation rate of 1.4. Slow evaporating solvents have evaporation rates of less than 0.8. Mineral spirits is a slow evaporating solvent with an evaporation rate of 0.1. In general, materials applied by brushing will use slower evaporating solvents and those that are sprayed will use faster evaporating solvents. Faster evaporating solvents are often added to brushed finishes that are applied at cooler ambient temperatures.

evaporative finish *n.* Any finish which hardens by the evaporation of its solvent, leaving behind the hard solute. Shellac and lacquer are examples of evaporative finishes. See also: lacquer, shellac.

Everclear *n.* Brand name of bottled grain alcohol (ethanol) intended for use as an alcoholic beverage. The product is available in 151 and 190 proof versions. The 190 proof (95% alcohol) is used as a solvent and thinner for shellac for French polishing. It can only be purchased retail in some states. See also: ethanol, French polish, shellac.

Everett, Kent Georgia USA guitar luthier and teacher.

explosion proof *adj.* Explosion proof fans and lights are used when spraying highly flammable materials such as lacquer and shellac.

extender *n.* see fretboard extender

external mold *n.* see outside mold

external lining *n.* Solid linings found on some bass viols that are attached to the outside of the ribs. Instruments with external linings generally also have internal linings. See also: lining, solid lining.

eye *n.* Any small round construction feature. The most common uses of the term in lutherie describe the surfaces at the center of the scroll spiral of violin family instruments (scroll eye), and the round drilled holes at the ends of the f-hole. See also: f hole, scroll.

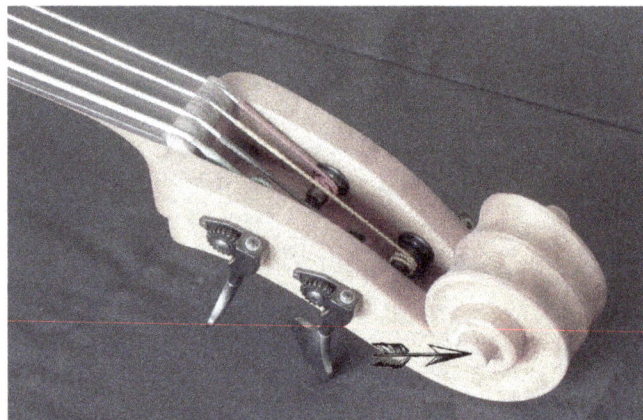

Eye of the scroll of an electric upright bass.

F

F clamp *n.* Bar clamp (British).

f hole *n.* The soundhole, shaped like a stylized 'f' character, used in most violin family instruments. F holes or variations on them are commonly used in mandolins and archtop guitars as well. Syn.: ff hole.

F style mandolin *n.* A mandolin with physical features similar to those of the Gibson F series of instruments. These include an asymmetrical body with a scroll at the upper left bout, and arched top and back plates.

Fabricatore, Gennaro Mid 18th to mid 19th century Italian guitar luthier from Naples.

Fabricatore, Gianbattista Baroque guitar builder from Naples. He was either the father or uncle of Gennaro Fabricatore.

fad *n.* see tampon

falcate brace *n.* Sickle-shaped brace.

fan brace *n.* see fan bracing

fan bracing *n.* A bracing pattern that uses a number of radially arranged braces to brace the area of the top below the soundhole. This is the most typical bracing

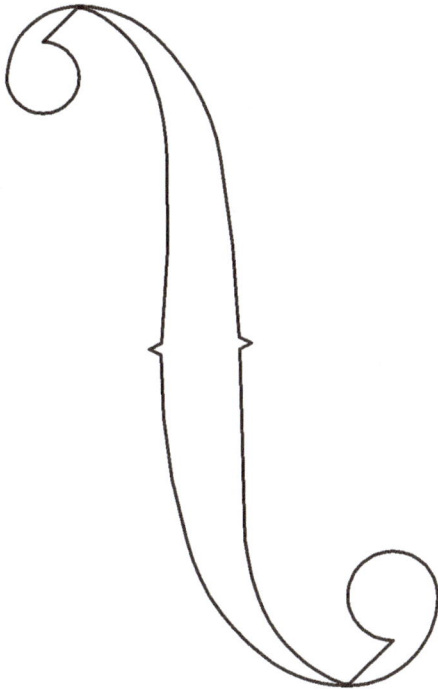

Outline of an f hole in the style of Stradivari.

Luthier begins carving the fan braces of the top of a classical guitar.

pattern for classical guitars, which generally use five to seven braces, but sometimes more or less. The typical bracing pattern uses a transverse brace above the soundhole, another transverse brace below the soundhole, and the fan braces below that. This pattern also often uses two diagonal cutoff bars below the fan braces. See also: A bracing, cutoff bar, ladder bracing, transverse brace, V bracing, X bracing.

fan fret *adj*. Describes a multiple scale length fretboard.

fan tuning machines *n*. see Preston tuning machines

FAS *n*. Originally an abbreviation for "Firsts and Seconds," this is the highest hardwood lumber grade in the National Hardwood Lumber Association (NHLA) hardwood lumber grading system. See also: National Hardwood Lumber Association.

fast Fourier transform *n*. Mathematical method for revealing frequency information from a sample of sound. Fast Fourier transforms are the basis of various frequency analysis devices and software packages. Syn.: FFT.

faux bound fretboard *n*. see self-bound fretboard

FE *abbr*. see first epoch

fecit *v*. (FEY-chit) Latin for "he made it." The word is often found in instrument labels following the name of the luthier.

Federation of European Producers of Abrasives *n*. European standards organization that provides the 'P' system standard for grading sandpaper grits. Note that 'P' grit numbers are roughly equivalent to Coated Abrasives Manufacturing Institute (CAMI) grits up to about 320. From that grit on up the 'P' grit numbers represent substantially coarser grits than the CAMI numbers, e.g. P1000 is approximately equal to CAMI 550. Syn.: FEPA See also: Coated Abrasives Manufacturing Institute, sandpaper grit.

feedback *n*. Howling tone from the amplifier of an instrument resulting from sympathetic vibration of the instrument's strings excited by the sound emitted from the amplifier. See also: feedback resistance.

feedback resistance *n*. Quality of an electric instrument, usually a guitar, which indicates how prone it is to acoustic feedback. Instruments with high feedback resistance such as solid body electric guitars can be played highly amplified without danger of acoustic feedback. See also: feedback, solid body.

Fellowship of European Luthiers *n*. Berlin based luthier organization. Published the lutherie magazine *Sustain*. Defunct.

felt block *n*. Small block made of felt used to rub out (buff or polish) a finish by hand. The block is used with a powdered abrasive such as pumice or rottenstone, and a lubricating oil such as paraffin oil. See also: paraffin oil, pumice, rottenstone.

Felt block used to buff a finish by hand.

felt buffing wheel *n*. Wheel made of compressed felt used to buff and polish hard wood parts such as guitar bridges and violin fittings, and also to polish metal.

Felt buffing wheel with green chromium oxide buffing compound, used to polish edge tools.

Fender, Leo (1909-1991) Fullerton CA, USA, guitar inventor and manufacturer. Generally considered the co-inventor, with George Fullerton, of the first mass-produced solid body electric guitar, the Fender Broadcaster (renamed the Fender Telecaster) in 1948. Founded the Fender Electric Instruments Co. Developed and produced that company's signature electric guitars and basses including the Precision Bass and Stratocaster, as well as various guitar and bass amplifiers.

FEPA *abbr*. see Federation of European Producers of Abrasives

ferrule *n*. Short metal cylinder with a top flange, used to line a drilled hole to prevent enlargement of the hole. There are three common types of ferrules used in lutherie: neck ferrules, string ferrules and string post ferrules.

ff hole *n*. see f hole

FFT *abbr*. see fast Fourier transform

fiber *n*. Sheet material made of wood fiber and resin. Fiber is used in place of wood veneer in lutherie for purfling lines or other fine lines that are so narrow that the substitution will not be noticeable. Fiber sheets and lines are generally available in white or black. Syn.: fiber veneer.

fiber saturation point *n*. In the drying of wood, the point at which all water not bound up in the wood fibers has evaporated, usually at about 20%-30% water weight. As wood dries there are no substantial dimensional changes until this point is reached, but dimensional changes do occur as wood dries below this point. Syn.: FSP.

fiddleback maple *n*. see curly maple

figure eight head *n*. Headstock with an outline in the shape of a figure eight. This shape was popular in 19th century and earlier guitars and other stringed instruments.

filetto *n*. (fee-LET-tow) Purfling (Italian).

F

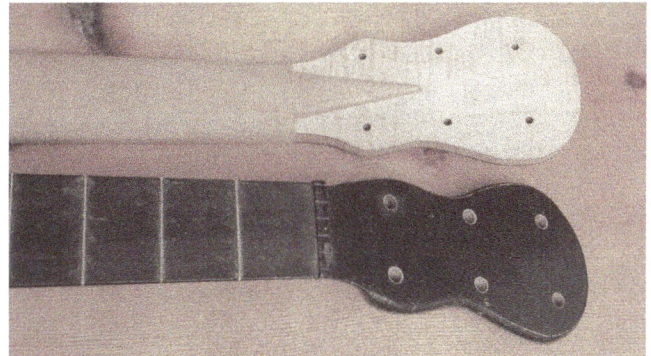

JAMES BUCKLAND

Two figure 8 head necks. The top one is from a guitar built by James Buckland. The bottom one is from an anonymous Mirecourt school guitar from the early 19th century.

finger brace *n*. Small brace usually found on the top plate of steel string guitars. These are free standing braces — their ends are not pocketed into the linings but are sometimes butted against other structural components. They are often found in the area of the top between the main X braces. See also: X brace.

finger joint *n*. Wood joint composed of many small fingers and spaces on each piece which fit together. This joint provides a large glue area. Taylor guitars use this joint to join headstock to neck shaft.

finger plane *n*. A small plane that is held in the fingers. Finger planes are used for the final stages of construction of arched plates of violins and other small instruments.

fingerboard *n*. The playing surface of a stringed instrument. The surface of the neck onto which the strings are pressed to stop them to different lengths. In general, the construction of the neck of an instrument makes use of a separate fingerboard, made of a material more resistant to abrasion than that of the neck shaft. Some instruments like Fender electric guitars and basses with necks made of hard maple do not use a separate fingerboard. On fretted instruments the fingerboard is also called the fretboard. Syn.: fretboard.

fingerboard extension *n*. The part of the fingerboard that extends over the body of the instrument.

fingerboard radius *n*. The playing surface of the fingerboard of some instruments is cambered, arched to provide a more comfortable position for the fingers when barring. The fingerboard radius is the radius of the arc of this cambering.

finish compatibility *n*. Indicates whether or not a coat of a finishing material can be used over a different finishing material. For example, there are a number of waterborne finishing products which are not compatible with oil varnish. Shellac on the other hand is compatible with most other finishes.

finish planing *v*. Lumber surface preparation. The board is planed completely smooth, to a specified thickness.

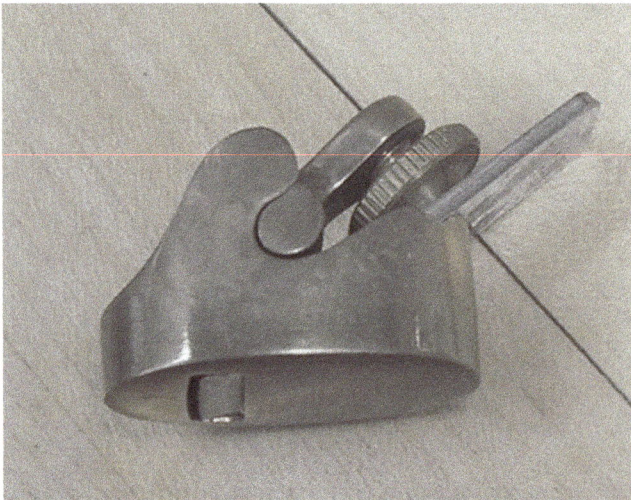

Finger plane.

Fingerboard extension of a classical guitar.

finite element analysis *n.* A method of computer based structural analysis that divides the structure into a number of small nodes. Each of these nodes has the properties of the material of the structure at that node. By limiting the scope of structural analysis to each individual node it is possible to simplify the analysis process for complex structures, such as musical instruments. Finite element analysis has been used to analyze response of an instrument to both the static forces imposed by string tension and to the dynamic forces of string vibration. Syn.: FEA, FEM, finite element method.

first epoch *n.* In his book *Antonio de Torres, Guitarmaker - His Life and Work*, José Romanillos cataloged the work of Torres divided into two epochs. The first epoch was from 1854 through 1868. Syn.: FE. See also: José Romanillos, second epoch, Antonio de Torres Jurado.

fish eye *n.* Cratering or pock marking of sprayed finish due to lack of adhesion of the finish to the wood. Fish eye is often the result of silicone contamination of the wood or work area from products containing silicone oil, such as polishes. Individual craters can be fixed by drop filling. Fish eye can be controlled by the addition of a small amount of silicone oil (generally sold as fish eye remover/additive) to the lacquer, but doing so further contaminates the work area and generally commits the user to always using this additive. Scrupulous cleaning of the work area will generally clear up the problem of fish eye over time.

fish glue *n.* Collagen glue made from fish scales and bones. Water soluble, with high tack and a long open time. Some luthiers prefer fish glue over liquid hide glue, considering it to be harder and having a longer shelf life.

five course guitar *n.* Early guitar with five strings or five courses of two strings each.

Fixed bridge glued to the top of a steel string guitar.

fixed bridge *n.* The two basic types of instrument bridges are fixed and floating. Fixed bridges are glued to the top of the instrument. They are found mostly on flattop instruments. See also: floating bridge.

fixture *n.* Any kind of special-purpose tool used for holding or positioning an instrument or component during construction. See also: jig.

flamed maple *n.* see curly maple

flamenca blanca *n.* (fla-MEN-cah BLAHN-cah) Flamenco guitar with light colored back and sides, usually made of cypress. Blanca is Spanish for white. See also: flamenca negra, flamenco guitar.

flamenco guitar *n.* A Spanish style guitar of classical construction built for use in flamenco. Although there is no real consensus on the differences between classical and flamenco guitars, there are some structural differences that are common. Flamenco guitars are often made of cypress wood, they often use tuning pegs rather

Fixture for holding a guitar in a vertical orientation.

than tuning machines, and they almost always have plastic tap plates called golpeadores glued to the top. The latter protect the top from damage due to the rhythmic drumming of the fingers on the top that is common in flamenco playing. Flamenco guitars often have bodies that are a bit shallower than those of classical guitars. Action is often lower than on classical guitars as well. See also: classical guitar, golpeador.

flamenca negra *n.* (flah-MEN-cah NEG-rah) Flamenco guitar with dark colored back and sides, usually made of rosewood. Negra is Spanish for black. See also: flamenca blanca, flamenco guitar.

flamenco peg *n.* A straight wood tuning peg of the type used in violins, common on some flamenco guitars.

flat sawn *n.* A board that is sawn so that, when viewed from the end grain, the grain lines run more or less parallel with the width of the board. Wood is flat sawn (as opposed to quarter sawn) for two reasons: 1. It is easier to saw; 2. some species look better when sawed this way. Syn.: back sawn, slab sawn. See also: quarter sawn, rift sawn.

End grain of flat sawn cherry.

flat top *n.* see flattop

flattened oval *adj.* Typical cross section profile of the neck of a guitar or other plucked instrument. The flattened oval neck profile is self-descriptive. See also: boat neck, D neck.

flattop *adj.* Describes a stringed instrument with plates which are essentially flat. Classical and steel string guitars are flattop instruments, as are some acoustic bass guitars and some mandolins. This modifier is generally used to differentiate instruments with essentially flat plates from those with carved arched plates. Most modern flattop instruments do not have plates which are actually flat. The plates of these instruments usually are slightly domed. See also: archtop.

flattop bass *n.* Flattop acoustic bass guitar. See also: acoustic bass guitar, flattop.

flattop guitar *n.* A guitar with thin, essentially flat, braced plates. One way to divide up acoustic steel string guitars

This steel string guitar is a flattop instrument.

for identification purposes is whether they are flattop or archtop. See also: flattop.

flatwork *n.* The flat fiber plates used in the construction of magnetic pickups. The plates form the top and bottom surfaces of the pickup assembly.

flatwound string *n.* A steel string, typically for guitar or bass guitar, which consists of a steel core wound with flat metal ribbon. The flat windings provide a smooth feel. Note that although most wound strings for orchestral instruments are also wound with metal ribbon, they are generally not referred to as flat wound strings. This term is generally only used to distinguish strings by their winding type, that is, to differentiate strings wound with flat metal ribbon from those wound with round metal wire.

Fleta, Ignacio (1897-1977) Barcelona Spain violin and guitar luthier. One of the Spanish classical guitar luthiers attributed with moving from the light construction of Torres to a heavier and more heavily braced guitar.

Fletcher, Neville H. Researcher of musical instrument acoustics. Coauthor of the book *The Physics of Musical Instruments*.

flexible heater *n.* see silicone heating blanket

flitch *n.* A series of boards or veneer slices stored in the order they were sawn from the log. Adjacent boards/slices in a flitch are bookmatched. See also: bookmatched.

flitch order *n.* Sequential order of boards or slices in a flitch.

floating bridge *n.* The two basic types of instrument bridges are fixed and floating. Floating bridges are not glued to the top of the instrument and are held in place by string tension. They are found mostly on archtop instruments. Floating bridges may be of solid construction or adjustable for height. See also: fixed bridge.

F

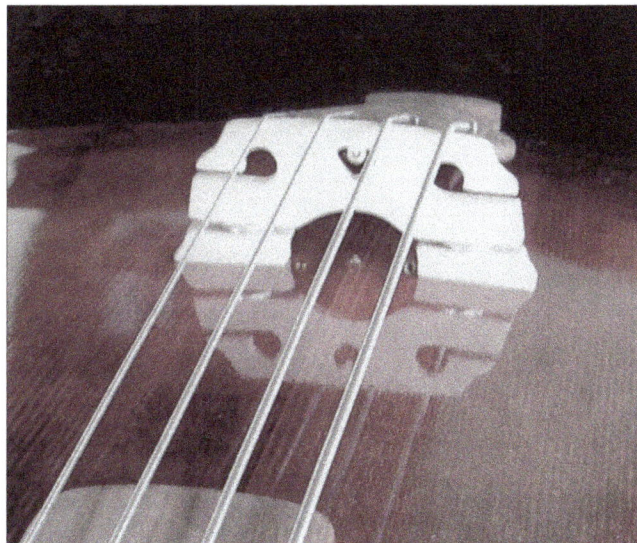

This floating bridge is not glued to the top of this archtop acoustic bass guitar.

floating fingerboard *n.* Fingerboard extension that is not attached to the body of the instrument. The term is generally used only when describing an instrument such as the flattop guitar that usually does have the extension glued or otherwise attached to the top. See also: fingerboard extension.

Florentine cutaway *n.* Cutaway styles divide into two major types, depending on the curve of the point or horn of the cutaway. The horn of the Florentine cutaway is pointed in shape, while that of the Venetian cutaway is rounded. See also: cutaway, Venetian cutaway.

floss core *adj.* Describes the core material of a wound string. The core is made of fine strands of material, usually nylon. See also: solid core.

floss sanding *v.* see sandpaper pull sanding

F

Guitar with Florentine cutaway.

flowout *n.* A property of finishing materials. The rate at which applied finishing material levels out. Brushed finishes for example will show brush marks immediately after application. These brush marks will disappear quickly for materials with good flowout (a high flowout rate), and will disappear slowly or not at all for finishing materials with a low flowout rate. Flowout often shows an inverse relationship to material viscosity and to the thickness of a finish coat.

Floyd Rose tremolo *n.* Brand name of an electric guitar vibrato bar (whammy bar) system invented by Floyd D. Rose. The package includes a locking nut and a vibrato tailpiece with locking string anchors. These string locking features allow the system to be used for deep string slackening effects, generally known as dive bombs.

fluid adjustment screw *n.* The part of a spray gun which regulates maximum fluid flow. The fluid tip contains an orifice in which the fluid needle is located. The rate of flow of fluid is regulated by how far the fluid needle is removed from the fluid tip. The fluid adjustment screw determines how far the fluid needle can be removed, thus limiting maximum fluid flow. See also: fluid needle, fluid tip.

Fluid adjustment screw on a gravity feed spray gun.

fluid needle *n*. The part of a spray gun which regulates fluid flow. The fluid tip contains an orifice in which the fluid needle is located. The rate of flow of fluid is regulated by how far the fluid needle is removed from the fluid tip. See also: fluid tip.

fluid tip *n*. The part of a spray gun from which fluid flows to be atomized. The fluid tip contains an orifice in which the fluid needle is located. The rate of flow of fluid is regulated by how far the fluid needle is removed from the fluid tip. See also: fluid needle.

fluorocarbon guitar strings *n*. Classical guitar strings making use of fluorocarbon polymer in place of nylon. The material has greater axial stiffness than nylon and so must be reduced in diameter to tune up at the same tension. Strings made of this material are generally considered to provide more high frequency content.

flying brace *n*. A brace that is only attached to a plate near the brace's ends. Syn.: Strut.

folk harp *n*. see Celtic harp

fond *n*. (fohn) Back plate (French).

fondo *n*. (FOWN-do) Back plate (Italian, Spanish).

foot *n*. 1. The part of a floating bridge which contacts the top of the instrument. 2. The part of the heel of the neck of a classical or flamenco guitar that is inside the body and contacts the inside of the back. See also: floating bridge, Spanish heel.

forced response *n*. A system such as the body of a stringed instrument will vibrate at whatever frequency is driving it. Instrument bodies are driven by the vibrations of the strings, even though these vibrations are at frequencies that are not necessarily resonant frequencies of the body. This is forced response and it is why instruments produce sound at all frequencies at which the strings are capable of vibrating.

Forderer, James (1943-2016) California USA guitar collector and historian. He made rare instruments available for examination and playing by luthiers and musicians at a number of Guild of American Luthiers conventions.

Forest Stewardship Council An independent, non-governmental, not for profit organization established to promote the responsible management of the world's forests. The organization provides certification of forest management, chain of custody, and of controlled wood. Syn.: FSC.

forêt à archet (for-AY a ahr-SHAY) see bow drill

form *n*. see mold

formant *n*. A resonant peak in the frequency spectrum of an instrument or room. The pattern of formants contributes to the unique sonic characteristics of classes of instruments and of individual instruments within a class.

Fourier analysis *n*. (FOOR-ee-ay) A general area of mathematics that involves the application of Fourier series. It is also a shorthand term used in signal analysis to mean signal analysis by means of Fourier transforms. Lutherie applications include spectrum analysis, where energy in different frequency bands is plotted over time.

forward shifted bracing *n*. Top bracing of an X braced instrument in which the main braces have been moved forward toward the soundhole. See also: X bracing.

Fox side bender *n*. A simple side bending machine that makes use of a heated inside mold. The machine was invented by Charles Fox. See also: Charles Fox, side bending machine.

Fox, Charles Portland OR, USA, guitar luthier, author and educator. Founder and director of the American School of Lutherie. Inventor of the Fox side bender machine and other lutherie tools and jigs. See also: Fox side bender.

F

frame body construction *n.* Body construction featuring a heavy rigid internal frame which attaches to the ribs and supports the top. This construction frees the top from some static load and provides a heavy and rigid boundary for the edges of the top. Syn.: frame construction.

FRC *abbr.* see frequency response curve

free plate *n.* A plate (top or back) that is not yet attached to the rest of the instrument.

free plate tuning *n.* The process of measurement and modification of the free plate (a plate that is not yet attached to the rest of the instrument) with the intent of optimizing some characteristic(s) of the tone of the finished instrument. The most common measurement methods include various types of tap tuning, and the measurement of the frequencies and/or shapes of the modes of vibration of the plate. Modifications involve removing wood from the plate and/or its braces. See also: tap tuning.

free stroke *n.* Finger style plucking motion where the plucking finger remains in the air (not touching the adjacent string) following the pluck. Generally produces a somewhat quieter sound than that of the rest stroke. Syn.: tirando. See also: rest stroke.

French bow *n.* Bow type for cello and double bass. French bows are played with the bowing hand over the bow. See also: German bow.

French polish *n.* A hand applied shellac finish. French polish is built up in many layers using a hand held cloth pad called a rubber, tampon or muñeca. The shellac is dissolved in alcohol and then padded on. The major steps in the process include sealing, grain filling, bodying, spiriting off, and glazing. See also: bodying, glazing, grain filler, sealer, shellac, spiriting off, tampon.

French polishing *v.* The process of applying French polish.

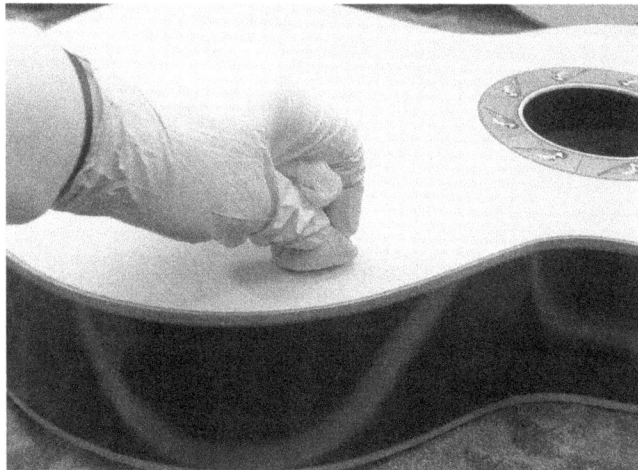

French polishing the top of a classical guitar.

French, (Richard) Mark Professor of mechanical engineering technology at Purdue University, Mark French is the author of the books *Engineering the Guitar: Theory and Practice*; and *Technology of the Guitar*. He is a luthier and has published research on the physics and construction of the guitar.

frequency of vibration *n.* The number of complete wave cycles (vibrations) occurring in a period of time. Frequency of sound waves is measured in cycles per second, generally expressed in units Hertz (abbreviated Hz). 1 Hz = 1 cycle per second. Frequency of sound waves is directly related to musical pitch. See also: Hertz.

frequency response curve *n.* A plot of an instrument's output signal level over frequency. There are two typical ways to obtain this. In the first, the instrument is excited by a constant level signal from a signal generator. The frequency is swept through some range while the output level is measured with a microphone. The second method involves making a digital recording through a microphone while the instrument is excited impulsively,

F

by being tapped with a hammer or finger. Fourier analysis of the recording will yield the frequency response plot. Syn.: FRC. See also: Fourier analysis, signal generator, frequency response function.

frequency response function *n*. Theoretical mathematical function describing an instrument's output signal level over frequency. Plotting the function produces a frequency response curve. In practice this term and frequency response curve are interchangeable. Syn.: FRF, transfer function. See also: frequency response curve.

fresco powder *n*. see dry pigment

fret *n*. A raised feature on the fingerboard of an instrument that provides a positive stop for shortening the vibrating length of the string. Early instruments used tied frets made of gut. Later instruments used metal frets made of thin metal bars called bar frets, or metal frets made of fret wire with a cross section that has a thin tang and a larger bead, head or crown. See also: bar fret, fret wire, gut, tied fret.

fret buck *n*. Massive metal plate used in the process of hammering in frets to the fingerboard extension of a completed guitar. The fret buck is inserted into the guitar through the soundhole and held in place under the fingerboard extension while frets are hammered in. See also: fingerboard extension.

fret crown *n*. The apex of the bead of the fret. The cross section of a fret usually shows a rounded bead, and the crown is the top of that rounded bead. See also: fret.

fret crowning file *n*. A small file with a concave surface, used to restore the crown to a fret after fret leveling has flattened it. Fret crowning files are special purpose tools available from lutherie suppliers. See also: fret crown, fret leveling.

fret dressing *v*. Preparing the frets of an instrument for optimal playing. Fret dressing includes leveling the frets,

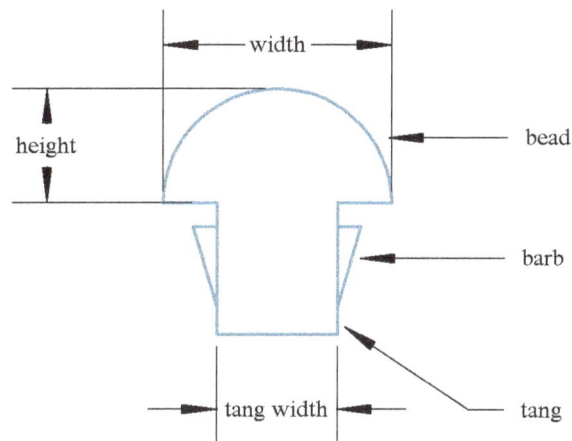

Fret cross section, showing parts of the fret.

recrowning them, and then polishing. It may also include other operations such as fret end rounding. See also: fret end rounding, fret leveling, fret recrowning.

fret end beveling *v*. The ends of the frets are generally beveled slightly for playability. After the frets are installed they are filed flush to the sides of the fingerboard and then they are beveled with the file.

fret end rounding *v*. The sharp edges at the ends of the frets are generally slightly rounded over a bit with a file to prevent them from cutting the players fingers. An

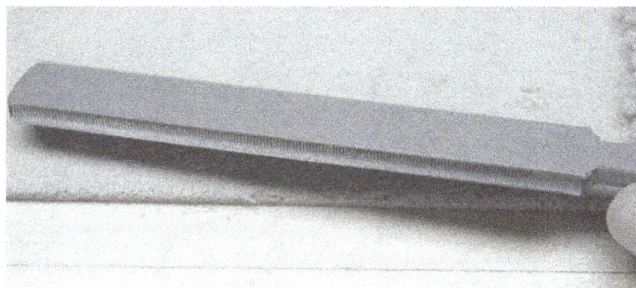

Fret crowning file.

exception to this is found on the classical guitar. Not all (and possibly not most) classical guitar builders round over the edges of the frets at the ends, as proper classical guitar playing form keeps the fingers away from the ends of the frets.

fret file *n.* A broad mill file used to level the frets. See also: fret leveling, mill file.

fret interval *n.* The space between two adjacent frets. See also: fret scale.

fret leveling *v.* After frets are installed they are leveled using a flat file or stone. This is done to even out any discrepancies in fret height due to discrepancies in fingerboard surface height or fret installation height. Frets are usually recrowned following leveling.

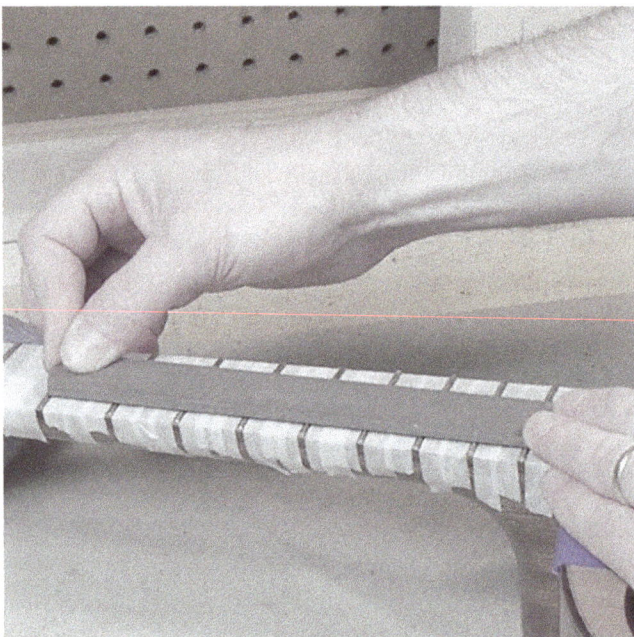

Fret file is used to level the frets of this guitar.

fret marker *n.* A marker on the playing surface of an instrument fingerboard. Dot markers are probably the most common type of position marker as they fit into a drilled hole and are thus easy to install, but fret markers can also be made in any shape and any size that will fit. Fret markers are typically made of plastic or shell. See also: dot marker.

fret nipper *n.* Flush cutting pliers used to cut fret wire to approximate length and to cut the fret ends flush to the sides of the fretboard after the frets are installed.

fret position *n.* Location of a fret relative to the nut or nominal bridge position. Fret position can be calculated based on the fret scale or can be determined by using a fret scale rule. Syn.: fret location. See also: fret scale, fret scale rule.

fret position constant *n.* A value which, when the scale length of the instrument is divided by it, yields the location of the first fret as an offset from the nut. That distance can be subtracted from the scale length and the resulting value can be divided by the fret position constant to yield the distance from the first fret to the

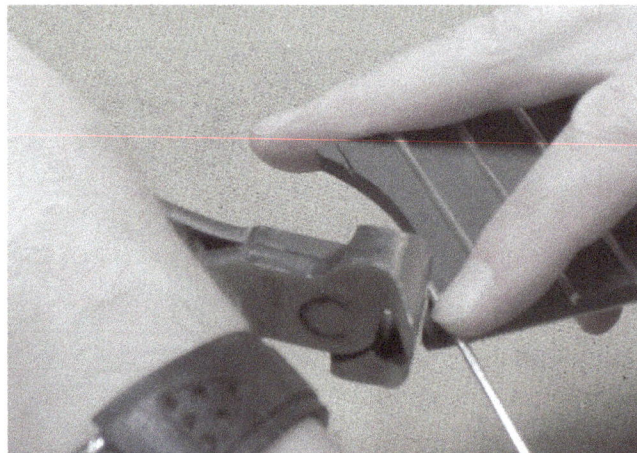

Using a fret nipper to cut a fret on the end of a classical guitar fretboard.

second fret. The process can be repeated for all frets. The traditional fret position constant was 18, specified by the rule of 18. A more modern constant is 17.817, which is derived from the 12th root of 2. Syn.: fret location constant. See also: 12th root of 2, rule of 18.

fret recrowning *n*. Filing a curved crown back onto the bead of a fret that has been flattened during the fret leveling process. Fret recrowning can be done with either a special fret crowning file or with a small triangular file. See also: fret crown, fret crowning file, fret leveling.

fret rocker *n*. Short straight edge used to check for a high fret. The tool is used to bridge three frets. If it can be rocked back and forth then the center fret of the group is higher than the other two.

fret scale *n*. The nut position, fret positions for each fret, and nominal bridge saddle position for a given scale length. Syn.: fret spacing. See also: fret position, scale length.

fret scale rule *n*. A rule which indicates nut location, each fret location and nominal bridge saddle location for a given scale length.

fret slot *n*. Slot in the fretboard into which the tang of a fret is inserted. Fret slots are generally sawn just a bit wider and a bit deeper than the dimensions of the fret tang. For bar frets the slot is quite wide as it must accommodate the full thickness of the bar stock. See also: bar fret, fret tang

fret slot cleaning tool *n*. A thin gouging tool used to clean debris out of fret slots. Fretboards are generally sanded after the fret slots are cut, and this sanding fills the slots with sanding dust. Because the tolerances between the fret slot and the fret tang are so small, all debris must be cleaned from the fret slots before the frets are installed. See also: fret slot, fret tang.

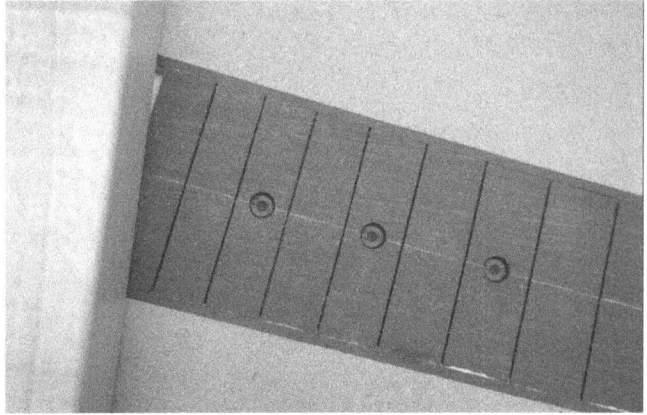

Fret slots (and holes for dot markers) in a guitar fretboard during construction.

fret slotting miter box *n*. A special miter box used to cut fret slots by hand. The slotting miter box usually has facilities for limiting the depth of cut so all fret slots will be of uniform depth. Some fret slotting miter boxes are made to be used with fret spacing templates so that fret slots can be accurately positioned on the fretboard. See also: fret slot, fret spacing template.

fret slotting saw *n*. A small back saw used to cut fret slots in fretboards. Fret slotting saws have the teeth set so the width of the slot is just a bit wider than the

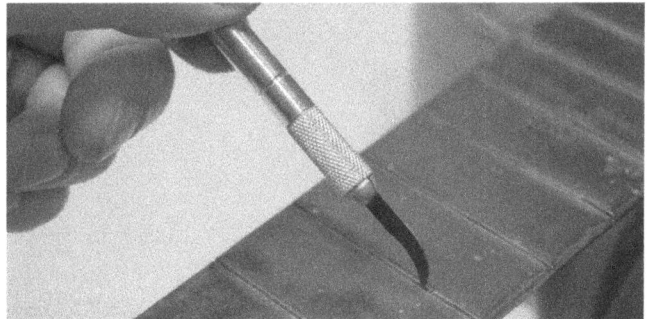

Fret slot cleaning tool.

thickness of the tang of the fret wire used, generally 0.022″ (0.56mm). See also: fret slot, fret tang, fret wire.

fret spacing *n*. see fret scale

fret spacing template *n*. A template that marks the location of each fret relative to the nut position. Fret spacing templates are used to mark fret positions for sawing fret slots or are used in fret slotting miter boxes or with a table saw and miter gauge to directly locate and cut fret slots in fretboards. See also: fret scale rule.

fret tang *n*. The part of a fret that, when the fret is installed in the fretboard, goes into the fret slot and ends up below the playing surface of the fretboard. See also: fret, fret slot.

fret tang nipper *n*. Tool to cut off a piece of the tang of a fret. In one style of bound fretboard, the binding is attached to the fretboard after it is slotted but before the frets are installed. Installing frets require that their tangs be short enough to fit in the fret slots, but the bead part of the frets must be a bit longer to go over the binding. The fret tang nipper is used to cut off a small piece of the tang on each end of the fret. See also: binding, fret slot, fret tang.

F

fret wire *n*. Metal wire with an end profile suitable for use as instrument frets. The profile consists of a bead and a narrower barbed tang. Installed, the tang fits into the fret slot in the fretboard and the bead remains above the fretboard playing surface. Fret wire comes in rolls and is cut to length as needed for each fret. See also: bead, fret, fretboard, fret slot, fret tang, playing surface.

fretboard *n*. The fingerboard of a fretted instrument. For fretted instruments the terms fingerboard and fretboard are used interchangeably. See also: fingerboard.

fretboard arching plane *n*. Steel string guitar fretboards usually have the playing surface cambered with a slight arch intended to improve playability. A fretboard arching plane is a special purpose tool for cambering (arching) the playing surface. See also: radius sanding block.

fretboard extender *n*. An extension to the fretboard for only some of the strings, usually the treble strings.

fretboard markers *n*. see fret marker

fretless bass *n*. An electric bass or an acoustic bass guitar with a fingerboard that doesn't have frets. Fretless fingerboards may be either plain or lined. In the latter case the playing surface of the fingerboard has contrasting lines inlayed where the frets would be.

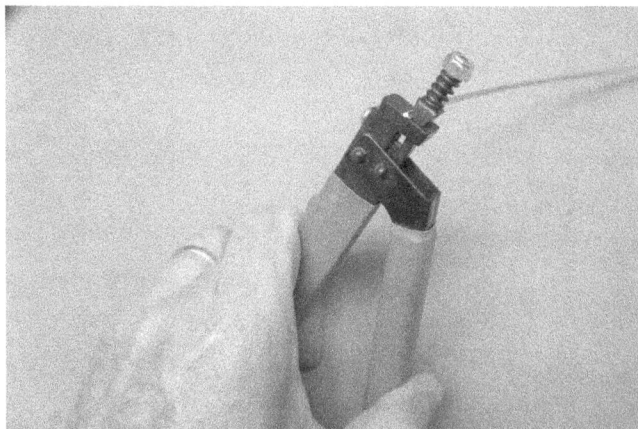

Cutting off a piece of the tang using a fret tang nipper tool.

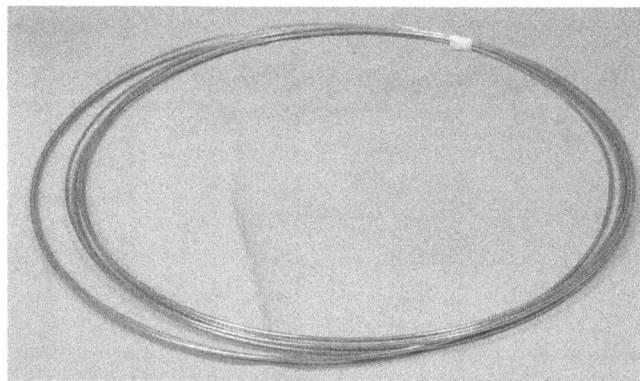

A short roll of fret wire.

Right handed and left handed fretless electric basses.

***Frets* magazine** Short-lived magazine with articles about acoustic guitars and playing. It was published by G.P.I. and ceased publication in 1989.

fretted wood rosette *n.* Soundhole decoration of early guitars and other instruments with round holes. Consists of a thin wood disc that fits in the soundhole. The disc is cut out in decorative patterns using a saw and knife.

fretting out *v.* see noting out

fretting press *n.* A press used to install frets into a fretboard. Syn.: fret press. See also: arbor press.

FRF *abbr.* see frequency response function

friction peg *n.* A tuning peg that relies on friction to keep it from turning backwards due to string tension. Friction pegs were used on early instruments and are used in violins. They are also used in some banjos and flamenco guitars. See also: tuning peg.

Fritz, Claudia Université Paris research scientist specializing in musical instrument psychoacoustics. Her landmark research in player preferences between new and old violins is considered a milestone in the field. See also: psychoacoustics.

frog *n.* 1. The part of the bow of a violin that anchors the hair at the end that is held in the bowing hand. 2. The part of a hand plane that clamps the blade down to the plane body. Syn.: nut. See also: bow.

front *n.* The body of stringed musical instruments has two large plates. The one that supports the bridge and has the soundhole(s) in it is called the top or belly or front. Of these three terms, the one most used to describe this plate for violin family instruments is belly. But the term front is also used, especially for the double bass and the cello, possibly due to their vertical playing orientation.

front bow *n.* String tension on the neck of a stringed instrument tends to bend the neck to the front of the instrument, bowing the fingerboard into a lengthwise concavity. This generally undesired condition is called front bow. A certain amount of front bow is desirable in fretted instruments as it provides space for the displacement of the vibrating strings. Any desired front bow is called relief. See also: relief, back bow.

FSC *abbr.* see Forest Stewardship Council

fundamental frequency *n.* The lowest frequency at which a vibrating system will vibrate. Vibrating systems will vibrate simultaneously at different frequencies, generally referred to as partials. Syn.: fundamental. See also: partial.

furniture powder *n.* see dry pigment

F

G

G clamp *n*. C clamp (British).

"G" Thang *n*. Acoustic guitar design software.

GAL *abbr*. see Guild of American Luthiers

Galloup, Bryan Big Rapids MI, USA, guitar luthier and teacher.

gamba corner *n*. Refers to the style of the corners of the body of the double bass. Gamba corners are plain, like those of the viola da gamba from which the name comes. They do not pinch out in the acute manner of violin corners. Syn.: viol corner. See also: soft corner, violin corner.

gamut *n*. The complete range of musical notes.

garland *n*. The assembled rib, lining and block subassembly of a stringed musical instrument.

garnet *n*. Sanding abrasive. It is orange in color and is found on sandpaper products generally suited for hand sanding wood.

geared tuning peg *n*. A tuning peg that uses internal gears (usually planetary gears) to provide fine tuning capability. Geared tuning pegs replace friction pegs in a number of instruments. They are commonly found in banjos.

gear ratio *n*. The ratio of shaft turns in a geared system such as a guitar tuning machine. Guitar machines generally have gear ratios of between 12:1 to 18:1. A 12:1 ratio for example requires twelve turns of the tuning machine knob to make the string post or roller turn once.

gekkin *n*. Japanese guitar-like instrument.

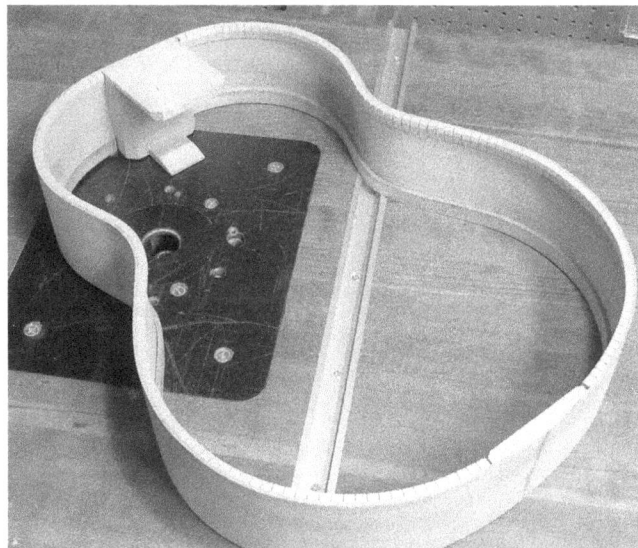

The garland is the rib, block and linings assembly.

gel varnish *n*. Oil based varnish thickened with a thixotropic additive, intended to be applied with a pad. See also: thixotropic.

Geppetto *adj*. The name of the woodworker father in the story of Pinocchio is often used as an adjective to describe a shop, tool or jig that is evocative of traditional woodworking. For example guitar luthier Kent Everett has described his "Geppetto room", a room in his shop that has no power tools but does include a lot of traditional woodworking hand tools. See also: Kent Everett.

German bow *n*. Bow type for cello and double bass. German bows are played with the bowing hand under the bow. Syn.: Butler bow. See also: French bow.

German silver *n*. see nickel silver

German spruce *n*. see *Picea abies*

Gesù, Giuseppe del see Guarneri, Giuseppe Bartolomeo

ghodi *n*. Bridge of the sitar or similar instrument. Syn.: jawari. See also: closed jawari, open jawari.

ghosting *n, v*. In lutherie this term is most often used to refer to the appearance of the pattern of the top braces on the outside of the top of a guitar or similar instrument.

Gibson, Orville (1894-1920) Founder of what was to become the Gibson Mandolin-Guitar Manufacturing Company in Kalamazoo MI, USA. Gibson made archtop mandolins and guitars. He sold his business to a group of investors in 1902 and continued working with the company as a consultant until 1904.

gigue *n*. Name for all musical instruments. Middle Ages.

Gilet, Gerard Australian luthier and coauthor of the book *Contemporary Acoustic Guitar Design and Build*.

gittern *n*. Medieval and Renaissance plucked instrument with a teardrop-shaped body. Syn.: gyterne, guisterne, guitarre, guiterne, guiterre, quinterne, quitaire, quitarre, quinterne, chitarino, chitarra or guitarra.

Giustiniani guitar *n*. One of the five guitars known to be built by Stradivari. Built in 1681, the guitar is currently in a private collection in Milan, Italy.

glazing *v*. 1. The final step in French polishing. Glazing fills the scratches left by leveling of the finish after bodying. 2. A wood finishing technique. Solid pigment stain is wiped onto the piece quite dry, which leaves behind a layer of color that tends to build in crevices and not build on outside edges. Creates a worn or well used look. Glazing is rarely used in lutherie except to emulate the look of an old finish. See also: bodying, French polish.

Gleason, Robert (Bob) Hawaii USA ukulele luthier and materials supplier.

glitter *n*. Small particles of reflective Mylar, available as a powder for crafts and decoration. Glitter is used in vibration analysis of the plates of instruments. The plate is sprinkled with glitter, then induced to vibrate by a speaker connected to an amplifier and signal generator. The glitter moves to the nodes — areas of low vibration of the plate. See also: Chladni pattern.

Gluck, Evan New York City USA guitar repair person, lecturer and guitar repair teacher.

glue block *n*. see tentellón

glue pot *n*. A heated pot used for hot hide glue. Hot hide glue must be kept hot to be spreadable, so glue is mixed and then put in the glue pot for use. Modern glue pots generally have electric heaters and thermostats, and some are configured to heat the glue in a water bath. The water bath provides even heat, and the hot water can be used to thin the glue as well. See also: hot hide glue.

Glue pot used to heat and hold hot hide glue.

G

glue squeeze out *n*. see squeeze out

glue syringe *n*. Syringe used to apply glue into tight places. See also: transfer pipette.

glued-in neck *n*. see set neck

go bar *n*. A semi flexible rod used to provide clamping pressure in a go bar deck. See also: go bar deck.

go bar deck *n*. A clamping fixture consisting of two shelf-like platforms held parallel to each other. The item to be clamped is placed on the lower platform (the floor) and one or more semi-flexible rods called go bars are wedged between the item to be clamped and the upper shelf (ceiling). The rods are a bit longer than will fit between the shelves and so have to be bent to fit. The go bar deck is a simple and inexpensive way to clamp long and thin pieces like braces that would otherwise require a lot of special purpose clamps.

golden mean *n*. Also called the golden ratio or golden section. An irrational number with the approximate value of 1.6180339887, the golden mean is often denoted by the Greek letter phi (ϕ). The value can be calculated as $(1 + sqrt(5)) / 2$. This value has been used by artists and architects since the Renaissance to proportion elements of their work, and is considered by those that use it to represent a natural esthetic proportion. Analysis of historical instruments have indicated that this ratio was used extensively, but most such studies are methodologically flawed and only partially supported by historical evidence. A number of modern luthiers use this ratio to proportion elements of their instruments. Syn.: golden ratio, golden section, phi.

golden ratio *n*. see golden mean

golden section *n*. see golden mean

golpeador *n*. (goal-pay-ah-DOHR) Thin plastic plate glued to the top of flamenco guitars to protect the top from damage from the rhythmic drumming of the fingers common in flamenco playing. Syn.: tap plate.

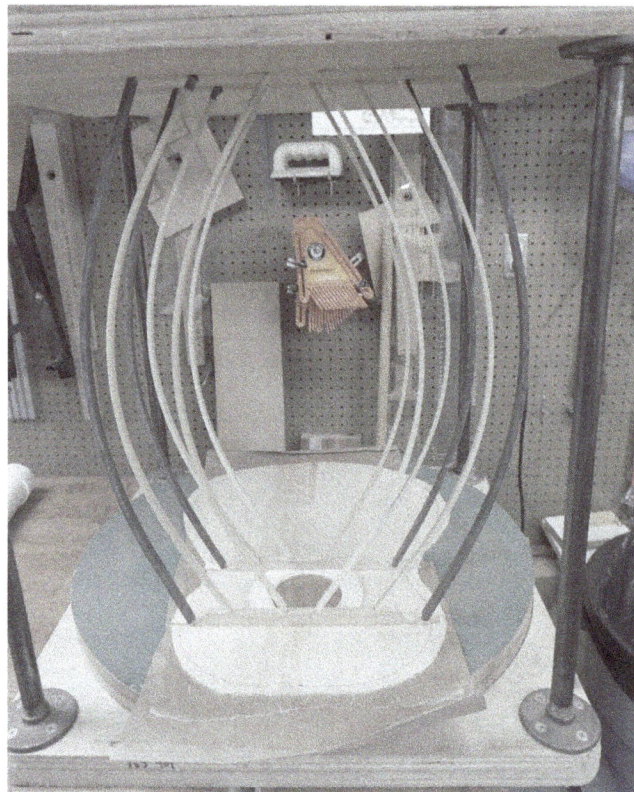

Go bar deck and go bars used to clamp transverse braces to the top of a guitar.

gooseneck scraper *n*. A curved card scraper with a profile of varying radius curves. See also: card scraper.

Gore, Trevor Australian luthier and coauthor of the book *Contemporary Acoustic Guitar Design and Build*.

graduate *v*. The process of carving a plate, usually of an archtop instrument, so that it ends up with varying thickness. It is common to carve arched plates so they are thinner at the edges and thicker near the center.

graduation *n*. The variability in thickness of (usually) arched plates. It is common to carve arched plates so they are thinner at the edges and thicker near the center.

graft *n.* Any connection (joint) between two pieces of wood or two subassemblies is a graft. In lutherie the noun generally refers to the end graft, a decorative feature of flattop guitars. See also: end graft.

graft *v.* To connect two pieces of wood or two subassemblies.

grain *n.* 1. The primary orientation of the fibers of wood. 2. The unit of coarseness of a rasp, which run from 1 (coarse) to 15 (fine).

grain filler *n.* Any substance that is used to fill the pores on the surface of wood so that a subsequent application of finishing material will result in a smooth finish. Many different types of grain filler are used in lutherie. Commercial paste wood filler (oil based grain filler) is a mixture of dilute varnish, tint, and finely ground sand. Commercial water based grain filler is based on a waterborne polymer. Traditional French polishing makes use of a grain filler of pumice and shellac. Epoxy is used as a grain filler by many hand builders. Syn.: pore filler. See also: epoxy, French polish, paste wood filler, pumice, shellac, varnish.

gram strength *n.* Measure of strength of cured hot hide glue. The larger the number, the stronger the cured glue. Numbers range from approx. 135 to 379. Values are obtained using a laboratory device called a gelometer. See also: hot hide glue.

gramil *n.* A cutting gauge used to mark out purfling channels and the rabbets for guitar binding. Syn.: purfling cutter. See also: purfling channel, purfling cutter.

grand auditorium size guitar *n.* One of the general size classifications for steel string guitars, adopted from C.F. Martin size designations. The body of a grand auditorium size guitar is approximately 20.125″ long and 16″ wide at the lower bout. Syn.: M.

Gramil.

grand concert size guitar *n.* One of the general size classifications for steel string guitars, adopted from C.F. Martin size designations. The body of a grand concert size guitar is approximately 19.625″ long and 14.125″ wide at the lower bout. Syn.: OO.

gravity feed spray gun *n.* Spray gun in which the material to be sprayed flows into the gun via gravity. The material cup for such a gun is mounted on top of the gun. See also: siphon feed spray gun.

green rouge *n.* see chromium oxide buffing compound

green wood *n.* Freshly cut wood or wood with a moisture content close to that of freshly cut wood. See also: dry wood.

Greven, John *n.* Portland OR, USA, guitar luthier, known for prolific production using a minimum of special-purpose tooling.

grimel *n.* see gramil

grip *n.* Part of the bow of violin family instruments. The grip is composed of a wrapping of the stick near the frog and a thumb cushion, usually made of leather.

G

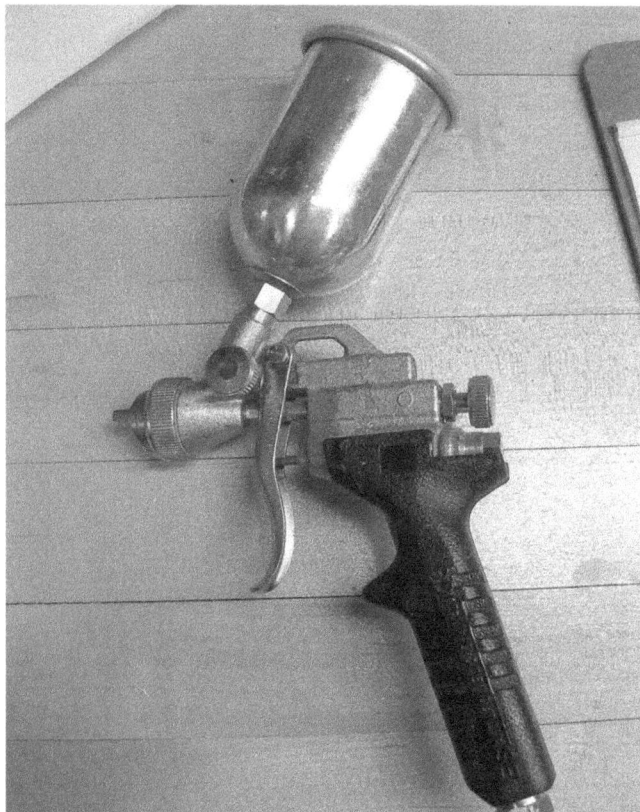

Gravity feed spray gun.

grit *n.* see sandpaper grit

ground *n.* Base layer of a multilayer wood finish.

ground wound string *n.* A wound steel string, typically for an electric bass guitar. The steel core is wound with steel wire, and then the outside of the windings are ground flat. Ground wound strings are intended to provide the smooth feel of a flatwound string with some of the bright sound of a roundwound string. See also: flatwound string, round wound string.

grub screw *n.* Set screw (British).

Gruhn, George Owner of Gruhn Guitars, and a well known historian and dealer in vintage and collectable stringed instruments in Nashville. He was a designer at Guild guitars and was involved with design at Tacoma Guitars. He is coauthor of the books *Gruhn's Guide to Vintage Guitars*, *Acoustic Guitars and Other Fretted Instruments*, and *Electric Guitars and Basses*.

Guadagnini, Giovanni Battista (1711-1786) Italian violin luthier. His father Lorenzo worked in the shop of Stradivari. He is a significant member of the Guadagnini lutherie family, the shop of which produced violins, guitars and mandolins until 1948.

Guarneri, Andrea 17th century Cremonese violin maker, was apprenticed to Nicolò Amati. See also: Nicolò Amati.

Guarneri, Giuseppe Bartolomeo (1698-1744) (del Gesù) Son of Andrea Guarneri. 18th century Cremonese violin maker, considered by most to be the finest violin maker ever. Syn.: Giuseppe del Gesù.

Guarneri, Giuseppe Giovanni Battista (*filius* Andrea) Son of Andrea Guarneri. 17th-18th century Cremonese violin maker.

Guibourtia demeusei *n.* Bubinga, African rosewood. These common names denote two species, *Guibourtia demeusei* and *Didelotia africana*. Not a true rosewood (*Dalbergia*), this wood is pinkish in color when freshly cut and oxidizes to brown over time. It is used for flattop guitar backs and sides and also for fingerboards and headplates. It has a typical specific gravity (dry) of 0.89 and a modulus of elasticity of 18.4 GPa.

Guild of American Luthiers *n.* Founded in 1972 by Tim Olsen, the Guild of American Luthiers is the largest and oldest organization of luthiers worldwide. Based in Tacoma WA, USA, the GAL publishes the quarterly journal *American Lutherie* as well a number of lutherie books and plans, and hosts a lutherie convention. Syn.: GAL. See also: Tim Olsen.

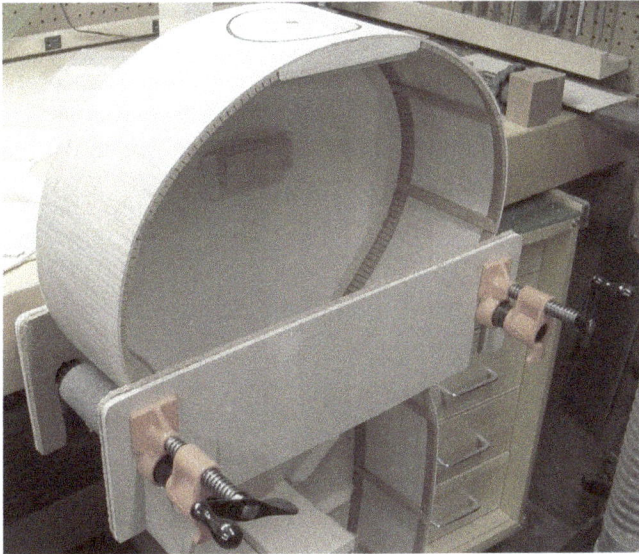

Guitar body vise.

guitar body vise *n.* Vise, usually shop built, for holding guitar during assembly.

guitar cradle *n.* A fixture for holding a guitar during assembly or for repair.

guittar *n.* see English guittar

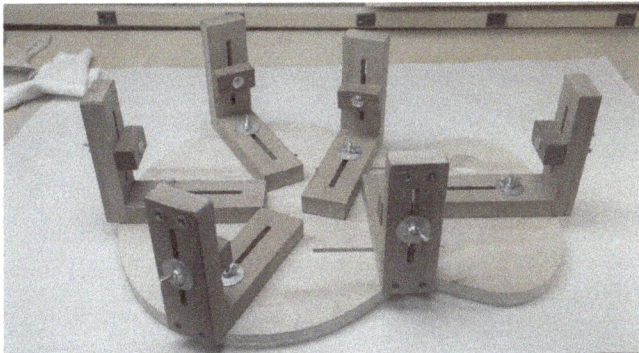

Guitar cradle.

guitarra flamenca *n.* (gee-TAR-rah flam-EN-cah) see flamenco guitar (Spanish).

guitarrero *n.* (gee-tar-RARE-oh) Guitar maker (Spanish).

guitarrón n. (gee-tar-ROAN) Mexican acoustic bass guitar with a deep body with a highly vaulted back. It is generally tuned A D G C E A.

gum *n.* Any vegetable secretion that hardens with exposure to air and is soluble in water. Gums are often used as components of spirit varnishes, usually as a secondary resin. See also: spirit varnish.

gum elemi *n.* A resin used in the production of violin varnish. Gum elemi comes from trees of the family *Burseraceae.*

gunstock oil *n.* Generic name for oil varnish intended to be applied by padding. This is a traditional finish for wooden gunstocks. See also: Tru-oil.

Gurian, Michael Currently a manufacturer of inlay and decorative wood trim, Michael Gurian is a self-taught guitar maker who first set up shop in New York City in 1965.

gut *n.* Cord made from the intestines of animals. Gut strings are used in antique instruments and in some instruments of the violin family.

G

H

Hacklinger gauge *n*. Brand of magnetic thickness gauge used to measure the thickness of instrument ribs and plates. The gauge has two parts, a magnet which is inserted inside the instrument and the gauge part which remains completely on the outside of the instrument. This gauge can be used to measure wood thickness in places that are not accessible to a caliper. See also: magnetic thickness gauge.

haléotides n. (HAL-ay-oh-teed) Abalone (French).

Ham, James Bass builder from Victoria BC, Canada. Ham is best known for innovative design, construction and construction techniques, including the use of balsa and carbon fiber.

hammered dulcimer *n*. A large trapezoidal instrument that is played on a stand or table. The strings are hit with special spoon shaped hammers.

Handroanthus **spp**. South and Central American tree generally called ipe or Brazilian walnut. The wood sees limited use in lutherie but is sometimes used for classical guitar backs and sides. It is very dense and stiff. It machines well but tends to dull tools. Specific gravity (dry) 1.10. Modulus of elasticity is 22.1 GPa. Shrinkage (radial, tangential): 5.9%, 7.2%.

hand-applied sunburst *n*. Sunburst color pattern that has been applied by hand, with dyes rubbed directly onto the wood. This is the historical method for applying sunbursts, used before spray equipment was available. Modern sunbursts are generally sprayed. Syn.: hand-rubbed sunburst.

hand-stitched rasp *n*. A rasp in which the teeth are raised by hand, rather than by machine. Hand stitched rasps are considered to cut smoother because the tooth pattern is more random than those on machine made rasps. See also: rasp.

Hand-stitched rasp.

hard maple *n*. see *Acer saccharum*

Hardanger fiddle *n*. A Norwegian fiddle, very similar in construction to the violin but with (usually) eight strings — four bowed strings and four or more sympathetic strings underneath the bowed strings. The instruments are usually ornately decorated. See also: sympathetic string.

hardingfele *n*. see Hardanger fiddle

hardtail bridge *n*. A non-vibrato bridge for the electric guitar.

hardwood *n*. Wood from deciduous trees, trees with broad leaves. The term does not necessarily have anything to do with the hardness of the wood - there are hardwoods that are softer than some softwoods.

harmonic *n*. Oscillation at a frequency that is an integer multiple of some fundamental frequency. Musical instrument strings (nearly) vibrate in a harmonic fashion, vibrating simultaneously at the fundamental frequency, at 2 times the fundamental frequency, 3 times ... The fundamental frequency is called the first harmonic. The entire series is called a harmonic series. See also: inharmonicity, harmonic series.

harmonic bar *n*. see transverse brace

harmonic series *n*. A fundamental frequency of vibration and simultaneous vibration at integer multiples of the fundamental. See also: harmonic.

Harmony Chicago IL, USA, manufacturer of inexpensive stringed instruments, founded in 1892 by Wilhelm Schultz. The company was at one time the largest USA manufacturer of stringed instruments. They manufactured guitars, violins, ukuleles, and mandolins. Harmony was an early supplier to Sears, Roebuck and Company, and Sears bought Harmony in 1916. Harmony instruments were sold under a number of names including Vogue, Valencia, Johnny Marvin, Monterey and Stella. Sears used the name Supertone among others. Production of instruments peaked during the mid-1960s but competition from foreign manufacturers eventually led to the company's demise in 1975.

harp guitar *n*. A guitar with additional non-fretted strings. Some models of harp guitars include a separate sound box for the non-fretted harp strings.

harp lute *n*. Late 18th century fretted instrument invented by Edward Light. Each string features a sharping lever that can be operated by the players thumb, which raises whatever note played on that string by a semitone.

Hauser, Hermann (1882–1952) German builder of classical guitars and other stringed instruments. Considered one of the greatest classical guitar makers. His instruments were used by Segovia. His family continues to produce instruments - his son (HH II) and grandson (HH III) retained the family business.

hazelfichte *n*. (HAYS-el-fich-teh) see bearclaw

Head (headstock) of an archtop guitar.

head *n*. Name for part of an instrument, bow or amplifier. 1. Section of an instrument at the end of the neck that usually supports the tuning pegs or machines, also called the headstock. 2. The skin or plastic top of a banjo. 3. The pointed end of a bow for violin family instruments, to which the hair is attached, also called the bow tip or point. 4. The part of a guitar amplifier that contains the electronics, in amplifiers where the electronics and the speakers are found in separate cabinets. Syn.: headstock (1). See also: banjo, bow, headless.

head plate *n*. The fronts of the heads of some instruments are covered with a veneer of decorative wood called the head plate.

head slot *n*. There are two types of tuning machines. In one type, the posts that the strings are wound on protrude out the front of the head and are perpendicular to the front surface. In the second type the posts are accessible through slots cut into the head, and do not protrude at all. The slots that provide access to the posts in the latter style of machines are called head slots. Syn.: slot. See also: slotted peghead, tuning machine.

H

Guitar with ebony headplate over a mahogany headstock.

headless *adj.* Describing an instrument that does not have a headstock. Headless instruments put the tuning machines on the body, at or below the bridge. This approach was popularized by electric guitars and basses made by Ned Steinberger. See also: Ned Steinberger.

headroom *n.* In stringed instruments this term describes how much harder an instrument can be played above a conventional upper limit and still produce useful musical sound.

headstock *n.* see head

headstock angle *n.* Nominal angle between the top surface of the headstock and the plane of the fingerboard playing surface of a guitar or similar instrument. Headstock angles for acoustic guitars range from approximately 12 to 20 degrees. Headstock angles for lutes and ouds can approach 90 degrees.

headstock cap *n.* see head plate

heartwood *n.* The central part of the log. See also: sapwood.

heat treatment (wood) *n.* Heat treated wood is used primarily in lutherie for guitar tops and braces. Heat treatment techniques vary, but generally involve heating the wood for some period of time. Some processes control humidity and/or available oxygen during treatment. Heat treating affects a number of physical properties of the wood. The wood ends up darker in color, stiffer, heavier, and with reduced breaking strength and ability to take up moisture. This latter property makes the wood more dimensionally stable with changes in humidity. There are various "brand names" of heat treatment. The most commonly known is Torrefaction. Brand names of heat treated wood include Perdure, Thermowood, Stellac and Platowood. In lutherie contexts a common generic term for such heat treatment is torrefication. Syn.: torrefication.

heating blanket *n.* see silicone heating blanket

heel *n.* The part of the instrument neck that connects to the body.

heel block *n.* see neck block

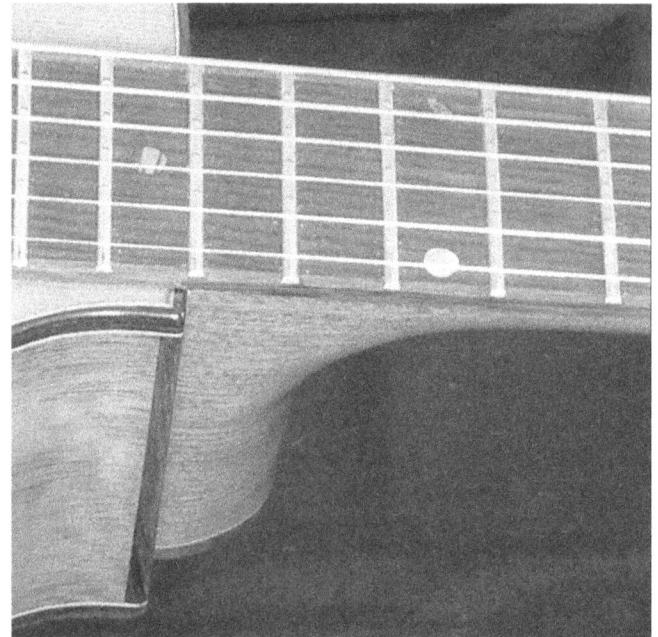

Heel of the neck of an acoustic guitar.

Guitar with rosewood heel cap on mahogany neck.

heel cap *n.* Decorative piece of wood that covers the bottom of the heel of the neck of an acoustic guitar or similar instrument. See also: button.

heel stack *n.* see stacked heel

Helmholtz motion *n.* The motion of a bowed violin string, first described by Hermann von Helmholtz. The motion includes two parts, the first in which the string "sticks" to the hair of the bow and is displaced laterally in the direction of bow motion. At some point the restoring force overcomes that of sticking and the string quickly jumps back to its original position. See also: Hermann von Helmholtz.

Helmholtz pitch notation *n.* Archaic system of alphabetic pitch notation. Pitches are designated by the letters C-B and appropriate accidentals, but letter case and additional subscript or superscript prime marks are used to designate octaves. So C0-B0 are notated $C_{\prime\prime}$-$B_{\prime\prime}$; C1-B1 are notated $C_{\prime}$-$B_{\prime}$; C2-B2 are notated C-B ; C3-B3 are notated c-b ; C4 (middle C)-B4 are notated c'-b' ; C5-B5 are notated c''-b'' ; etc. See also: Note Frequency pitch notation, Scientific pitch notation.

Helmholtz resonance *n.* The lowest sound-producing mode of vibration of the enclosed air inside a musical instrument. The resonator is composed of the air enclosed in the body of the instrument functioning like a spring, and the air in and around the soundhole functioning like a mass attached to that spring. Its frequency is a function of the volume of air enclosed by the instrument body and the size of the soundhole. This resonance coupled with vibrational modes of the plates forms the main air resonance. In a frequency response curve the Helmholtz resonance is usually identified as the lowest frequency valley. See also: air resonance, frequency response curve, Hermann von Helmholtz, main air resonance.

Helmholtz tube *n.* A tube fitted into a soundhole to extend its depth, to lower the resonant frequency and Q of the instrument's Helmholtz resonance. See also: Helmholtz resonance, Q, tornovoz.

Helmholtz, Hermann von (1821–1894) German physicist Helmholtz was trained as a medical doctor but did substantial research in other areas including the human perception of sound. For his investigations he had built a series of tuned acoustic filters, now known as Helmholtz resonators.

HEPA *abbr.* see high efficiency particulate air

Hernández, Santos (1873-1942) Spanish guitar luthier. Worked for Manuel Ramírez until Ramírez' death in 1920, then opened his own shop in Madrid. See also: Manuel Ramírez.

Heron-Allen, Ed Author of the book *Violin Making as it was and is*. The book is probably the first comprehensive lutherie instruction manual, first published in 1885.

Hertz *n.* Unit of frequency of vibration. 1 Hertz = 1 cycle (1 complete vibration) per second. Syn.: Hz. See also: frequency of vibration.

H

herringbone *n.* A pattern used in purfling and back strips that resembles the backbone and ribs of a fish. See also: purfling, back strip.

hide glue *n.* Glue made from the hides of animals. Hide glue is probably the earliest lutherie glue and is used today by some luthiers. There are two generally available forms of hide glue, hot hide glue and liquid hide glue. Due to its short shelf life, liquid hide glue is not often used in lutherie. Glue joints made with hide glue can be reversed with the application of water and heat or alcohol and mechanical pressure. This means the glue is not ideal for applications that will subject the joint to a hot wet environment. However it is a very useful glue for applications where the finished joint must be reversible at some time in the future. It is used extensively for repair and restoration of antique instruments and is used exclusively by most makers of violin family instruments. See also: hot hide glue, liquid hide glue.

high angle plane *n.* Plane with a higher than normal angle between the blade and the sole of the plane. High angle planes are useful when planing highly figured wood.

high efficiency particulate air *adj.* Describes a filter used to filter dust particles from air. Describes some filters in vacuums and dust collectors and also in dust masks. Syn.: HEPA.

highpass filter *n.* An electrical circuit or an acoustic system which passes high frequencies relatively intact but attenuates lower frequencies. See also: bandpass filter, lowpass filter.

high pressure laminate *n.* Sheet material made by laminating a paper and phenolic resin backing with a melamine covered paper image. The material is best known by one of its trademarked product names, Formica. High pressure laminates are used in the construction of lutherie jigs and fixtures. They have been used by some manufacturers for guitar tops, backs and sides. Syn.: HPL.

Hill guitar *n.* One of the five guitars known to be built by Stradivari. Built in 1688, the instrument is currently in the collection of the Ashmolean museum in Oxford, UK.

hit-or-miss planing *v.* Surface preparation for lumber. Rough sawn boards are run through the planer just once. The resulting surface may still have unplaned areas, but the surface is generally smooth enough to be able to see what the wood will look like once it is finish planed. See also: finish planing.

holiday *n.* Defect in the application of a coat of finishing material. A holiday is a missed spot, a spot in which finish was inadvertently not applied.

hollow body *adj.* Electric guitars and similar instruments can be classified by general construction of the body. A hollow body instrument has a body constructed in similar fashion to that of an acoustic guitar. See also: semi-hollow body, solid body.

hollow radius form *n.* see dished workboard

holography *n.* Generally, the making of three dimensional images. Holography is used in musical instrument acoustics research to image the motion of plates and of sound radiation.

Honduras mahogany *n.* see *Swietenia macrophylla*

honing *v.* A loosely defined term which specifies a phase of the process of sharpening edge tools. In the most general use the term honing refers to the process of refining the sharpness of the edge without the removal of much metal.

horizontal belt sander *n.* Stationary belt sander in which the belt and platen are fixed in a horizontal position. Horizontal belt sanders are often used in lutherie shops for shaping of small parts, finish sanding small flat pieces

Horizontal belt sander.

such as headstock surfaces, and for truing up the ribs of guitars and other similarly sized instruments.

horn *n*. If a body cutaway is considered to be the removal of material from the shoulder area of the body of an instrument then the material that remains after the cutaway is made is called a horn. The cutaways of some solid body electric guitars are so stylized that this may not be easy to visualize. Electric guitars often have double cutaways and in this case the two remaining horns are called the upper horn and the lower horn. The upper horn is the one closest to the player's head when the instrument is held in playing position. See also: cutaway.

Hornbostel-Sachs system *n*. System for the classification of musical instruments, developed by Erich Moritz von Hornbostel and Curt Sachs and first published in 1914. In this system the major division of instruments is by the way they produce sound.

hot *adj*. Describing solvents and glues that dry very quickly.

hot hide glue *n*. One of the two common forms of hide glue. Hot hide glue is available commercially as dry flakes. These are soaked in water and then heated to make a syrupy glue. It is kept hot in a glue pot. Hot hide glue gels quickly as it cools, which makes it ideal for the assembly of parts which require a fast "grab" time. The pot life of hot hide glue is not that long, and most shops make a fresh batch each day. See also: glue pot, hide glue.

house brand *n*. Brand name of a retailer. House branded instruments are built by an instrument manufacturer but have the brand name of the retailer selling them. These instruments are often built to the retailers specifications but are also often re-branded instruments from the manufacturer's own product line. The existence of housed branded instruments complicates historical identification and organology. See also: organology.

HPL *abbr*. see high pressure laminate

hum *n*. Electromagnetic noise induced into magnetic pickups from alternating current power lines. Power line current alternates polarity at either 50 or 60 Hz depending on country, inducing a characteristic humming noise. See also: electromagnetic noise.

humbucking pickup *n*. A two coil magnetic pickup with each coil wound in the opposite direction, one around a top north magnet and the other around a top south magnet. The combination of winding direction and magnetic polarity difference means that both pickups will produce signals that are in phase in response to string movement, but the coils will have high common mode rejection for signals that are induced into them such as those from electrical hum. See also: common mode rejection.

humidity gauge *n*. see hygrometer

Humphrey, Thomas (1948-2008) USA classical guitar luthier, most famous for his Millennium model which featured a raised fretboard.

H

Humbucking bridge pickup.

Hurd, David Hawaiian classical guitar and ukulele builder and author. David Hurd is author of the book *Left Brain Lutherie* and a proponent of using deflection analysis of instrument tops as a way of yielding good and consistent tone and structural integrity. See also: deflection analysis.

hurdy-gurdy *n.* A popular Renaissance stringed instrument with a sound like bagpipes. The hurdy-gurdy strings are vibrated by means of a rosined wheel which is turned with a crank at the tail end of the instrument. The strings are fretted using keys in a key box, which both shorten the vibrating length of the strings and push them in contact with the rotating wheel. Most instrument include one or more drone strings as well as the melody strings.

Hutchins, Carleen (1911-2009) American violin maker and musical instrument acoustics researcher. She is generally credited with reviving interest in musical instrument acoustics research. Starting with work by 19th century musical instrument acoustics researchers, she developed techniques of free plate tuning intended to optimize violin tone. She also developed the violin octet, a family of scaled instruments. Hutchins was

instrumental in the founding of the Catgut Acoustical Society. See also: Catgut Acoustical Society, free plate tuning, violin octet.

HVLP *abbr, adj.* High Volume Low Pressure. A type of spray gun that moves a lot of air at lower than usual pressure. The advantage of guns of this type is less waste of material. The lowered pressure results in less material bouncing off the object sprayed.

hybrid bass strings *n.* Double bass strings suitable for both arco and pizzicato playing. Double bass strings are constructed with internal damping so that they start vibrating when bowed. But this damping makes for a dull sound when played pizzicato, so strings sets are available for pizz-only playing that have less damping. Hybrid strings have enough damping to start to the bow but not so much that they sound dull when played pizz.

hygrometer *n.* A gauge for measuring the relative humidity of air. Stringed instruments are often built in a temperature and humidity controlled environment because extremes in both temperature and humidity can have adverse effects on the structure of instruments. A hygrometer (humidity gauge) is useful in maintaining shop humidity.

hygroscopic *adj.* Absorbing water. Wood is a hygroscopic material.

Hz *abbr.* see Hertz

I

Ibáñez, Salvador (1854-1920) Spanish guitar luthier from Valencia.

ice cream cone heel *n.* see cone heel

impedance *n.* Measure of the amount of force which must be applied to a medium which conducts waves to produce waves of a given measure of motion. In musical instrument acoustics, the measure of the opposition to the flow of vibrational energy, the inverse of admittance. In electronics, resistance to the flow of alternating current. See also: admittance.

impedance matching *v.* Generally used in the description of electrical circuits such as amplifiers and tone modifying electronics. In an electrical circuit all components of the circuit affect the behavior of the circuit. It is usually easier to design complex circuits as connected simple circuits, but this can only be done when making such a connection would not affect the behavior of the two circuits connected. For the kinds of circuitry typically used in instrument electronics this can be accomplished by being sure the impedance of the driving circuit is substantially lower than that of the driven circuit. Designing for this is called impedance matching. See also: impedance.

impreg *abbr.* see resin impregnated wood

in situ *adj.* (in SITE-you) Latin phrase which means in place. In lutherie the term generally refers to parts of an instrument in need of repair. A part often cannot be easily removed from the instrument for repair and thus has to be repaired *in situ.*

in the air construction *n.* see archaic construction

in-cannel gouge *n.* A gouge that has the bevel ground on the inside of the curve. Syn.: inside bevel gouge. See also: out-cannel gouge.

The bevel on the blade of an in-cannel gouge is cut on the inside surface of the gouge.

Indian rosewood *n.* see *Dalbergia latifolia*

indigo *n.* Plant dye from genus *Indigofera.* Used as a blue colorant in some traditional varnishes.

individual tuning machines *n.* Tuning machines that are not combined on a single mounting plate. See also: plated tuning machines.

inductance *n.* Fundamental property of electrical components that opposes a change of current flow. In musical instrument electronics this property is of consequence in coils of wire such as those found in magnetic pickups. The overall tone of a pickup is related to its resonant peak which is affected by the values of inductance, capacitance and resistance of the pickup and surrounding circuitry. The unit of inductance is the Henry (H). Increasing the number of turns of wire on a coil increases its inductance. See also: capacitance, magnetic pickup, resistance, resonant peak.

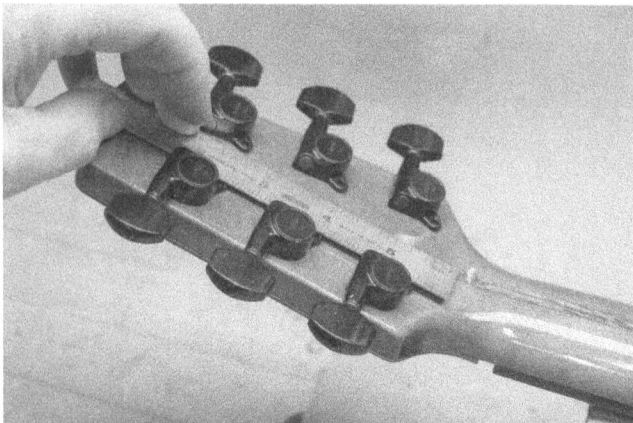

Aligning individual guitar tuning machines during installation.

inertia *n*. A property of matter by which it remains at rest or in uniform motion in the same straight line unless acted upon by some external force.

inflection point *n*. A point in a complex curve at which curvature changes sign. Curves such as the transverse arching profile of a violin plate from the nadir of the recurve to the apex of arching at the centerline contain a single point of inflection. Moving along the curve from the nadir of the recurve toward the apex, the slope at each point of the curve increases until the inflection point is reached. Continuing along the curve from here, the slope at each point of the curve decreases. Syn.: inflexion point, point of inflexion.

inflection point

Inflection point.

inharmonicity *n*. The extent to which the partials of a vibrating string depart from a true harmonic series. An ideal string would simultaneously vibrate at its fundamental frequency and also at other frequencies which are integer multiples of the fundamental frequency (i.e. at 2x, 3x, 4x, 5x, ...). Real strings exhibit inharmonicity and so the frequencies of the partials are not true integer multiples of the fundamental, tending to skew sharp. The extent of inharmonicity is primarily a function of the bending stiffness of the string.

ink *n*. Coloring solution made of pigment mixed with a vehicle to form an emulsion. Ink is used to color an absorbent material or to color very fine engraved lines in hard materials like pearl. See also: dye, dye solution, pigment, vehicle.

ink-drawn purfling *n*. Decorative purfling that is drawn on the surface of the instrument plates with ink, rather than being inlaid strips of wood. This style of purfling was found on some plucked instruments until about the middle of the 19th century. See also: purfling

inlay *n*. Any work involving the insertion of one material into pockets cut into the surface of another. Inlay common to lutherie include pearl inlay and wood inlay. Inlay features include fret markers, decorative headstock inlay, and purfling and back strips.

inner form *n*. see inside mold

inside bevel gouge *n*. see in-cannel gouge

inside mold *n*. A mold used in the construction of the garland (rib and block assembly) of stringed instruments. The inside mold fits inside the garland. Another way to put this is the garland is built around the mold. Inside molds are used extensively in the production of violin family instruments. Note that this definition is common in North America and in some other parts of the world. Unfortunately in other places the term means the exact opposite. Disambiguation often must be done by context. Due to the ambiguity of the term it is best to not use it

Pearl inlay and its pocket in a headplate for a guitar made by the author.

but instead to describe where the mold fits in relation to the garland. Syn.: inner form, internal form, internal mold. See also: garland, mold, outside mold.

inspection camera *n*. Device for looking inside of and photographing the insides of confined spaces. Modern devices usually attach to a computer, phone or similar device via USB and provide a thin probe that can be inserted into sound holes and other small holes. Syn.: borescope, endoscope.

A USB inspection camera connected to a phone.

inspection lamp *n*. see inspection light

inspection light *n*. A light used for the inspection of the inside of an instrument. Most inspection lights are built on the principle of the drop light, a light at the end of a flexible wire. Instrument inspection lights must be small enough to be introduced into the instrument through a sound hole. Strings of Christmas tree lights are often used as inspection lights.

inspection mirror *n*. A small mirror on the end of a flexible or articulated stick used to view the inside of an instrument. Dental exam mirrors are often used for instrument inspection mirrors.

Inspection mirror inserted into the soundhole of a guitar.

integral bridge saddle *n*. Guitars of Louis Panormo featured bridges where the leading edge was a raised lip that served as the saddle. This style of bridge was a transition between the saddle-less lute style bridge and the modern bridge which has a separate saddle located in a slot in the bridge. See also: Louis Panormo.

intensity *n*. In acoustics, the measure of sound strength. Measured as rate of flow per unit of area.

internal mold *n*. see inside mold

in-the-white *adj*. Describes a fully assembled but unfinished instrument.

I

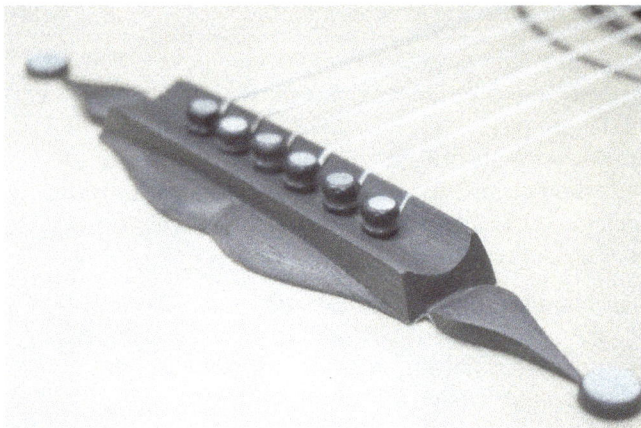

Integral bridge saddle of the bridge of a replica Panormo guitar. The front edge of the bridge itself serves as the saddle.

intonating *v*. To adjust intonation.

intonation *n*. The accuracy of pitch of a fretted instrument. Although luthiers generally do not attempt to adjust fret placement to achieve more accurate intonation, adjustments are often made to placement of the bridge saddle(s) and sometimes the nut. Adjustment of intonation is easy for instruments like electric guitars which have individually adjustable saddles.

ipe (EE-pay) see *Handroanthus* spp.

Irish bouzouki *n*. An instrument with four courses of double strings often tuned GDAD at an octave below the mandolin. Irish bouzoukis are variations on Greek bouzoukis and generally feature "flat" top and back with a floating bridge and a tailpiece to anchor the strings.

Irish harp *n*. see Celtic harp

iron *n*. Metal part. In lutherie this term generally refers to a part of a plane; either the blade itself, or the cap iron which holds and stiffens the blade. See also: cap iron.

iron oxide *n*. Rust. Identified in the finishes of old violins. Possibly used as a drier and/or pigment (Venetian red).

isotropic *adj*. Uniform in all directions. As applies to materials this means the material properties are uniform in all directions through the material. Metal is an isotropic material. Its stiffness is the same in all directions. Wood is not an isotropic material. It is stiffer along the grain than it is across the grain. See also: anisotropic.

ivoroid *n*. Synthetic ivory, made of plastic, usually celluloid, PVC or polyester.

Ivoroid tuning machine buttons.

ivory *n*. Animal tusk material, traditionally used for instrument nut and saddle and often used for trim. Use of this material from non-extinct animals is essentially banned for new instruments due to international regulations.

J

jack *n*. Mechanical device for pushing two parts apart. Functionally a jack it the opposite of a clamp.

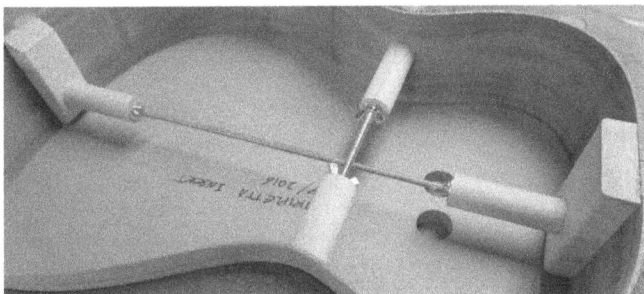

These special purpose rib jacks expand to hold the ribs of a guitar in place in the mold during assembly.

Japan dryer *n*. Drying agent for oil varnish, usually containing a mix of metallic dryer, thinner, and some resin. See also: metallic dryer.

Japanese pull saw *n*. A class of woodworking saws that generally feature thin, replaceable blades that cut on the pull direction. The most common saws in this class are the double edge Ryoba, used for general cross-cutting and ripping, the single edge Kataha, and the Dozuki backsaw. See also: Dozuki, Kataha, Ryoba.

jawari *v*. Process of shaping the top of the saddle of the sitar or similar instrument. These instruments do not provide a definite termination for the string at the saddle but rather a smooth hump. This gives the buzzy sound characteristic of instruments of this family. See also: closed jawari, ghodi, open jawari.

Japanese pull saw being used to trim the back reinforcement strip of a guitar back.

jeweler's saw *n*. A small handsaw with a frame supporting a thin blade. Jeweler's saws are used in lutherie for cutting out inlay materials like mother of pearl.

Jewitt, Jeff Strongsville OH, USA, guitar luthier and wood finishing expert. Jeff has written a number of books and produced instructional videos on wood finishing, including one on guitar finishing.

jig *n*. Any shop-built device used to hold work and/or tools during a construction process. The use of jigs generally improves accuracy, consistency and speed of a process. See also: fixture.

Jeweler's saw being used to cut an inlay from a sheet of shell.

JND *abbr.* see just noticeable difference

join *v.* To glue or otherwise permanently attach two boards to each other at an edge.

Preparing to join the two bookmatched halves of a guitar top.

joint *n.* The location of a wood-to-wood connection, e.g. the neck joint.

joint *v.* To plane straight the edges of boards that will be glued together.

jointer *n.* A stationary power tool for planing straight board edges.

jointer knife *n.* The cutter of a jointer. See also: jointer

Jonge, Sergei de Ottawa Canada classical and steel string guitar luthier and teacher.

jumbo *adj, n.* One of the "standard" acoustic steel string guitar body shapes. The jumbo shape is characterized by a large body, relatively square shoulders, a tight waist and a rounded tail end. The Gibson J-200 is the iconic jumbo guitar.

just intonation *n.* Musical tuning in which scale tones are related to each other by simple whole number ratios.

Body outline of jumbo guitar.

just noticeable difference *n.* In musical psychoacoustics, the minimal difference in some aspect of a musical tone that is reliably detectable by human listeners. Syn.: difference limen. See also: psychoacoustics.

K

kamanche *n*. A Persian (Iranian) bowed instrument, also called a spike fiddle. The modern instrument has four metal strings and a rounded bowl-like body which is covered with a skin sounding board. The instrument is played in the upright position.

Kasha, Michael Physical chemist and classical guitar designer. His classical guitar design was based on what was known about guitar acoustics at the time and focused on improving efficiency of the instrument. He collaborated with luthier Richard Schneider, who built instruments from his designs. See also: Richard Schneider.

kataha *n*. Japanese pull saw used for general cutting. See also: Japanese pull saw.

katalox *n*. see *Swartzia cubensis*

kauri wood *n*. see *Agathis australis*

Kay Musical Instrument Company *n*. see Stromberg Voisinet

kerf lining *n*. see kerfed lining

kerfed lining *n*. Lining material used primarily in guitars and mandolins. It consists of wood strips that are kerfed (cut almost all the way through) at close regular intervals. The kerfs allow the lining to be bent cold, which speeds assembly time. Syn.: kerfing, kerf lining See also: laminated lining, lining, reverse kerfed lining, solid lining.

kerfing *n*. see kerfed lining

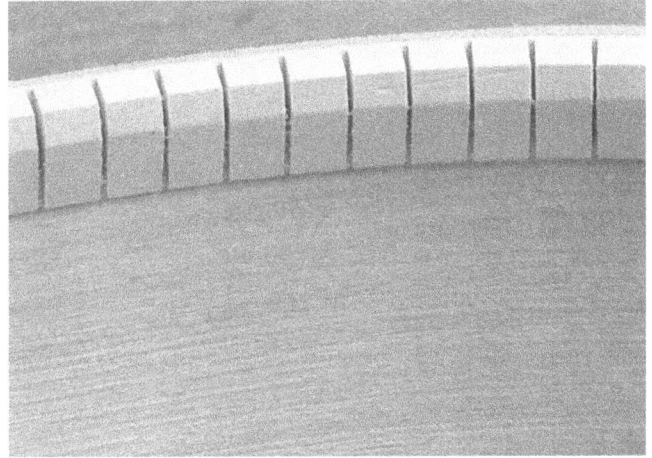

Kerfed lining.

key tuning machine *n*. Tuning machine that features a metal key "handle" instead of a button. See also: tuning machine.

kick off *v*. Setting of cyanoacrylate glue. See also: cyanoacrylate glue.

kiln dried wood *n*. Wood that has been dried with the application of heat. Kiln dried wood is dried in an oven or kiln. Kiln drying takes considerably less time than air drying, but is thought to result in less dimensionally stable wood. See also: air dried wood.

kin *n*. Japanese instrument. A small size koto. See also: koto.

King William pine *n*. see *Athrotaxis selaginoides*

kit *n*. Tiny fiddle used by 17th and 18th century dance instructors. Syn.: dancing master's fiddle, pochette, pocket fiddle.

kithara *n*. Ancient Greek lyre family instrument consisting of a rectangular box with two curved arms. A cross piece at the top of the arms anchors the strings.

Klein, Steve USA electric and acoustic guitar luthier.

K

knot shadow *n*. A defect in wood. The effect of a knot on the grain of wood can usually be seen quite a distance away from the knot. The grain may show localized bending and in quartered pieces the grain may be tilted at the shadow. Knot shadows are usually quite visible under finish even if they don't look like much on unfinished wood.

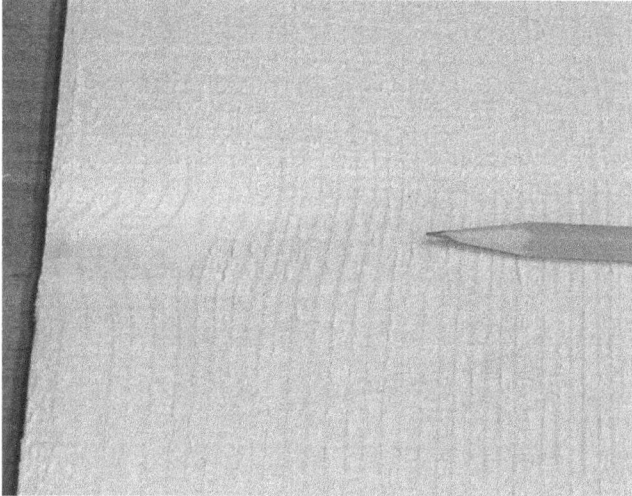

Japanese koto.

Knot shadow on a spruce soundboard to the left of the pencil.

Kuronen put together a collection of instruments for the show at the museum entitled "Dangerous Curves: The Art of the Guitar" and authored a book of the same name.

Kyvelos, Peter Massachusetts USA luthier and repairman specializing in Middle Eastern instruments. Noted for his ouds. Deceased 2017.

koa *n*. see *Acacia koa*

Kohno, Masaru (1926-1998) Japanese classical guitar maker. Founded the guitar company that bears his name. Began building guitars in 1948 and studied guitar making in Spain in 1960.

koto *n*. Japanese zither-like instrument with silk strings. See also: zither

khula *n*. see open jawari

K

Kuronen, Darcy Curator of the musical instrument collection at the Boston Museum of Fine Arts, Mr.

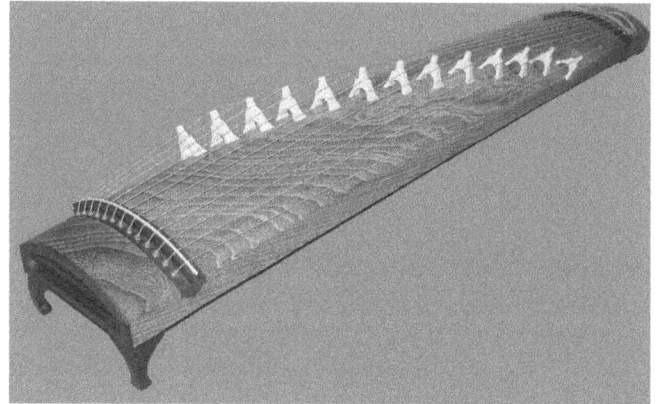

L

L-0 *n*. Gibson steel string flattop guitar built between 1926 and 1942. Initially introduced at 13.5″ wide at the lower bout, it expanded in width in 1930 to 14.75″. In early examples the neck joined the body at the 12th fret. Instruments with the neck joined to the body at the 14th fret were introduced in 1932. The guitars were available in various years with spruce or mahogany tops, and birch, maple and mahogany backs and sides.

L-00 *n*. Gibson steel string flattop guitar built between 1929 and 1945. Generally the same as the L-0 but with less decoration. See also: L-0.

L-1 *n*. Gibson steel string flattop guitar built between 1926 and 1937. Generally the same as the L-0 but with better materials and decoration. See also: L-0.

L-2 *n*. Gibson steel string flattop guitar built between 1929 and 1935. Generally similar to the L-0 but with better materials and decoration. This was the top of the line L series instrument. It originally featured a 13 fret neck, but this was changed to 12 fret in 1931, then back to 13 again in 1932. 1934 instruments featured a 14 fret neck. The 1932 instrument featured a trapeze tailpiece and adjustable bridge. See also: L-0.

L-5 *n*. Gibson steel string archtop guitar, introduced in 1923 and originally intended for use in mandolin orchestras. This is the iconic jazz guitar originally applied to that musical style during the transition from banjo to guitar as the big band rhythm instrument in the 1920s and popularized by Eddie Lang. The L-5 features f-holes, a 14 fret neck and a 16″ wide lower bout.

label wrinkler *n*. Humorous name for back reinforcing strip, so called because, if it wasn't there, the inside surface of the back of a flattop guitar would provide a smooth surface onto which the label could be glued. Syn.: back reinforcing strip.

Lace Sensor *n*. Brand name of a passive magnetic guitar pickup. This is a single coil pickup which makes use of magnetic shielding to reduce noise.

Lacey Act *n*. U.S. act intended to prevent abuse and overuse of plants and wildlife. The act prohibits taking and trading in illegally taken plants and animals. It is administered by the Departments of the Interior, Commerce, and Agriculture. Lutherie interest in the act and its enforcement relates mostly to wood and shell materials, particularly those that were potentially harvested illegally, including those from other countries.

Lacôte, René-François (1785-1855) French guitar maker, likely born in or near Paris.

lacquer *n*. The term generally refers to any fast drying alcohol thinned finish, usually sprayed on. In lutherie the word when unqualified (as opposed to qualified terms such as acrylic lacquer, waterborne lacquer, etc.) usually refers to nitrocellulose lacquer, which is made from highly refined cellulose in a vehicle of alcohol, to which other volatile compounds are added. Lacquers are high burn-in finishes. Each coat melts into the previous coats forming an unlayered mass. See also: brushing lacquer, burn-in.

ladder bracing *n*. A bracing pattern that makes use of braces that are parallel to each other and perpendicular to the instrument centerline. Ladder bracing was commonly used on the tops of all flattop stringed instruments before the use of fan bracing and X bracing and is still the most common bracing pattern for backs. See also: A bracing, fan bracing, V bracing, X bracing.

lake pigment *n*. A pigment made by combining a dye and an opaque binder. The binder is usually white and highly

L

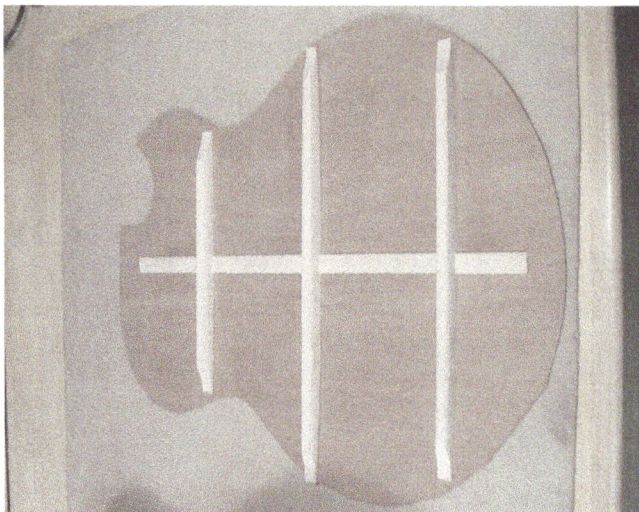

Ladder bracing on a guitar back.

Laminate trimmer.

reflective and, in modern pigments, is usually a metallic salt. The color of the pigment comes from the color of the dye.

laminate *n*. Any material made of multiple layers. A number of types of laminate are commonly used in stringed instruments. The most common is laminated wood. These are used for backs, sides and even tops in inexpensive instruments. There are also wood/carbon fiber laminates, used in the construction of braces. Various other laminated materials are used by some builders as well.

laminate trimmer *n*. A small router originally intended for trimming high pressure laminates like Formica. These are often used in lutherie when a small router is required, such as when routing binding channels.

laminated *adj*. Describes something made of thin layers of material, usually wood veneer, glued together. Some instruments make use of laminated sides, plates, linings or necks.

laminated lining *n*. Linings made of laminated strips of solid material. The strips may be pre-bent before lamination/installation, or in some cases may be cold laminated. See also: lining, kerfed lining, solid lining.

laminated neck *n*. Instrument neck made up of a number of strips of wood laminated together. This construction is often used for strictly decorative purposes. It is also used to increase the long term stability of the instrument neck.

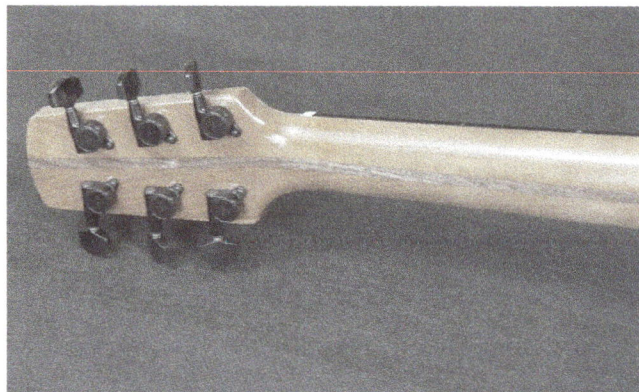

Laminated guitar neck constructed of two pieces of cherry with a center laminate of walnut.

landing / takeoff stroke *n.* Characteristic motion used in the application of finish by French polishing and in the leveling of finish by hand. In French polishing the tampon is moved to come in contact with the instrument as a plane lands, that is, in a gliding motion that just softly touches down on the surface while moving. The stroke continues with the tampon moving across the surface until near the far edge, at which point it is gradually lifted from the surface while moving, in the same manner as a plane taking off. This prevents finish from being squeegeed off the tampon by the edge of the instrument, which prevents buildup of a ridge of finish at the edge. Level sanding and rubbing out is done with similar motion. See also: French polishing, level sanding, rubbing out.

lap *v.* To flatten metal, generally by rubbing two pieces together with abrasives between them. In lutherie the term refers to the general flattening of a metal part or tool, like the back of a chisel or plane iron.

lap joint *n.* A woodworking joint in which the two pieces to be joined are overlapped for gluing.

lap steel *n.* An electric guitar that is played in the lap of the sitting musician. It is played with a slide in the manner of the pedal steel guitar.

Larrivée, Jean Canadian guitar maker, builds classical, steel string acoustic and electric guitars.

Larson, Carl and August Early 20th century guitar manufacturers in Chicago IL, USA. The Larson brothers produced few instruments under their own name, but manufactured brand name instruments under the names Maurer, Prairie State and Euphonon. They also built "house brand" instruments for retailers such as William C. Stahl and William J. Dyer. Syn.: Maurer, Prairie State, Euphonon. See also: William J. Dyer, William C. Stahl.

laser cutting machine *n.* CNC machine that moves a laser cutter. Laser cutting machines have some advantages over CNC routers because the laser does not physically touch the material and so they require less robust material clamping. The cutting area is very thin so little material is sacrificed to the cut. For example a laser cutting machine can cut a sheet of veneer into purfling lines with little waste and without the need to secure the veneer sheet firmly to the machine base. These machines are found in larger guitar shops and in some small shops as well. See also: CNC machine.

Laskin, William "Grit" USA steel string and classical guitar luthier, known for highly detailed inlay work and armrest bevels.

late wood *n.* The harder, heavier, less porous and slower growing part of the annular ring or grain of wood. See also: early wood.

laterally tapered fingerboard *n.* Fingerboard that tapers down from nut end to body end but tapers more on the bass side. This provides for a little higher action for the bass strings to provide needed clearance for their vibration, while maintaining an even height of the bridge saddle across all strings. This construction feature is found almost exclusively on the classical guitar. See also: tapered fingerboard.

lattice bracing *n.* A bracing pattern used for the top plate of some flattop guitars. The pattern consists of an orthogonal pattern of struts that look like a lattice. Lattice bracing is generally attributed to Greg Smallman and is sometimes called Smallman style bracing. See also: bracing pattern, Greg Smallman.

lavender spike oil *n.* Botanical oil distilled from the herb *Lavandula latifolia*. It is a component of a number of traditional violin varnish recipes.

lead *n.* Heavy metal, identified in the finishes of old violins. Possibly used as a drier or pigment.

L

L

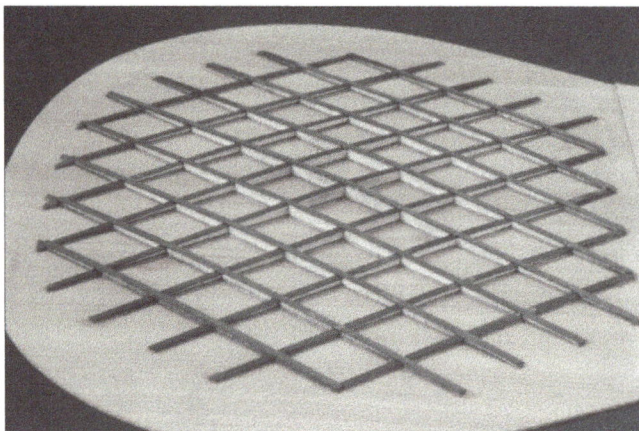

Lattice bracing on guitar top by Greg Smallman.

lead zirconate titanate *n*. Piezoelectric ceramic crystal material used in the construction of piezo pickups. Syn.: PZT. See also: piezoelectric.

lemon oil *n*. The oil of the skin of the lemon fruit. It is a light weight oil and is often used as a wood polish. Commercial lemon oil wood polish is usually made of lemon scented mineral oil.

Leonardo Guitar Research Project *n*. Nonprofit partnership involved in research and promotion of alternatives to tropical wood species used in lutherie.

level sanding *v*. The sanding of cured finish to level out the surface. It is generally done using fine grits of sandpaper on a felt, soft rubber or cork block. Level sanding can be done wet or dry. Wet sanding uses water, oil, or solvent as a lubricant. Dry sanding uses stearated sandpaper to prevent corning of the sanding dust. See also: corning, dry sanding, stearated sandpaper, wet sanding.

lever harp *n*. see Celtic harp

Liberon Finishing Oil Brand name of a commercial finishing product used by some guitar luthiers. See also: Tru-oil.

lignin *n*. (LIG-nin) Part of the microstructure of wood. The "glue" which holds the microstructural components of wood together.

lime wood *n*. see *Tilia americana*

linden *n*. see *Tilia americana*

lined fretless bass *n*. Fretless bass guitar with lines on the playing surface of the fretboard which indicate fret positions. See also: fretless bass.

lining *n*. Strips or blocks of wood at the junction of the ribs and plates of most stringed instruments. The purpose of the linings is to increase the gluing area at the rib/plate joint. See also: kerfed lining, laminated lining, solid lining, tentellón.

lining clamp *n*. Clamp used to glue the linings to the rib of an instrument. Most luthiers use some kind of small spring clamp, either a commercial spring clamp or a spring-type clothes pin.

linseed oil *n*. A drying oil that is used alone as a finish or as a component of varnishes. Linseed oil comes from the seeds of the flax plant. It is used in lutherie primarily as a

Lining clamps used to clamp kerfed lining.

finish for the neck shaft of violin family instruments. Syn.: raw linseed oil. See also: boiled linseed oil, drying oil.

lipstick tube pickup *n*. A single coil magnetic guitar pickup with a cylindrical metal cover that has the look of a lipstick tube. Originally featured on guitars made by Danelectro. See also: single coil pickup.

liquid hide glue *n*. A form of hide glue that is commercially available in ready to use liquid form. It is as strong, hard, and heat resistant as hot hide glue. Like hot hide glue, it is not very water resistant. It can be used to make a joint which is readily reversible. Its major advantage is that it takes a long time before it begins to harden, which makes it useful in applications that require the assembly pieces to be manipulated after the glue has been applied. Its major disadvantage is that it has a relatively short shelf life (approx. 1 year) and considerably degrades after that time. It is not often used in lutherie. See also: hide glue, hot hide glue.

Liriodendron tulipifera *n*. North American tree generally called yellow poplar, tulip poplar or just poplar. It is not a true poplar. The wood sees limited use in lutherie but is sometimes used for electric guitar bodies that will be painted. It is moderately dense and moderately stiff. It machines well but tends to be fuzzy when sanded. Specific gravity (dry) 0.46. Modulus of elasticity is 10.9 GPa. Shrinkage (radial, tangential): 4.6%, 8.2%.

liver of sulfur *n*. Sulfides of potassium. Used to synthetically age copper and brass. See also: relicing

Loar, Lloyd (1886-1943) USA engineer and instrument designer. Worked for Gibson in the early 20th century. Designed guitars, mandolins and pickups.

logarithmic decrement *n*. A measure of damping in a system, the logarithmic decrement is the natural log of the ratio of the amplitudes of two successive peaks.

long oil varnish *n*. Oil varnish containing a relatively large quantity of non-drying oil. Long oil varnishes dry softer than short oil varnishes. Long oil varnishes are not generally used for finishing stringed instruments. See also: oil varnish, short oil varnish.

longitudinal *adj*. Referring to the length of an instrument or component. The longitudinal centerline of an instrument is the center of the instrument along its length. Longitudinal stiffness of wood is its stiffness along its length.

longitudinal arch *n*. Profile of the arching of a plate of an archtop instrument such as a violin family instrument along the plate centerline.

longitudinal bar *n*. see longitudinal brace

longitudinal brace *n*. A brace that is oriented more or less in parallel with the centerline of the instrument.

longitudinal stiffness *n*. Stiffness along the long dimension of a part.

longitudinal vibration *n*. Strings vibrate in three distinct modes: transverse, longitudinal and torsional. Although transverse vibration produces most and sometimes all of the sound produced by an instrument, longitudinal vibration can produced a small but audible high pitched clang tone in the bass strings of certain instruments. Longitudinal vibration manifests as a compression wave moving end to end along the string. It is generally of no concern to the designers and builders of acoustic instruments but it can be detectible by piezoelectric bridge pickups. See also: clang tone, torsional vibration, transverse vibration.

loop end *adj*. Strings can be classified by the termination features at the string anchor end. Loop end strings terminate in a loop of the core material. String anchors for this type of string contain a hook over which the loop is hung. See also: ball end.

L

L

Lospennato, Leonardo Berlin Germany based luthier, author, and editor of the magazine *Sustain*, from the Fellowship of European Luthiers.

loudness *n*. Perceived strength of sound. When used as a general quality of a musical instrument, this term generally refers to the perceived intensity of the sound of the instrument from close to the instrument. See also: intensity, projection.

loudness level *n*. Comparative loudness.

Lover, Seth Patented a design for a humbucking guitar pickup in 1955 while working for Gibson. See also: humbucking pickup.

low angle plane *n*. A plane with its blade set at a low angle to its sole. Low angle planes are better at planing end grain but worse at planing with the grain.

lower bout *n*. The lowest and usually the widest part of the profile of a guitar or violin family instrument.

lower transverse brace *n*. Transverse bracc of the top of the acoustic flattop guitar. Classical guitars will often use a lower transverse brace located just below the soundhole. Steel string guitars often have two lower transverse braces, located between the bridge plate and the tail block and positioned somewhat diagonally. See also: transverse brace.

Lower transverse brace of the top of a classical guitar.

lowpass filter *n*. An electrical circuit or an acoustic system which passes low frequencies relatively intact but attenuates higher frequencies. See also: bandpass filter, highpass filter.

lozenge *n*. Decorative squashed square shape used for inlay. Rosettes of early guitars often featured alternating lozenges and squares of pearl on a dark background.

lp *abbr*. Les Paul.

Lucchi wood elasticity tester *n*. (LOO-key) Also referred to as a Lucchi meter. An electronic device used to measure the speed of sound in wood. Syn.: Lucchi meter.

Lundberg, Robert (1948-2001) USA luthier and author, best known for lutes and instruments of the lute family.

lute *n*. Renaissance/baroque instrument featuring a teardrop-shaped body with a rounded staved back and a pegbox tilted back on the neck shaft at a severe angle. Lutes generally use tied frets and are strung with gut strings. Many varieties have existed, including long and short neck lutes, instruments of various sizes and pitchs, and instruments with extended pitch range, some featuring additional harp-like bass strings. See also: tied fret.

lute guitar *n*. A hybrid instrument dating from the 19th century that features guitar neck and strings and a lute body.

lute rose *n*. The decorative insert in the soundhole of a lute.

luth *v*. To build stringed musical instruments (slang).

lutherie *n*. (LOO-ther-ee) The craft of constructing stringed musical instruments. The term is generally used to describe the construction of bowed and plucked instruments.

lutherie school *n*. School that teaches lutherie. See also: lutherie.

luthier *n.* (LOO-thee-er) Person that builds or repairs stringed musical instruments. The word is French (pronounced loo-tea-AY) but the common anglicized pronunciation is given. Its original definition is a person (and specifically a male) that makes lutes, but it is currently used in the USA to indicate any person that builds any kind of stringed musical instrument.

luthière n. (loo-ti-AIR) Feminine form of the French word luthier. This word is not in common English usage.

Lutz spruce *n.* Hybrid spruce from the Pacific Northwest of North America. It is a hybrid of Sitka spruce (*Picea sitchensis*), Engelmann spruce (*Picea engelmannii*) and white spruce (*Picea glauca*). Syn.: Roche spruce. See also: *Picea engelmannii, Picea glauca, Picea sitchensis*.

Lyman, Frederick C. (1925-2011) American double bass builder and author. In addition to his instruments Lyman is known for his article (*American Lutherie #24, #25*) and plans for an inexpensive upright bass, available from the Guild of American Luthiers.

Lyon and Healy Late 19th to early 20th century guitar and mandolin manufacturer based in Chicago IL, USA. Founded by George Washburn Lyon and Patrick Joseph Healy. This company was originally a retailer for and a spin off of the Boston MA sheet music company Oliver Ditson Co. They began instrument production by contracting out work to other builders, but eventually built instruments in house as well. They were the largest manufacturer of guitars by the start of the 20th century. Their top of the line instruments were sold under the Washburn name. Syn.: Washburn.

lyra *n.* Simple ancient Greek instrument with a small soundbox usually made of tortoise shell.

lyra viol *n.* Baritone range viol. See also: viol.

IMAGE IS IN THE PUBLIC DOMAIN

Image on vase of muse playing ancient Greek lyra.

lyre *n.* Folk instrument taken from the ancient Greek lyra. It is like a small harp with strings attached to an open frame.

lyre guitar *n.* A guitar with a shape similar to the lyre. The body of the lyre guitar has two arms which emerge from the upper bout/shoulders area and connect to the neck at or near the headstock. See also: lyre.

M

M *adj*. One of the "standard" acoustic steel string guitar body shapes. The M shape is a large body with a lower bout width of approx. 16 inches. The designation comes from the original Martin M series guitars, which Martin calls "grand auditorium" size. Syn.: grand auditorium.

Macassar ebony *n*. see *Diospyros celebica*

Maccaferri guitar *n*. see Selmer Maccaferri guitar

Maccaferri, Mario (1900-1993) Italian guitarist and luthier born in Cento, near Bologna, Italy. Best known for the design of what are now know as Selmer Maccaferri style guitars for Selmer in Paris. He also manufactured his own line of inexpensive guitars and ukuleles in the USA which made extensive use of injection molded styrene plastic. See also: Selmer Maccaferri guitar.

***Machaerium* spp**. *n*. Pao ferro, Bolivian rosewood, morado, palo santo, caviuna, santos rosewood, Brazilian ironwood. Not a true rosewood (*Dalbergia*), this is a hard, heavy and stiff wood used for fingerboards and guitar backs and sides. Dry wood has a specific gravity of 0.87 and a modulus of elasticity of 10.86 GPa.

machete *n*. Portuguese guitar and ancestor of the ukulele.

machine head *n*. see tuning machine

Madagascar rosewood *n*. see *Dalbergia baronii*

madder *n*. Red pigment from the roots of the Eurasian shrub *Rubia tinctorum*.

Maggini, Paolo (1580-c.1630) Italian violin luthier from Brescia, considered to be one of the earliest makers of the violin.

magnetic pickup *n*. A transducer that uses a permanent magnet or magnets and a coil of wire to convert string vibrations to electrical current. Magnetic pickups can be used only with strings composed of ferrous materials. The vibration of the string over the magnet displaces magnetic lines of force. This displacement induces current changes in the coil. Magnetic pickups are used primarily in electric guitars.

magnetic thickness gauge *n*. A gauge used to measure the thickness of components of an instrument *in situ*, in cases where complete access to the back side of the component is not possible and so calipers cannot be used. Magnetic thickness gauges are used to measure the thickness of violin and guitar plates without having to remove the plates from the instrument. The gauge is positioned on the outside surface of the plate and then a small but powerful rare earth magnet is slipped inside the instrument. The magnet sticks to the gauge but on the other side of the plate. When the gauge is moved, the magnet will move along with it. The gauge works by measuring the magnitude of the magnetic field, which varies with distance from the magnet. See also: caliper.

mahogany *n*. Wood from any of a number of species of *Swietenia*. The most commonly used mahogany in lutherie is *Swietenia macrophylla*, generally referred to as Honduras, true, or genuine mahogany. The term is also used to describe other species with wood that is similar in appearance. See also: *Swietenia macrophylla*.

main air resonance *n*. The lowest peak in the frequency response curve of a stringed instrument, the main air resonance is the result of the coupling of the Helmholtz resonance and resonances of the plates. Its frequency is lower than that of the Helmholtz resonance. The resonance serves to support the lowest notes of the instrument. In most instruments the main air resonance is found near to the lowest note the instrument is capable of producing. An exception to this is the double bass, where it is generally located between the notes of the lowest two strings. See also: frequency response curve, Helmholtz resonance.

mains voltage *n*. Line voltage (British).

manche *n*. (monsh) Neck, neck shaft (French).

mandolin *n*. Soprano voice instrument strung in four courses of two wire strings each. Tuning is the same as that of the violin. Mandolins are generally played with a pick. The most common styles of mandolins are the Neapolitan or round backed, the archtop, and the flattop.

mandolin family *n*. Gibson and other manufacturers produced mandolin family instruments in the early part of the 20th century. The instruments are analogous to those of the violin (string) quartet and include the mandolin, mandola and mandocello. Mandobass instruments also were made. These instruments were played in small ensembles and also in larger mandolin orchestras. Note that early 20th century USA mandolin orchestras differ from northern European mandolin orchestras, which are composed of mandolin, octave mandola and classical guitar. See also: mandolin.

mango *n*. Neck shaft (Spanish).

manico *n*. (MAN-ee-co) Neck or neck shaft (Italian).

Manouche guitar *n*. see Selmer Maccaferri guitar

Manzanero, Felix *n*. Spanish guitarmaker from Madrid; also a collector of Spanish guitars.

Manzer, Linda *n*. Canadian luthier, builder of archtop and flattop guitars. She is known for introducing a wedge-shaped guitar body, intended to enhance ergonomics, and for a multi-neck harp style guitar inspired by paintings by the artist Picasso.

maple *n*. see *Acer*

Marchione, Stephen Texas USA guitar luthier specializing in archtop and classical guitars built using traditional Italian building methods.

marking gauge *n*. A tool used to scribe an offset line from a reference edge of a board. The traditional design is a block of wood with a movable stick mounted in a hole. The end of the stick contains a scribing point. A newer design is all metal and uses a sharpened wheel to scribe the line.

Markneukirchen German city known as a traditional manufacturing center of musical instruments. The city is the birthplace of Christian Frederick Martin, and the home of Rubner tuning machines.

marquetry *n*. Pictures or patterns made from inlaid wood veneer. Marquetry is sometimes used as a decorative technique on stringed musical instruments. Marquetry strips are wood strips with decorative patterns such as herringbone or stripes. These are used as guitar purfling and back strips. See also: purfling, back strip.

marriage strip *n*. see back reinforcing strip

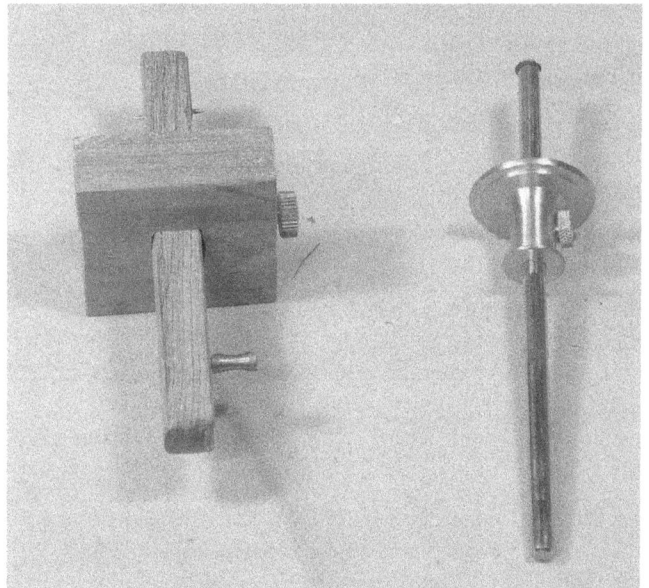

Traditional wood and modern metal marking gauges.

M

Martin, Christian Frederick (1796-1873) German guitarmaker and founder of the C.F. Martin company. Martin was an apprentice of Austrian luthier Johann Stauffer. Martin moved to New York City in 1833 and opened a retail shop and small manufacturing facility. The company moved to Nazareth PA in 1838. Martin popularized the steel string flattop guitar. See also: Johann Stauffer.

Martin Jr., Christian Frederick (1825-1888) Business partner of his father beginning in 1857, he ran the C.F. Martin Guitar Co. upon his father's death in 1873 and until his own death in 1888.

Martin III, Christian Frederick (1894-1986) Took control of the C.F. Martin Co. upon the death of his father, Frank Henry Martin. Expanded production facilities and expanded the product line to include banjos, drums and strings.

Martin IV, Christian Frederick "Chris" (1955-) Grandson of Christian Frederick Martin III, he ran the C.F. Martin Co. starting in 1986. Known for introducing modern production methods.

Martin, Frank Henry (1866-1948) Ran the C.F. Martin Guitar Co. following the death of his father, Christian Frederick Martin Jr. During his tenure mandolins and ukuleles were introduced to the Martin product line as well as dreadnought guitars. See also: dreadnought.

Martin, Douglas Boat builder and experimental violin maker from Maine USA. Martin is noted for a series of experimental violins made mostly from balsa. He also is noted for a rapid prototyping technique that makes the production of experimental instruments both fast and inexpensive.

masking *n.* Psychoacoustic effect where one sound reduces the perception of another sound. Loud sounds can mask softer ones or ones of a higher pitch that occur simultaneously, but can also mask softer sounds that occur after and even before the louder sounds. See also: psychoacoustics.

mass *n.* A property of materials, mass is a fundamental measure of the amount of matter in an object. For most lutherie purposes mass is equivalent to weight. Mass is one of three material properties which affect a physical vibrating system, such as a string or instrument top. The others are stiffness and damping. See also: stiffness, damping.

mass loading *v.* Adding mass to a vibrating system to change its vibratory characteristics. In lutherie this is generally done as either an investigative technique or less frequently as a construction technique. Adding mass to a vibrating system lowers the frequency at which the system vibrates and also the Q of resonance. Small weights are sometimes temporarily added to parts of an instrument to lower the frequency of vibration and to ascertain the effect on the instrument. Mass is also sometimes permanently added to an instrument. Wound strings are an example of mass loading — the windings increase the mass of the string while retaining much of the flexibility of the core. See also: Q.

mass per unit length *n.* Description of the mass of a vibrating string, used in calculations of vibrating frequency and string length. Syn.: unit weight.

Mastertone banjo *n.* Banjo made by Gibson, considered to be the standard bluegrass banjo.

mastic *n.* 1. A resin from the mastic tree (*Pistacia lentiscus*) used as a component of violin varnishes. 2. Any thick, hardening mixture of binder and pigment materials, used as a surround for decorative inlay. Mastics were often made of hide glue and ebony dust, or shellac and wood dust or mineral pigment. A common use of mastics was as the background material for shell inlays used to decorate the soundholes of guitars.

mástil *n.* (MAS-teel) Neck (Spanish).

Shell inlay in mastic rosette of a Mirecourt school guitar restored by James Buckland.

material safety data sheet *n*. A general information sheet containing data on various aspects of safety of hazardous industrial products and materials. These must be made available by manufacturers and sellers of these materials. Syn.: MSDS.

mathematical model *n*. Mathematical description of the behavior of a system. In lutherie mathematical models are used to describe things like the relationship between the frequency of vibration of a string and string tension, length and mass. Models of such physical systems are often only approximate, and their practical utility depends a lot on their accuracy. Syn.: model.

Maurer see Larson, Carl and August

MC *abbr*. see moisture content

McDonald, Graham Australian author and luthier. McDonald builds mandolins, ukuleles and Irish bouzoukis as well as other instruments and is author of the books *The Bouzouki Book*, *The Mandolin Project*, and *The Ukulele:An Illustrated Workshop Manual*.

McNally, Bob New Jersey USA luthier and designer of the Martin Backpacker guitar and the Strumstick, a reduced body dulcimer.

McRostie, Don Athens OH, USA, mandolin luthier and lutherie tool designer.

meander pattern *n*. A pattern used in decorative wood inlay. The meander looks like a rectangular spiral.

Meander pattern strips for the back strip of a Torres replica guitar by Federico Sheppard.

mècanique *n*. (may-cahn-EEK) Tuning machine (French).

Meccano *n*. (British) Erector Set. European lutherie articles and books will often mention jigs and fixtures that look like they were constructed using it. The term is used tongue in cheek to indicate naive mechanical construction.

medullary ray *n*. Part of the structure of wood. Medullary rays appear as radial structures which run lengthwise through the tree. These structures are more prominent in some species than in others. They are most observable in wood that has been quarter sawn, i.e. where the grain lines are vertical to the wide surface of the board. Syn.: medullary. See also: quarter sawn.

mensure *n*. see scale length Syn.: mensur.

Mersenne's laws *n*. Laws concerning the vibration of a string, as codified by Marin Mersenne. The fundamental frequency of vibration of a string is inversely proportional to its length (i.e. Pythagoras' law), proportional to the square root of the tension, and inversely proportional to the square root of its mass per unit length. See also: Marin Mersenne, Pythagoras' law.

Mersenne, Marin (1588–1648) French mathematician and priest. He developed the equation which specifies the relationship of the frequency of vibration of a string and its mass per unit of length and its tension.

metalized dye *n*. Modern dye with better color fastness than aniline dye. See also: aniline dye.

metallic drier *n*. Various metal salts in chemical solution are added (or available to be added) to finishes like varnish to speed drying. Cobalt is probably the most commonly used metallic drier. Most commercial varnishes contain metallic driers. They are also available to be added to finishes by the user. Metallic driers speed drying by increasing oxidation. Too much drier can result in a wrinkled finish due to over drying of the surface of the finish. Syn.: cobalt dryer, dryer, Japan dryer, siccative.

methanol *n*. Also called methyl alcohol or wood alcohol, methanol is a toxic alcohol. It is not used directly in lutherie due to its toxicity. It is added to ethanol by manufacturers to render it undrinkable but still useful as a solvent. This combination is called denatured alcohol. See also: denatured alcohol.

methyl alcohol *n*. see methanol

methylated spirits *n*. see denatured alcohol

Mexican ebony *n*. see *Swartzia cubensis*

Micarta *n*. A brand name of sheet plastic made from phenolic resin impregnated cloth or paper fibers. This and other phenolic based plastics are often used for guitar nuts and bridge saddles.

Micromesh *n*. Brand name of graded sandpaper with very fine grits that is made by gluing abrasives to a thin foam backing material. It is used to rub out finishes and to polish frets. This product uses its own unique grit grading system. See also: sandpaper grit.

micron grit grade *n*. A grading system for sandpapers. In this system the size of the grit particles in microns is used, so the numbers get smaller as the grit particle size gets smaller. See also: sandpaper grit.

microphonic *adj*. Describes something that behaves like a microphone. This is generally used to describe a defect of magnetic pickups, usually caused by loose parts or windings.

mill file *n*. Single cut file with flat parallel surfaces, it has one set of parallel teeth. Mill files are used in lutherie to level frets and for other metal work.

Millettia laurentii *n*. Wenge. African wood often used for fingerboards, necks and sides of guitars. The wood is dark in color, hard, heavy and stiff. Dry wood has a specific gravity of 0.87 and a modulus of elasticity of 17.6 GPa.

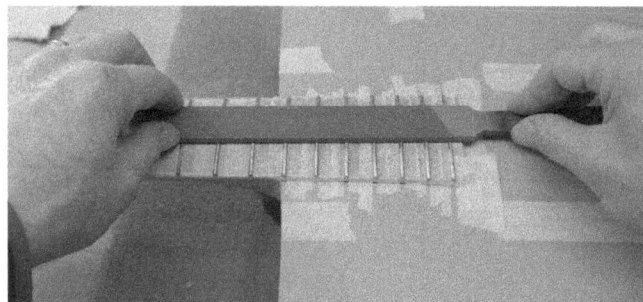

A mill file is used to level the fret tops following fret installation.

Minor, Gregg (1955–) USA plucked stringed instrument collector, scholar, recording artist and performer, best known for his work with harp guitars.

Mirecourt French city known as a historical manufacturing center of musical instruments, particularly of the violin family.

mise en place *n.* (meez on plas) French culinary term meaning "set in place" and referring to the process of having all ingredient preparation done and ready to go before starting to cook. The term is used in lutherie when referring to the preparation for finishing or gluing or other operations that need to be performed in a limited amount of time so that they can proceed smoothly.

mobility *n.* see admittance

mode *n.* In physics and in musical instrument acoustics, the term refers to a mode of vibration. Physical structures such as instruments vibrate in different modes, based on frequency. The mode patterns are based on the structure and materials of the instrument. There are different naming conventions used for these modes, but most combine a letter indicating a part of the instrument (such as 'A' for the air inside the instrument, 'T' for the instrument's top, 'B' for the whole body, etc.) and a mode number, with 0 or 1 being the lowest frequency mode for that part and successive numbers used for successively higher frequency modes.

modeler's iron *n.* A small electric iron with a straight handle, used for spot heating. It is often used in guitar repair to soften the glue under the fingerboard extension for removal of the neck.

model *n.* see mathematical model

modeling *adj.* Description of a digital device such as an effects processor or digital preamplifier or digital amplifier that simulates the sound qualities of an analog device by modifying the sound using a mathematical model of the qualities of the simulated device. See also: mathematical model.

modulus of elasticity *n.* A measure of the stiffness of an object, generally defined as stress over strain. Also called elastic modulus. In lutherie we are often concerned with both the stiffness and mass of structural components, as these two properties control the frequency at which the component will vibrate. Syn.: elastic modulus, Young's modulus.

MOE *abbr.* see modulus of elasticity

moisture content *n.* The percentage of the weight of wood that is water, expressed as a percentage of the dry weight of the wood. Green wood has a moisture content of approximately 70%. Wood that is dry enough for use has a nominal moisture content of 12%. See also: equilibrium moisture content.

moisture meter *n.* An electrical meter which measures the moisture content of wood. There are two basic types. Pin meters have two sharp pins which are plunged into the wood to take a reading. Pinless meters take readings without pricking the wood.

mold *n.* A form used to shape the ribs of an instrument. The mold will also often serve as an assembly fixture for gluing blocks and linings to the ribs to create the garland, and for gluing on the plates. There are two general types of mold, the inside mold and the outside mold. Syn.: form, mould. See also: block, garland, inside mold, lining, outside mold, plate, rib.

moment *n.* Engineering term denoting a static torque, it is a shortened form of the term moment of torque.

moment of inertia *n.* see second moment of area

Mönch, Edgar German classical guitar luthier. Moved to Canada. Teacher of Jean Larrivée. See also: Jean Larrivée.

An outside mold for a guitar body.

monochord *n.* A single-string instrument. Monochords are often built as experimental apparatus for string experiments.

monopole *n.* Vibrating element which contains a single area of vibration. In lutherie this is usually used to describe a mode of vibration of a plate, where the entire plate moves in and out. Monopoles are considered to be efficient radiators of sound. See also: dipole.

Monteleone, John USA luthier, builder of archtop guitars and mandolins. Monteleone is known for the inclusion of modern features in the context of traditional design.

Monterey cypress *n.* see *Cupressus macrocarpa*

MOP *abbr.* see mother of pearl

morado *n.* see *Machaerium* spp.

mordant *n.* A substance used to set dyes.

mortise *n.* A pocket cut into a piece of wood to accept a tenon. See also: mortise and tenon, tenon.

mortise and tenon *n.* A type of wood-to-wood joint. In lutherie, mortise and tenon joints are most often used as neck joints. The most common style is the dovetail joint, but straight-sided mortise and tenon joints are also sometimes used. See also: mortise, tenon, dovetail joint.

MOTS *abbr.* see mother of toilet seat

mother of pearl *n.* Also called nacre, mother of pearl is the smooth lining found on the inside of some mollusk shells. It is the same substance that pearls are made of. Mother of pearl is used as an inlay material. Syn.: MOP, nacre.

mother of toilet seat *n.* Fanciful name for imitation pearl material, usually made of celluloid or acetate. The term derives from one use of early celluloid plastics. The term is sometimes used derisively, sometimes ironically. Syn.: pearloid.

mould *n.* see mold

mountain dulcimer *n.* A diatonically fretted instrument with three or four strings and a thin hour glass shape. The instrument is played on the lap.

Mouradian, Jim Massachusetts USA guitar luthier and repairman. Specialized in electric bass guitars. Deceased 2017.

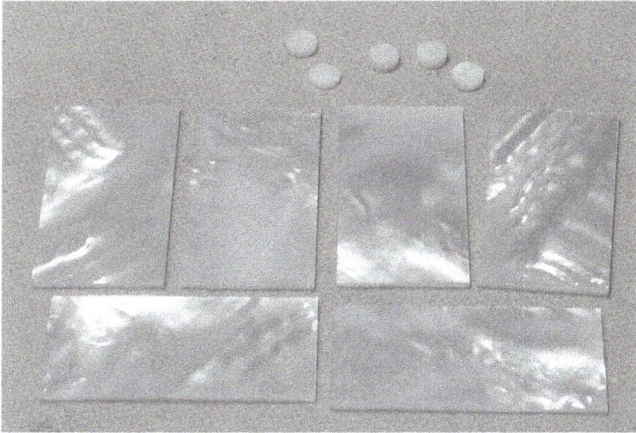

Mother of pearl sheets and dots.

COURTESY ALBERTO PAREDES

A Colombian bass bandola by Alberto Paredes featuring a multiple scale length fretboard.

moustache bridge *n.* A style of guitar bridge that features elongated wings that curl up or down in a decorative fashion, in the style of a 19th century moustache. See also: mustachio

MSDS *abbr.* see material safety data sheet

multi-scale fretboard *n.* see multiple scale length fretboard

multiple scale length fretboard *n.* A fretboard with frets placed in a skewed fashion so as to implement a different scale length for each string. Generally, multiple scale length fretboards have a shorter scale length for the treble strings and a longer length for the bass strings. This style of fretboard was first seen in the Renaissance orpharion and bandora. It is used for extended range instruments where a single scale length cannot yield decent intonation for the bass strings, or a short enough scale length for the treble strings to prevent those strings from breaking due to string tension. Some modern users of this type of fretboard claim ergonomic benefits as well. Syn.: fan fret. See also: bandora, orpharion.

multi-radius fretboard *n.* see conical section fretboard

muñeca *n.* (moon-YEA-kah) see tampon

music wire *n.* Steel wire used to make instrument strings. There are a number of different wire gauge conventions used to size this wire, but the most common is the Washburn & Moen Wire gauge. Music wire tends to have high yield strength.

musical instrument acoustics *n.* see musical instrument physics

musical instrument physics *n.* The study of the physics of the sound producing mechanisms of musical instruments. Syn.: musical instrument acoustics.

Musicman style pickup *n.* Form factor classification of a magnetic pickup for electric bass. This style of pickup has the shape of the pickup originally installed in the Musicman Stingray bass.

mustachio *n.* Decorative element of a guitar bridge. See also: moustache bridge.

Musurgia Universalis *n.* 17th century encyclopedia of music by Athanasius Kircher, containing descriptions and illustrations of musical instruments.

N

N95 *adj.* A rating for a commonly used dust mask from the National Institute for Occupational Safety and Health. An N95 mask is not resistant to oil and removes 95% of airborne particles in a standardized test. See also: National Institute for Occupational Safety and Health.

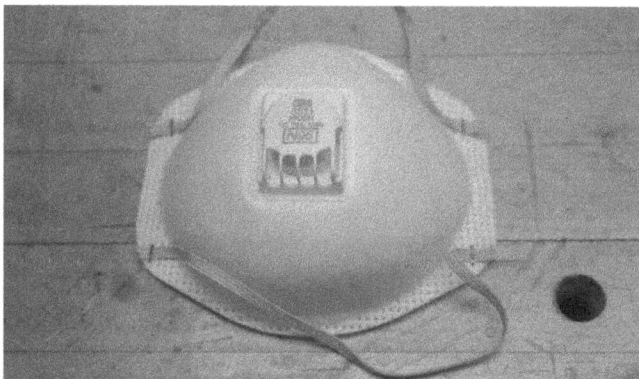

Typical N95 dust mask.

nacre *n.* see mother of pearl

nadir *n.* (nay-DEER) Lowest point. In lutherie this generally refers to the lowest point of a dish or an inverted arch. See also: apex.

NAMM *abbr.* see National Association of Music Merchants

Natelson, Jonathan Philadelphia PA, USA, classical guitar luthier and repairer and coauthor of the book *Guitarmaking Tradition and Technology*.

National Association of Music Merchants *n.* California USA based not-for-profit association for the global music products industry. The organization was founded in 1901. Syn.: NAMM.

National Hardwood Lumber Association *n.* Trade organization that provides the most commonly used visual grading system for hardwood lumber. Syn.: NHLA.

National Institute for Occupational Safety and Health *n.* USA federal government institute that issues standards for safety equipment. For luthiers the most frequently encountered of these standards is the one that rates the effectiveness of dust masks and respirators. These ratings indicate both the efficiency of the filter and its resistance to airborne oil particles, and are composed of a letter followed by a number. The letter is one of the following: N (not resistant to oil); R (resistant to oil); P (completely oil proof). The number indicates the percentage of airborne particles removed in a standardized test. A commonly used dust mask for moderate protection from wood dust is the N95 certified mask, which is not resistant to oil and removes 95% of airborne particles. Syn.: NIOSH.

natural frequency *n.* The fundamental frequency at which a vibrating system will vibrate once set into motion. See also: fundamental frequency.

Neapolitan mandolin *n.* Traditional teardrop shaped mandolin with a bowl back.

neck *n.* That part of a stringed instrument that separates the body from the pegbox or headstock, and supports the fingerboard.

neck angle *n.* The angle between the top surface of the fingerboard and the nominally flat surface of the top of the instrument at the ribs, when viewed from the side of the instrument. An instrument with a neck angle of 0 has the fingerboard and top surfaces parallel to each other. A positive neck angle indicates that the neck is tilted back relative to the top. This results in a higher bridge than would be the case with no neck angle. A negative neck angle indicates that the neck is tilted up relative to the top, and this results in a lower bridge than would be the case with no neck angle. Modern steel string guitars with domed tops generally have a small positive neck angle. Archtop instruments generally have a greater positive neck angle. Modern classical guitars sometimes have a negative neck angle.

neck block *n*. A block of wood inside the body of an instrument near the neck. The neck block is used as the structure that supports the attachment of the neck to the body.

neck extension *n*. Extension of the neck shaft over the top plate of some instruments. Archtop guitars and mandolins typically make use of a neck extension to support and stiffen the part of the fretboard that extends over the top plate.

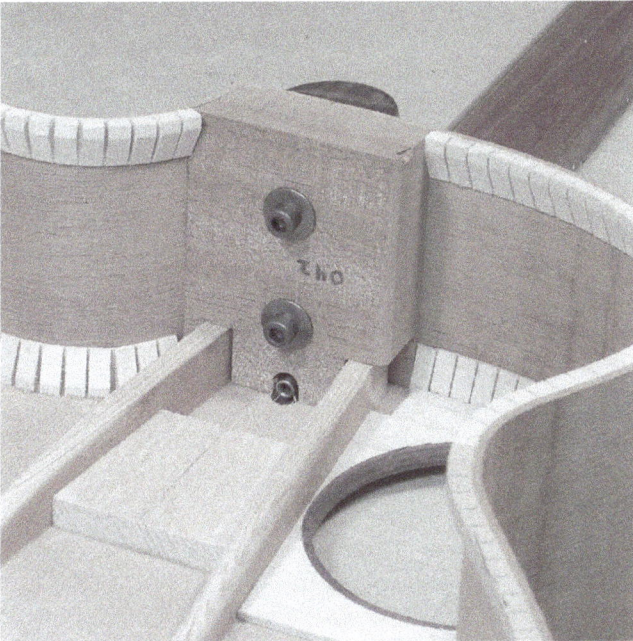

GRAHAM MCDONALD

Neck extension of a mandolin made by Graham McDonald.

neck facet *n*. When carving the shaft of an instrument neck, the transition from the rectangular cross section of the neck blank to the smooth contours of the finished neck can be effected by first carving the sharp edges of the blank profile down to flats. The resulting intermediate profile will not be smooth but faceted, that is, made up of flat sections. Each of these flat sections is called a neck facet.

neck ferrule *n*. An alternate method of preventing the screw heads of a bolt-on neck from damaging the back of an electric guitar body. Each neck attachment screw

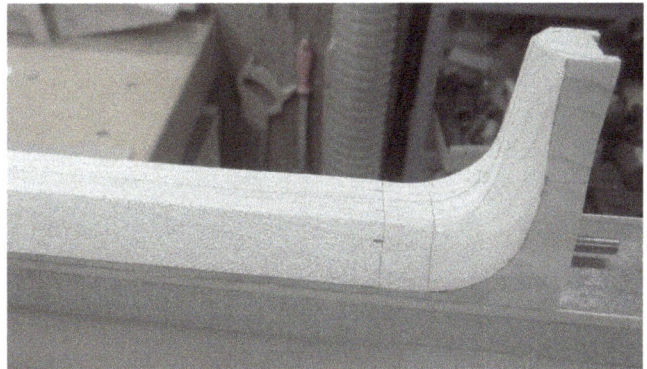

Neck block of a guitar with a bolt-on neck.

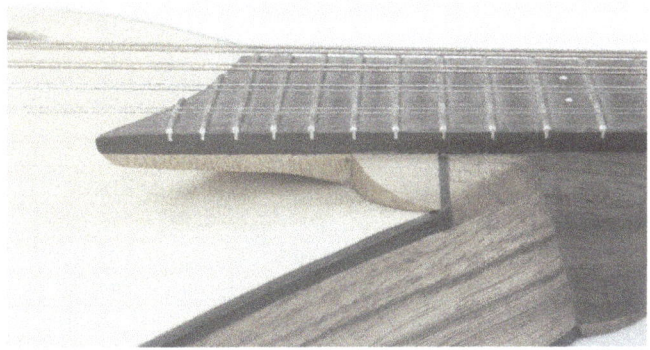

Primary neck facet of a guitar neck under construction.

passes through a ferrule countersunk into the heel. See also: neck plate, ferrule.

neck jig *n*. Any jig for cutting and aligning the neck to body joint of a stringed musical instrument. Syn.: neck angle jig.

neck joint *n*. The joint between the neck and the body of a stringed instrument. The most common types of neck joints for acoustic instruments are some variation of the mortise and tenon joint, and some variation of the bolt-on neck joint. Butt joints are also sometimes used. Solid body electric guitars also sometimes employ a "neck through" neck joint, where the shaft of the neck simply continues into and through the body. See also: bolt-on neck joint, mortise and tenon, neck through construction.

neck pickup *n*. Indication of placement of a pickup on an electric guitar. Electric guitars with two pickups identified by location include the bridge pickup (the pickup located near the instrument bridge) and the neck pickup (the pickup located near the instrument neck) See also: bridge pickup.

neck plate *n*. Metal plate used to attach the neck of a typical bolt-on neck electric guitar. The plate has holes through which the screws that attach the neck to the body are placed. See also: neck ferrules.

neck pocket *n*. The pocket in the body of a solid body electric guitar into which the neck is bolted.

neck relief *n*. When viewed from the side the playing surface of the fingerboard of most well set up instruments is not flat but slightly concave, that is, the fingerboard exhibits a small amount of front bow. The concavity provides space in which the strings can vibrate without touching the playing surface and creating buzzing noises. This concavity is called neck relief or simply relief. Relief is generally measured by fretting on the first fret and the fret at the body join, and then measuring the height of the strings above the middle fret in that range. Syn.: relief. See also: back bow, front bow.

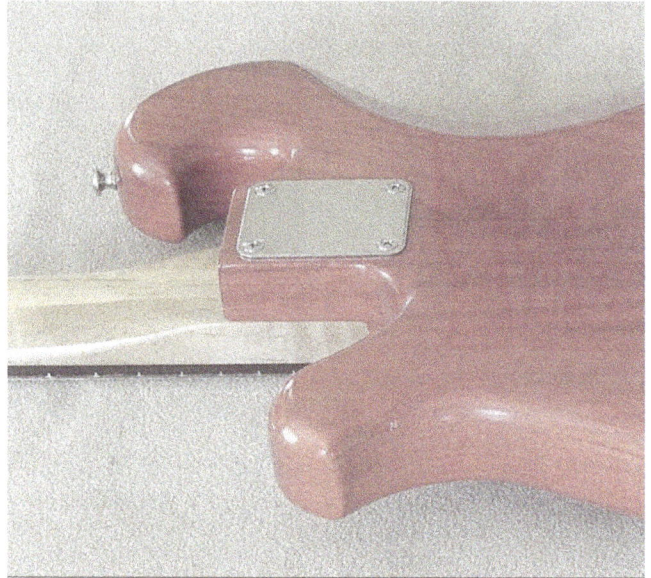

Neck plate of a solid body electric guitar.

neck reset *n*. Removing, then reattaching the neck of an instrument, changing the neck angle in the process. Neck resets are often done on flattop instruments after string tension has distorted the top enough to cause the action to raise enough to make the instrument unplayable. See also: action, neck angle.

neck resetting *v*. Changing the angle at which the neck joins the body of an instrument.

neck through construction *n*. A type of neck joint used on solid body guitars and basses. In neck through construction the neck shaft enters and continues right through the body. See also: bolt-on neck, set neck.

neutral axis *n*. The axis in the cross section of a beam on which there is no longitudinal stress and strain. Consider a simple beam, simply supported at its ends, supporting a weight at its center and deflecting under that weight. The upper surface of the beam is in compression and the lower surface is in tension. The axis through the beam between these surfaces that is neither in tension nor compression is the neutral axis. Syn.: elastic axis.

new violin family *n*. An octet of scaled violin family instruments, originally designed and built by Carleen Hutchins. See also: Carleen Hutchins.

NFPA 704 diamond *n*. A safety symbol in the shape of a diamond that provides general safety information on the hazardousness of a material. The symbol uses a simple numeric scale of 0-4 in each of three colored boxes to indicate level of health hazard (blue box), fire hazard (red box) and reactivity hazard (yellow box). The symbol includes an additional white box which is used to denote special hazards.

NHLA *abbr*. see National Hardwood Lumber Association

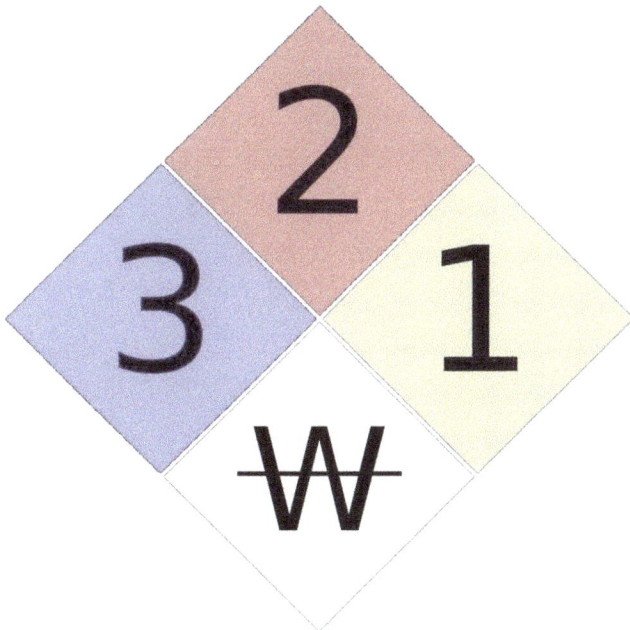

IMAGE IS IN THE PUBLIC DOMAIN.

NFPA 704 diamond.

nickel silver *n*. An alloy of copper, nickel and zinc. The material is used for fret wire and other metal parts. Syn.: German silver.

NIOSH *abbr*. see National Institute for Occupational Safety and Health

nitrocellulose lacquer *n*. Spray finishing material made from nitrocellulose refined from cotton, alcohol and other volatile solvents. Nitrocellulose lacquer is an evaporative finish that was used on electric and acoustic guitars from the 1920's on, and is still widely used today.

node *n*. An area of low displacement (movement) on a vibrating string, plate or air mass. See also: antinode

Nomex *n*. Brand name of fiber made of aramid polymers. Nomex is strong and light in weight. It is used in lutherie primarily in the form of a honeycomb material used as the center of a wood/Nomex/wood sandwich for guitar top plates.

nominal bridge location *n*. The location on the centerline of the instrument top that is the scale length distance from the nut. The actual bridge (saddle) location is usually a bit farther from the nut than the nominal bridge position for fretted instruments, because some compensation for string stretching and sharping during fretting is included when determining the actual bridge location. For most fretless instrument the nominal bridge location and the actual bridge location are the same. See also: actual bridge location, compensation.

nominal bridge position *n*. see nominal bridge location

nominal plane *n*. A plane used to describe or reference a more complex surface, when discussing the geometric relationship between the parts of an instrument. Examples include nominal plane of the top (of a flattop guitar) and nominal plane of the fingerboard (of a cambered fingerboard).

non-drying oil *n*. An oil that does not dry with exposure to air. Non-drying oils are sometimes used as components of varnishes. Olive oil is an example of a non-drying oil. See also: drying oil.

non-uniform rational b-spline *n*. Type of mathematical curve used in CAD and other drawing software to model complex smooth curves. Syn.: NURBS. See also: Bézier curve, spline curve.

Núñez, Sebastián Argentina born luthier known for lutes and other early stringed instruments, working in Utrecht, Netherlands.

NURBS *abbr*. see non-uniform rational b-spline

Norway spruce *n*. see *Picea abies*

note frequency pitch notation *n*. Pitch notation system commonly seen in scientific research papers. The letter name of the note is followed by the frequency of the note in Hertz. For example the note A above middle C is denoted A440 in this system.

noting out *v*. Problem that can occur during string bends on a guitar or other fretted instrument. If action is low enough it is possible for the string to contact a higher fret which in this configuration is "up hill" from the fretted fret. The contact will cause a buzzing sound or will quickly damp the note altogether. Raising the action slightly cures this problem. Syn.: fretting out. See also: action.

nut *n*. The termination structure for the vibrating part of the strings of a stringed musical instrument. The nut usually contains a slot for each string. The walls of the slot laterally locate the string, and the floor of the slot locates the string in relation to the top of the fingerboard or frets. Nuts are typically made of a variety of materials for steel string and electric guitars. The nuts of bowed instruments are traditionally made of ebony, and the nuts of early guitars and classical guitars are traditionally made of ivory or bone.

nut compensation *n*. Compensation added to the nut (that is, moving the nut location closer to the instrument

bridge), intended to produce better intonation of the instrument. See also: compensation, nut.

nut file *n*. A special sized file used to slot a nut for a particular gauge string. Nut files are available for all typical string gauges. See also: nut.

Nut file is used to create a slot in the nut for a string.

nut slot *n*. A slot cut into the nut of an instrument to secure one of the strings. A nut slot can be cut using a razor saw and/or needle file, or using special purpose nut files. See also: nut, nut file.

nut slotting file *n*. see nut file

O

O *adj.* (oh) One of the "standard" acoustic steel string guitar body shapes. The O shape is a small body with a lower bout width of approx. 13 1/2" (343mm). The designation comes from the original Martin O series guitars, which Martin calls "concert" size. Note that to disambiguate this from the number zero, the phrase "single O" is often used.

O1 tool steel *n.* (oh one) The most common tool steel for knife and plane and other woodworking blades. O1 tool steel is oil hardened.

Oberlin workshops *n.* Workshops offered in various aspects of bowed instrument lutherie. The workshops are held at Oberlin College by the Violin Society of America. See also: Violin Society of America.

O'Brien, Robbie Parker CO, USA, guitar luthier and lutherie instructor. Noted for his use of video instruction.

Occupational Safety and Health Administration *n.* U.S. federal government administration tasked with assuring safe and healthful working conditions for working men and women by setting and enforcing standards and by providing training, outreach, education and assistance. OSHA sets permissible exposure limits (PELs) for various solvents and chemicals used in lutherie. Syn.: OSHA.

Ochroma pyramidale *n.* Balsa wood. Balsa is a hardwood tree which grows from southern Brazil to southern Mexico. The tree is large and fast growing. The lumber is soft, light in color and extremely light in weight. Specific gravity of dry wood is 0.15. Modulus of elasticity is 3.7 GPa. Balsa finds use in lutherie primarily in the lattice bracing of some classical guitar tops. In this application the wood lattice is covered with carbon fiber material to make a strong, light bracing structure. Maine violin maker Douglas Martin has made a series of violins constructed mostly of balsa and other violin makers are experimenting with this material as well. See also: lattice bracing, Douglas Martin.

octave guitar *n.* Small guitar, typically with a scale length of 15.75" (400mm) and tuned an octave above the tuning of a standard guitar.

octobasse *n.* Giant three string double bass built by Vuillaume in 1849. See also: Jean Baptiste Vuillaume.

odor threshold *n.* The concentration of a substance just noticeable by smell. The quantity of vapors of a substance such as a solvent or adhesive when mixed with air can be represented as a concentration, usually expressed in parts per million (ppm). The concentration that is just noticeable by smell by most people is the odor threshold. Knowledge of the odor thresholds of various substances can be useful to help determine exposure levels to various substances and aid in maintaining a healthful workshop environment.

offset soundhole *n.* Soundhole that is located to one side of the centerline of the top of a guitar or similar instrument. Offset soundholes in the upper bout were popularized by some guitars built in the Kasha style and were featured in guitars built by Tacoma. See also: Michael Kasha.

oil finishes *n.* The so-called oil finishes consist of three major groups; non-drying oils, drying oils and wiping varnishes. All are applied with a pad. See also: drying oil, non-drying oil, wiping varnish.

oil varnish *n.* Varnish made from some kind of resin, polymerized and/or non-polymerized oil, and solvent. Oil varnishes are used primarily in violin family instruments but they are sometimes used for mandolins and guitars. The varnish is relatively slow drying and does not burn

Archtop guitar with offset round soundhole.

in. Applied coats do not melt into each other. See also: spirit varnish, varnish.

old growth timber *n*. Trees which are old enough to not have been planted by people, or at least not known to be planted by people. Old growth timber is generally preferred as it can be large enough to cut into wide boards, and it is often dense. The supply of old growth timer is of course diminishing rapidly.

Olsen, Tim USA guitar luthier, author and editor. Founder of the Guild of American Luthiers, he is also the publisher of the Guild's journal *American Lutherie*. See also: *American Lutherie*, Guild of American Luthiers.

OM *adj*. (oh em) One of the "standard" acoustic steel string guitar body shapes. The body of an orchestra model guitar is approximately 19 $^3/_8''$ (492mm) long with a lower bout width of approximately 15" (381mm). The designation comes from the original Martin OM series guitars, which Martin calls "orchestra" size.

on-board *adj*. Describes something built into an instrument that is not conventionally or historically found in the instrument. An example is a guitar with on-board electronics.

one hand clamp *n*. A type of bar clamp that can be positioned, clamped down and un-clamped using just one hand. Clamps of this type usually are configured in a pistol grip fashion. Repeatedly pulling the "trigger" tightens the clamp. Syn.: pistol grip clamp.

OO *adj*. (double oh) One of the "standard" acoustic steel string guitar body shapes. The OO shape is a medium body with a lower bout width of approx. 14 $^1/_4''$ (368mm). It is approximately the size of a modern classical guitar. The designation comes from the original Martin OO series guitars, which Martin calls "grand concert" size.

OOO *adj*. (triple oh) One of the "standard" acoustic steel string guitar body shapes. The OOO shape is a medium

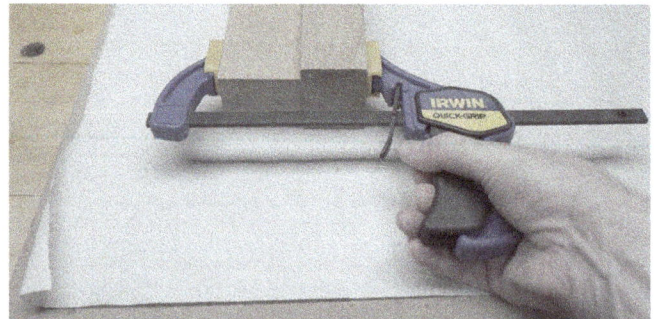
One hand clamp.

body with a lower bout width of approx. 15″ (381mm). The designation comes from the original Martin OOO series guitars, which Martin calls "auditorium" size.

open harmonic bar *n.* Transverse top brace that does not fully contact the plate along its entire length. Braces of this type have been used in some instruments by Torres and Romanillos, and are used regularly in guitars by Jeffrey Elliott. See also: Jeffrey Elliott, José Romanillos, Antonio Torres.

open string *n.* A string that is played without fretting.

open time *n.* The amount of time a glue or finishing material remains liquid and workable once its container is opened.

open jawari *n.* Relatively round shape of the top of the bridge of a sitar. Syn.: khula See also: closed jawari.

optical pickup *n.* Transducer that uses light to sense vibration of instrument strings or other vibrating components. Syn.: optical transducer.

orchestra size guitar *n.* see OM

orden *n.* (OR-den) Course of strings (Spanish). See also: course.

organology *n.* Study of the classification and development over time of musical instruments.

Oribe, José California USA classical and flamenco guitar luthier. Author of the book *The Fine Guitar*.

orpharion *n.* Renaissance plucked instrument of the cittern family, similar to but smaller than the bandora. It features wire strings and metal frets, often on a multiple scale length fretboard. See also: bandora, multiple scale length fretboard.

orpiment *n.* Arsenic sulfide. Yellow pigment used in traditional violin varnishes.

OSHA *abbr.* see Occupational Safety and Health Administration

oud *n.* Middle Eastern fretless bowl back plucked instrument, similar to and related to the lute. Syn.: ud, ood oud.

Middle Eastern oud by Peter Kyvelos.

ouïe n. (oo-WE) F-hole (French).

out-cannel gouge n. A gouge with the bevel ground on the outside of the blade. This is the "conventional" gouge bevel grind, i.e. unless otherwise specified, this is the way a gouge will be ground. Syn.: outside bevel gouge See also: in-cannel gouge.

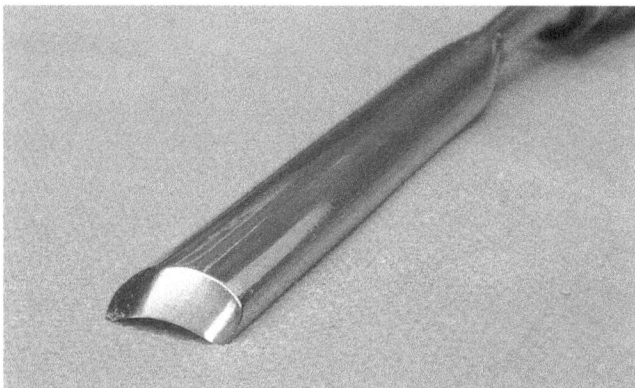

Out cannel gouge.

outside bevel gouge n. see out-cannel gouge

outside mold n. Assembly jig used to hold the ribs and blocks (garland) of an instrument in shape during assembly. An outside mold is positioned around the outside of the ribs. Guitars are often built using outside molds. Note that this definition is common in North America and in some other parts of the world. Unfortunately in other places the term means the exact opposite. Disambiguation often must be done by context. Due to the ambiguity of the term it is best to not use it but instead to describe where the mold fits in relation to the garland. Syn.: external form, external mold. See also: inside mold, garland.

overarm router n. Routing machine consisting of a router mounted on an arm extending over a flat table. The router can be moved vertically only. The table features a pin that is concentric with the router's cutter. Overarm routers are typically used for cutting out parts using a pattern. The pattern is attached to the back of the work piece and contacts the pin during operation. Syn.: pin router.

over braced adj. Referring to an instrument, usually a guitar or other plucked instrument, with a top that is thicker and/or more heavily braced than is required to support string tension. The term usually has a negative connotation and implies that the additional mass and stiffness of the top makes for less than optimal tone.

Overholtzer, Arthur Classical guitar luthier, teacher and author of the book *Classical Guitar Making.* Overholtzer built Spanish style guitars using what are generally considered to be very unconventional methods. He taught guitarmaking at Chico State College in California. A number of contemporary luthiers credit him as an influence.

overspun string n. see wound string

overstand n. The distance between the bottom surface of the fingerboard and the surface of the top of the instrument, measured at the neck to body join. The term is used mostly to describe this distance for violin family instruments. Given a fixed bridge height, more overstand will result in a smaller breakover angle of the strings at the bridge. See also: breakover angle.

overtone n. Vibration at some frequency in addition to the fundamental frequency. The vibration of musical instrument strings include a fundamental frequency as well as a number of approximately harmonic higher frequency partials. See also: harmonic, partial.

oxalic acid n. Chemical compound used as a wood bleach.

P

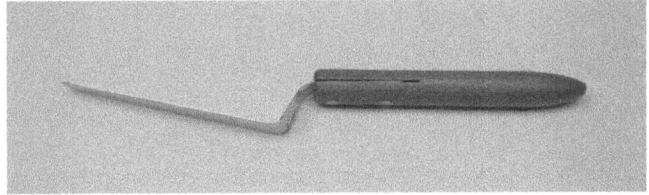

Palette knife.

P-90 pickup *n*. A single coil magnetic pickup for electric guitars originally built by Gibson.

P grade *n*. Sandpaper grit grading system of the Federation of European Producers of Abrasives (FEPA). See also: sandpaper grit.

Pa *abbr*. see Pascal

packer *n*. Shim (British).

pad *n*. A folded piece of cloth, used as an applicator for wood finish. Varnish and some waterborne finishes can be applied with a pad. In French polishing a pad is sometimes used to get finish into tight inside corners.

pad *v*. To apply finish with a pad. Finish applied with a pad generally goes on more smoothly than finish applied with a brush.

Padding, Koen Twentieth century manufacturer of violin finishing products and researcher on historical violin finishing materials and techniques.

paddle headstock *n*. Prebuilt and replacement guitar necks often come with an unshaped headstock so that the builder can cut this to a custom shape. These headstocks are generally called paddle headstocks.

PAF *abbr*. see patent applied for

Pagés, José Early 19th century Spanish guitar luthier. Made use of fan braced tops. See also: fan bracing.

palette knife *n*. Small offset handled knife originally intended for mixing and applying paint to an artist's palette. It is used by luthiers for repair work because its thin flexible blade can be worked into tight crevices.

palisander *n*. see *Dalbergia baronii*

palo santo *n*. see *Machaerium* spp.

pandoura *n*. Assyrian name for early plucked string instrument.

pan pot *n*. An electric guitar control that provides volume panning between two pickups. Pan pots are generally found in instruments that use active electronics and are more often found in electric basses than electric guitars. Syn.: blend pot. See also: active electronics.

Panormo *Fecit* *n*. Label name of one of the two lines of guitars made by Louis Panormo. These instruments generally featured ladder braced tops and generally had black painted necks. Backs and sides were usually of maple, sometimes satinwood. See also: *fecit*, Louis Panormo.

Panormo, George Lewis Nephew and successor of Louis Panormo, worked in his uncle's shop.

Panormo, Louis (1816-1860) London based violin and guitar luthier. He was the son of Sicilian violin luthier Vincenzo Panormo. His guitars feature the narrow bodies typical of his time, and have a distinctive crescent-topped headstock made of maple, and a pin bridge. Panormo's guitars are built using the Spanish style neck/body joint and have either fan or ladder braced tops. He built two lines of instruments. Panormo *Fecit* instruments featured ladder bracing, maple bodies and black painted necks. Louis Panormo "in the Spanish style" instruments featured fan bracing, rosewood bodies and naturally finished necks.

P

Panormo, Vincenzo (1734-1813) Italian violin luthier. Born in Palermo, he worked in Cremona, Turin, Marseille, Paris and London. Father of Louis Panormo. See also: Louis Panormo

pantograph router *n.* see carving machine

pantograph *n.* A mechanical linkage that renders movement in space at one point on the linkage to another point on the linkage. Pantographs are used to duplicate drawings at enlarged or reduced size. A stylus attached to one point on the device is used to trace the drawing, while a pen attached to the other point duplicates it on another sheet. Another common lutherie use of this device is in the duplication of carved plates. The contours of a model plate are followed with a stylus attached to one point of the pantograph, while a router attached to the other point routs those contours into another plate. These machines are also called plate duplicators or carving machines. See also: carving machine.

pao ferro *n.* see *Machaerium* spp.

paper linings *n.* Lutes and guitars often used paper for linings and the reinforcement of other body joints.

PAPR *abbr.* see powered air purifying respirator

parabolic bracing *n.* A bracing strategy for guitar tops in which the braces are carved to a nominally parabolic profile, both in cross section and across their lengths.

Paracho knife *n.* Woodworking knife featuring a curved blade and used by Mexican guitar builders. The knife is named after a town in Mexico famous as a guitar making center.

paraffin oil *n.* A light odorless petroleum oil used with abrasives to rub out finishes. The abrasives traditionally used are 2F pumice followed by rottenstone. See also: pumice, rottenstone, rubbing out.

parallel bracing *n.* One of the common bracing patterns, typically found in mandolins and archtop guitars. It consists of two braces that are approximately parallel but diverge from near the neck block to near the tail block. See also: bracing pattern.

parametric solid modeling *adj.* Describes CAD software that renders solid models from a combination of 2D drawings and tables of arithmetic values.

parchment *n.* Paper made from animal skin. Syn.: parchment paper.

parchment rosette *n.* Soundhole decoration for early guitars made of paper and inserted in the soundhole. Parchment rosettes were usually made of a number of decoratively cut layers that look like an inverted wedding cake. They were usually gilded or painted. Syn.: parchment rose.

Paredes Rodriguez, Luis Alberto Colombian luthier best known for classical guitar copies of the works of the great historical luthiers and for instruments of the Andean region of Colombia, including the tiple and bandola, built using modern lutherie techniques. Author of the book *Guitarra Clásica Moderna — Historia, diseño y construcción*. See also: bandola, tiple.

Parker, Ken Gloucester MA, USA, archtop guitar luthier. Ken Parker has developed a number of innovative instruments including the Parker Fly guitar, Nightfly, and Fly Bass.

parlor guitar *n.* General designation for any guitar that is narrower than current standards. Romantic period guitars and early 20th century guitars generally can be described as parlor guitars, as can modern narrow body instruments built in the style of 19th and early 20th century instruments.

partial *n.* Vibrating systems such as strings have multiple simultaneous modes of vibration. The frequencies of the modes are called partials. In some systems the frequency of vibration of the partials are nominally harmonic, that is, they are integer multiples of the fundamental frequency. In vibrating strings the partials are nearly harmonic but skew sharp.

Pascal *n*. Unit of pressure. 1 Pascal = 1 Newton per square meter. Abbreviation: Pa.

passive electronics *n*. Guitar electronics that do not use power from an onboard battery or other source. Traditional electric guitars make use of passive electronics.

passive pickup *n*. Magnetic pickup without a preamplifier inside the pickup case. If a magnetic pickup is not explicitly identified as an active pickup it is usually a passive pickup. See also: active pickup.

paste wood filler *n*. Ready to use grain filler made of ground quartz and pigment in a varnish binder. Syn.: grain filler.

patch *n*. General term for any small, thin piece of wood glued to the inside of a plate or rib. The most common example is the bridge patch, a piece of veneer glued to the underside of the top plate just under the position of the bridge.

patent applied for *adj*. Full colloquial name of early Gibson humbucking pickup. The term was originally used to differentiate the original pickups from later models, the originals bearing a label with this phrase printed on it. The term is now also used to identify reproduction pickups of the originals. Syn.: PAF.

patrón n. (pah-TROWN) In lutherie this is usually translated as pattern or model or template (Spanish).

pattern *v*. Refers to whether or not the pattern for an instrument plate can be cut from a particular board. Plate boards are generally rectangular and often contain defects and irregularities that should not impact their use because these defects will not appear inside the template of the plate of the finished instrument. A board with no defects is easy to pattern — the template for the plate can be positioned anywhere on it. A board with a lot of defects may be difficult to pattern — the template may only fit in one place that provides elimination of all defects. And of course some boards will not pattern — there is no place on it the template can be placed that would eliminate all defects from the finished instrument plate.

pattern bit *n*. A router bit equipped with a ball bearing on one end or the other. The bearing is the same diameter as the cutter. The pattern bit is used with a routing template. The bearing rides on the edge of the template and the cutter cuts the same profile in the material. See also: routing template.

peacock tuning machines *n*. see Preston tuning machines

pearl *n*. see mother of pearl

pearloid *n*. Any fake mother of pearl material, usually made of plastic. Syn.: mother of toilet seat.

peg *n*. see tuning peg

peg compound *n*. Liquid or semi-solid dressing for tuning pegs.

peg hole bushing *n*. The holes that support tuning pegs eventually wear enough that even the use of oversize pegs will not provide adequate tuning. In this case the holes are drilled out with a large diameter bit and a plug of wood is glued into them. This plug is then drilled and reamed as for a new instrument. The drilled plug is called a peg hole bushing.

peg hole reamer *n*. Tool used to ream a taper into drilled peg holes.

peg shaper *n*. Tool used to shape the shafts of tuning pegs to match the taper of the peg holes. The peg shaper works like a pencil sharpener. Before use, the angle of the shaper cutting blade is adjusted to match the taper of

P

the peg hole reamer used to ream the peg holes. See also: peg hole reamer.

peg shaver *n.* see peg shaper

pegbox *n.* The part of violin family and other instruments that supports the tuning pegs. This is generally constructed as a box with an open top. The holes for the tuning pegs are drilled through the sides of the pegbox.

peghead *n.* see head

peghead joint *n.* The joint between the peghead and shaft of the neck.

PEL *abbr.* see permissible exposure limit

Peltogyne paniculata *n.* One of many species the wood of which is called purpleheart, violetwood, amaranth. Hardwood used for guitar backs and sides, fingerboards, binding and purfling strips and for headplates. The wood is bright purple in color when freshly cut, but exposure to light darkens the color to a dark brown. The wood is hard, heavy and stiff. The specific gravity of dry wood is 0.86. Modulus of elasticity is 20.3 GPa.

peón n. (pey-OWN) see tentellón. Plural: peones.

Perdure *n.* A brand of heat treated wood. See also: heat treatment (wood).

permissible exposure limit *n.* Value for maximum continuous exposure to a hazardous substance, usually issued by a safety and health organization or government agency. Permissible exposure limit information is contained in material safety data sheets (MSDSs). Syn.: PEL. See also: material safety data sheet.

pernambuco *n.* see *Caesalpinia echinata*

Pfeil, Victor (1900-1978) German born inventor of the electric violin. The patent for the instrument was filed in 1928. He lived and worked in New Jersey USA.

phantom power *n.* Power provided by professional audio equipment such as mixers and direct boxes, originally intended to power condenser microphones. Some electric instruments with active electronics can be powered by phantom power, but the more general case is to power the electronics with onboard batteries.

phase switch *n.* A switch that can alter the phase relationship between two magnetic pickups. See also: pickup phase.

phenolic *n.* (fen-OH-lick) see phenolic resin

phenolic resin *n.* Synthetic thermosetting resin made from phenols and formaldehyde. Phenolic resin is a component of some varnishes used in lutherie. It is also a component of a composite material made with paper or cloth that is often used as a substitute for ebony for fingerboards or fittings. Some instrument nuts are also made of this material. Two such products are Garolite and Richlite. The resin is also used in a wood product that is composed of wood impregnated with it. This wood is sometimes used for fingerboards as well. See also: resin impregnated wood.

phi *n.* (fahy) see golden mean

Picea abies *n.* The species generally known as German spruce, Norway spruce, or European spruce (also called Swiss, French, Yugoslavian and Italian spruce). A European softwood used for the tops on many instruments. This species was used in many old Spanish classical guitars and, as a local species, is used in many modern European instruments. It is imported into the USA and used by American luthiers as well. It grows throughout Europe. It is light in color with darker latewood bands. Specific gravity of dry wood is 0.41. Modulus of elasticity is 9.7 GPa.

Picea engelmannii *n.* Engelmann spruce. This softwood from the Pacific Northwest is used for the top plates of guitars and other acoustic instruments. It is light in color with darker latewood bands. The dry wood has an average specific gravity of 0.39 and a modulus of elasticity of 9.44 GPa.

Picea excelsa n. see *Picea abies*

Picea glauca n. White spruce. This softwood is from the northern areas of North America. It is not often used in lutherie but it is one of the species included in the hybrid called Lutz Spruce that is used for guitar tops. The wood is light in color and density. Specific gravity of dry wood is 0.43 and modulus of elasticity is 9.1 GPa.

Picea rubens n. Red or Adirondack spruce. A North American softwood used for tops of many instruments. This species was used in many pre-World-War-II Martin guitars and is preferred by a number of modern flattop guitar builders. It is one of three species commonly referred to as eastern Spruce. It grows primarily in New England and in the Appalachian mountains. Dry wood has a typical specific gravity of 0.43 and a modulus of elasticity of 10.8 GPa. Syn.: Adirondack spruce, red spruce.

Picea sitchensis n. Sitka spruce. Softwood from the Pacific Northwest of North America. Used primarily for steel string guitar and mandolin tops. The typical specific gravity of Sitka spruce is 0.40 for dry wood. The modulus of elasticity of Sitka spruce grown in the United States is 11 GPa. Syn.: Sitka spruce, yellow spruce.

Pickering, Norman USA engineer, violin maker and musical instrument physics researcher.

pickguard n. A plate attached to the top of an instrument to protect the top from being scratched up by playing the instrument with a pick. Pickguards are common features of instruments generally played with a pick such as electric guitars and steel string acoustic guitars.

pickup n. Electrical transducer that converts string vibration energy to electrical energy. Unless otherwise qualified the term usually refers to the magnetic pickup. Syn.: transducer.

pickup phase n. A relative indication of the relationship between the direction of movement of the string over a

Installing the pickguard on an acoustic steel string guitar.

magnetic pickup and the corresponding direction of signal change at the pickup's output terminals. There is no standard absolute indication of pickup phase. Phase is used to compare two pickups and as such these pickups can said to be either in phase or out of phase. In phase pickups will output a signal of the same polarity given a movement of the string over them. For example, if the string is displaced to the right over both pickups and both pickups output a positive moving pulse then the pickups are said to be in phase. Out of phase pickups will produce signals of opposite polarity given the same string displacement over them. Electric guitar pickups are generally wired in phase to avoid signal cancellation. But signal cancellation gives a distinctive sound and so some electric guitars are wired with a switch that can alter the pickups' phase relation. See also: phase switch.

pickup polarity n. The magnetic polarity of a single coil magnetic pickup, or of one coil of a humbucking pickup. The magnetic polarity is usually expressed in relation to the top of the pickup, and so would either be top north or top south.

pickup ring n. Mounting plate for electric guitar magnetic pickup.

pickup waxing v. Adding melted wax to a magnetic pickup to reduce vibration of component parts. Syn.: pickup potting. See also: microphonic, waxed pickup.

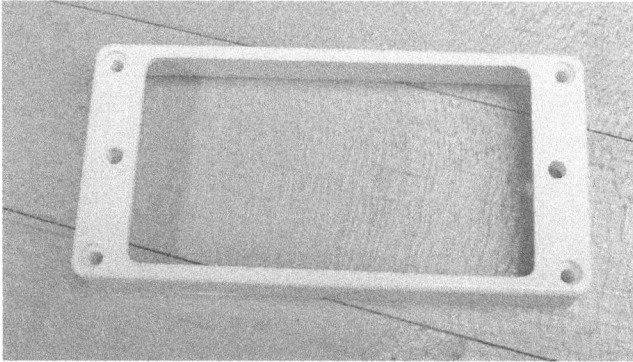

Pickup ring for a humbucking pickup.

P

pickup winder *n.* Machine for winding magnetic pickups.

pied du roi *n.* (pyeh dew ruah) Pre-revolutionary French unit of measurement, translated "royal foot." It was used by a number of instrument makers including those of the Voboam family. It is equal in length to 324.83mm.

piezoelectric *adj.* Pertaining to the generation of electricity by the mechanical stressing of a material. Only certain materials show the piezoelectric effect. Most of these are crystals but there are piezoelectric polymers as well. Piezoelectric transducers are used as pickups in some musical instruments such as violin family instruments and acoustic guitars.

piezo *abbr.* (PEE-eh-zoh, PEE-zoh) see piezoelectric

piezo cable *n.* Piezoelectric coaxial cable, often used as an under saddle transducer for acoustic guitars. The cable is constructed with an inner conductor wire surrounded by a tube of piezoelectric material, usually polyvinylidene fluoride (PVDF), which is covered with braided wire shielding, which in turn is covered by a protective plastic covering. See also: coaxial cable, piezoelectric, polyvinylidene fluoride, under saddle transducer.

piezo pickup *n.* Transducer that converts vibrational energy into an electrical signal by the piezoelectric effect. Certain substances will generate current when flexed or otherwise deformed. See also: piezoelectric.

pigment *n.* A substance that is used as a coloring agent. The particles of pigments are not soluble in the finishing material to which they are added. They impart color by reflecting light. Since they affect the transparency of the finishing material, the more pigment added, the more opaque the finish is. Pigments are used for solid opaque finishes and also for traditional transparent and translucent finishes such as those found on violin family instruments. See also: dye.

pillar drill *n.* Drill press (British).

pin prick method *n.* Technique for transferring lines from printed plans or drawings to wood. The drawing is positioned on the surface of the wood and then a series of pin pricks are made along the drawn lines, through the paper and into the wood.

pin bridge *n.* Describes a bridge that uses pins to anchor the ends of the strings in holes drilled through the bridge and the instrument top. Modern steel string acoustic guitars generally use pin bridges. See also: pinless bridge.

pin router *n.* see overarm router

pinless bridge *n.* Describes a bridge that does not use pins to anchor the string ends. See also: pin bridge, top-loaded bridge.

pipette *n.* see transfer pipette

pirolo *n.* (pea-ROH-low) Tuning peg (Italian).

pistol grip clamp *n.* see one hand clamp

pitch *n.* In lutherie the terms yaw, pitch, and roll, used to describe rotation of an object in space, are most often used to describe adjustments necessary to fit an instrument's neck onto its body. When the instrument is

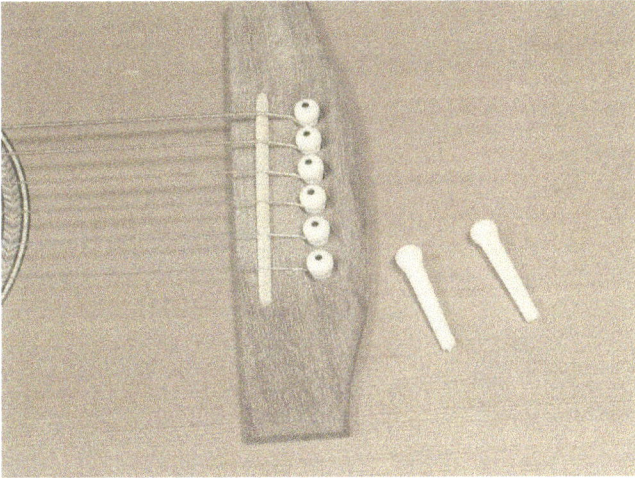

Pin bridge.

viewed from the side, pitch is up and down rotation of the neck about an axis extending from your eye to the neck/body join. See also: roll, yaw.

pitch pocket *n*. Defect in wood. An indentation filled with pitch or other soft material.

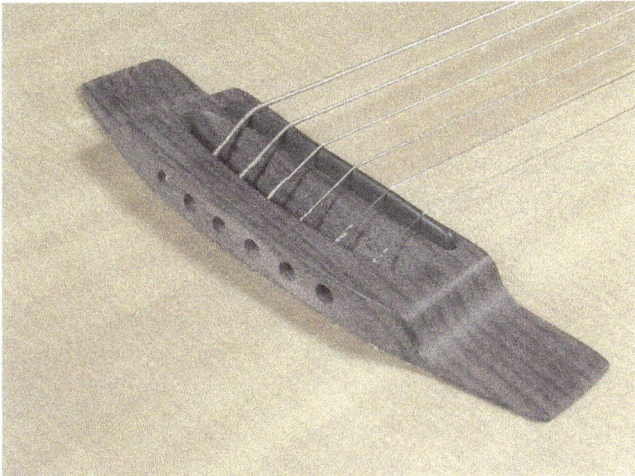

Pinless bridge.

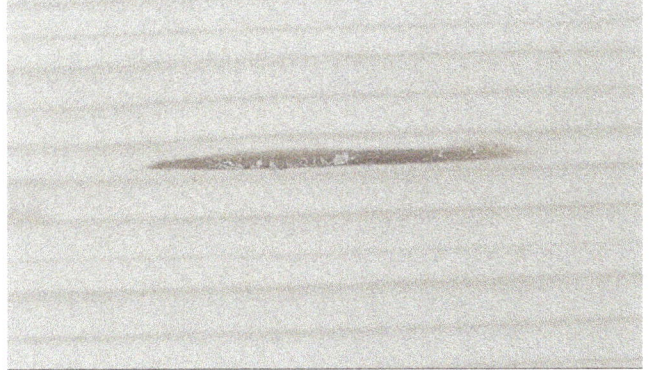

A pitch pocket in a Sitka spruce guitar top blank.

PJ pickups *n*. Pickup configuration for an electric bass guitar that has one Fender Precision Bass style pickup in the neck position and one Fender Jazz Bass style pickup in the bridge position.

plain sawn *n*. see flat sawn

plain string *n*. Strings can be classified by their general construction. A plain string is constructed from a unified piece of material, commonly metal wire, twisted gut, or nylon filament, without windings. See also: windings, wound string.

P

PJ pickups on a Fender Precision electric bass.

planetary gear tuning peg *n*. Tuning peg that contains internal gearing, intended to improve tuning accuracy. These generally fit in holes for standard straight tuning pegs. They are commonly used in banjos and ukuleles.

plantilla *n*. (plan-TEE-ya) The front view outline of the body of a guitar. This Spanish term is used mostly to describe Spanish (classical and flamenco) guitars.

plasticizer *n*. Material added to finishing material to make the cured finish more flexible. Non-drying resins or oils are typically used as plasticizers.

plate *n*. Acoustic stringed instruments have two large panels called plates. The top, front or belly plate is the one supporting the bridge. The back plate is on the opposite side of the instrument.

plate carving *n*. The process of shaping the plates of instruments with arched plates.

plate copier *n*. see carving machine

plate duplicator *n*. see carving machine

plate modes *n*. The modes of vibration of the plates of an instrument. These can be identified by exciting a plate into vibration at different frequencies.

plated tuning machines *n*. Multiple tuning machines attached to a single mounting plate. Tuning machines for classical guitars and mandolins typically use plated machines. See also: individual tuning machines.

Platowood *n*. A brand of heat treated wood. See also: heat treatment (wood).

playing surface *n*. On a fretless instrument, the surface of the fingerboard that the strings contact during playing. On a fretted instrument, this term is also used to denote the surface described by the tops of the frets.

Plek machine *n*. A special purpose automated fret leveling and dressing machine for guitars, manufactured by Plek / A+D Gitarrentechnologie GmbH in Germany.

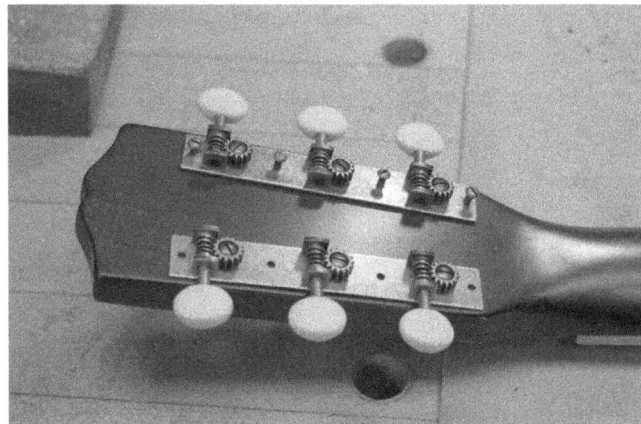

Plated tuning machines being attached to a steel string guitar.

pneumatic cylinder *n*. An actuator that converts air pressure to linear motion. Used in production machinery.

pocket *n*. In machining and other materials-forming operations, a pocket is an indentation in the surface of a material formed by removing (excavating) material. Pockets are typically flat-bottomed and have walls perpendicular to the bottom. See also: boss.

pocket *v*. To create a pocket.

polish *n*. see French polish

pole piece *n*. Part of a magnetic guitar pickup. A pickup with poles pieces generally has one for each string of the instrument, but some pickups will use more than one pole piece per string to retain signal level when strings are bent. The pole piece is a short length of metal rod that extends the field of the pickup magnet(s) closer to the strings. It is sometimes implemented as a screw so that distance from the top of the pole piece to the bottom of the string can be adjusted.

polyacrylate *n*. Polymer component of some two-part finishing materials. The substance is relatively hard and stiff and is therefore generally combined with polyester.

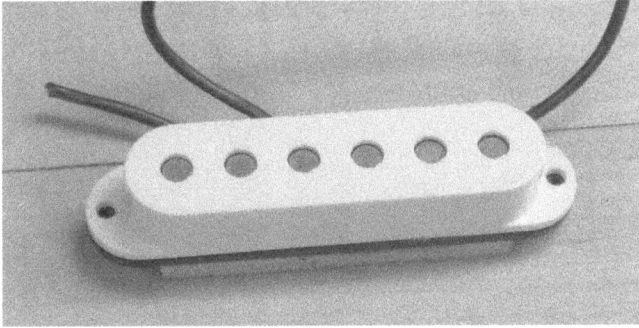

Single coil guitar pickup with six pole pieces.

polyester *n.* Polymer component of some two-part finishing materials. The substance is relatively soft and flexible and is therefore generally combined with polyacrylate.

polymerization *n.* The process of forming large molecular chains. Many finishing materials cure by polymerization.

polyurethane *n.* Polymer used in glues and finishing materials. It is tough and somewhat elastic. It does not find much use in glues and finishing materials used in lutherie.

polyvinyl acetate glue *n.* Generally referred to as white glue, it is generally not used in modern guitar lutherie having been superseded by aliphatic resin (yellow) glue, although formulations are available that are intended specifically for lutherie use. It is not used at all in violin lutherie.

polyvinyl chloride *n.* Plastic used for many plastic parts on guitars and similar instruments. Syn.: PVC.

polyvinylidene fluoride *n.* Polymer piezoelectric material used in pickups for musical instruments. The material can be molded into shapes and is available as a sheet material. Syn.: PVDF See also: piezoelectric.

ponding *v.* Storing wood for musical instruments under water for extensive lengths of time in an attempt to improve the sound qualities of instruments built with that wood. This term is mostly used as it applies to top wood for violin family instruments. The practice is controversial and the results are inconclusive.

ponte *n.* (POWN-tey) Bridge of a stringed instrument (Italian).

ponticello *n.* (pown-ti-CHEL-lo) see ponte

popsicle stick brace *n.* Transverse brace under the top plate of some flattop acoustic guitars. This brace is located between the neck block and the upper transverse brace. It is usually quite thin and often quite wide. The purpose of the brace is to provide cross grain support for the top to prevent it from cracking at the edges of the fretboard. See also: upper transverse brace.

poplar *n.* see *Populus* spp.

Populus **spp.** *n.* Commonly called poplar. This is a large genus with many species and subspecies which grow in Europe, Asia and North America. Lutherie use of poplar wood generally refers to European species commonly called black poplar or to hybrids of it. This has been used for blocks and linings for guitar and violin family instruments and also for backs of violin family

The low flat transverse brace on this guitar top under construction is the popsicle stick brace.

instruments. The wood has a light tan color with no pores. It is of medium density and stiffness. It should not be confused with the North American wood *Liriodendron tulipifera*, generally also called poplar although not a true poplar. Syn.: poplar. See also: *Liriodendron tulipifera*.

pore filler *n*. see grain filler

pore filling *v*. The process of filling the pores of open grained wood with some substance.

Portuguese guitarra *n*. Twelve string instrument with six courses of two steel strings each. The instrument evolved from the medieval citole and has a teardrop-shaped body. It is played finger style. It traditionally uses Preston style tuning machines. There are two distinct styles/sizes, Lisboa and Coimbra, with typical scale lengths of 445mm and 470mm respectively. Syn.: guitarra portuguesa, Portuguese guitar. See also citole, Preston tuning machines.

position marker *n*. see fret marker

post style bridge *n*. Bridge style typical of some Gibson style electric guitars. The bridge is mounted on metal

LUIS BENARD DA COSTA GHUDE

Lisboa style Portuguese guitarra played by António Chainho.

posts that are in turn mounted into the top of the instrument.

pot *abbr*. see potentiometer

pot life *n*. The amount of time a multipart glue or finishing material remains usable once mixed. The term is also used to specify the amount of time that hot hide glue can be left heated in the glue pot.

potassium dichromate *n*. Chemical coloring agent for wood. Unlike dyes and pigments, chemical coloring agents react with the wood to effect color change in the wood surface itself.

potassium feldspar *n*. A mineral identified in the finishes of old violins.

potassium permanganate *n*. Chemical used to emulate age-darkening of light colored woods such as spruce and maple.

potentiometer *n*. Variable resistor. This electronic component is used for volume, tone and blend controls for electric instruments. Syn.: pot

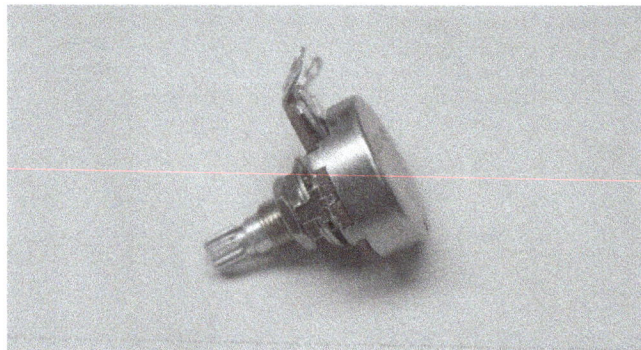

Potentiometer.

powered air purifying respirator *n*. Face mask/respirator that includes a fan to pump fresh air into the mask. These are used in harsh environments and by those that cannot achieve a tight fit using a passive mask. Syn.: PAPR.

Powers, Andy Principal luthier at Taylor Guitars.

ppm *abbr.* Parts per million.

Prairie State see Larson, Carl and William

Pratt and Lambert #38 varnish *n.* Commercial oil varnish (no longer in production) often used in hand finishing guitars.

preamp *abbr.* see preamplifier

preamplifier *n.* Active circuit used to increase signal from a low level source such as a pickup and/or for impedance matching. Preamplifier circuits are found in active magnetic pickups and in other active onboard guitar electronics, and also as the first stage of instrument amplifiers. See also: impedance matching.

pre-impregnated fabric *n.* Carbon fiber fabric that has been impregnated with epoxy. To mold the cloth into a part, the fabric can be cut to shape, placed in a mold and then heated to cure. Syn.: pre-preg. See also: carbon fiber.

prepared dye *n.* see dye solution

pre-preg *abbr.* see pre-impregnated fabric

pressure sensitive adhesive *n.* Adhesive backing often used on sandpaper to affix it to power sanders. Syn.: PSA.

Preston tuning machines *n.* Tuning machines typically used on the English cittern and Portuguese guitarra. These machines make use of a captive screw with a knurled head which is threaded into a small block constrained by a metal slot. As the tuning screw is turned the block moves within the slot. The string is attached to the block. Design of these tuners is generally attributed to John Preston in the late 18th century. Syn.: fan tuning machines, peacock tuning machines, watchkey tuning machines. See also: cittern, Portuguese guitarra.

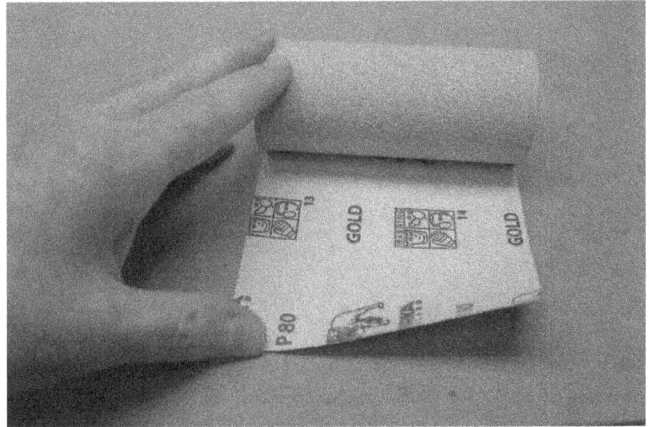

Sandpaper roll with pressure sensitive adhesive backing.

P

projection *n.* The quality of stringed instruments that describes audibility at distances far from the instrument. This differs from perceived loudness of the instrument, which generally describes its apparent loudness up close. Note that this term is generally ill-defined. See also: loudness.

PSA *abbr.* see pressure sensitive adhesive

Preston tuning machines on a Portuguese guitarra.

psaltery *n.* see zither

psychoacoustics *n.* Study of the perception of sound. Related to lutherie we are most interested in human perception of loudness and pitch. Syn.: psychophysics.

puente *n.* (PWEN-tay) Bridge (Spanish).

Puerto Rican tiple *n.* Small guitar family instrument with 3-5 single strings.

pulling over *v.* French polishing technique. During bodying, the polish is applied first with circular strokes and then with straight strokes to even out the application. This change to straight strokes is called pulling over. It tends to flatten out the shellac coating. See also: bodying, French polish.

P

pumice *n.* Powdered volcanic rock, used as an abrasive for rubbing out finishes and as a filler material for pore filling wood. Pumice comes in five grit grades, three of which are typically used in lutherie: 2F (medium), 3F (fine) and 4F (very fine). The 2F grade is generally used to rub out finishes in combination with paraffin oil or some other light oil. 3F or 4F pumice is used as a pore filler with shellac as a binder. See also: paraffin oil, pumice pore filler, rubbing out.

pumice pore filler *n.* Pumice and shellac are used as a traditional pore filler for oily dark woods such as rosewoods. This is often the pore filler used under French polish. Application involves coating the surface to be filled with shellac. When the shellac is dry, the polishing tampon is used with alcohol and a small bit of 4F pumice. The application motion is similar to that of French polishing. The alcohol dissolves some of the shellac during the process and also brings out some of the oily color from the wood. This, combined with the pumice and abraded wood fibers produces a colored slurry that fills the pores of the wood. See also: French polish, pumice, shellac, tampon.

punta *n.* (POON-ta) Violin corner (Italian).

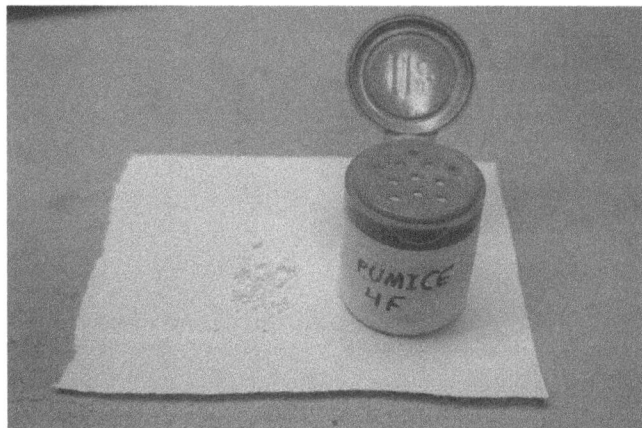

A small pile of 4F pumice next to a pumice shaker, for use in pumice pore filling.

purfling *n.* Decorative strips on the plates and possibly the ribs, near the edges. On guitars and similar instruments the purfling strips can be found between the bindings and the rest of the surface of the plate. Guitar purflings are composed of wood or fiber lines and also marquetry strips and shell pieces. Violin family instruments have no bindings and the purflings on these instruments are located just inboard of the edges of the plates. Violin purflings are always composed of simple lines. See also: bindings, marquetry, ink-drawn purfling.

purfling channel *n.* The routed channel into which purfling strips are inserted.

purfling cutter *n.* A hand tool used to cut purfling channels. The cutter has a blade which is indexed against the edge of the plate and so cuts at a fixed distance from the plate edge. To excavate a purfling channel using a purfling cutter, two such cuts are made and deepened. The distance between cuts is the width of the purfling channel. After these cuts are made the channel is excavated using a chisel or special purpose purfling groove cleaner. Syn.: gramil. See also: purfling channel, purfling groove cleaner.

Black and white purflings between binding and top of an acoustic guitar.

purfling groove cleaner *n.* A special purpose tool used to remove waste material between cuts made with a purfling cutter to create a purfling channel. See also: purfling channel, purfling cutter.

purfling groove cutter *n.* see purfling cutter

purfling line *n.* A thin and narrow strip of veneer used to create purfling. Purfling strips are usually composed of multiple pieces of wood. In the finished instrument these appear as lines.

purfling slot *n.* see purfling channel

purpleheart *n.* see *Peltogyne paniculata*

push back *v.* Varnishing technique used particularly for producing a sunburst finish on a violin family instrument. Following application of colored oil varnish of the base color, thin coats of colored varnish are applied to the instrument. Following application of a color coat the varnish is "pushed back" away from the central area of the plate while still wet, which leaves the instrument with deeper coloration at the edges. Generally many color coats are required to yield a smooth sunburst effect. See also: sunburst finish.

PVA glue *n.* see polyvinyl acetate glue

PVC *abbr.* see polyvinyl chloride

pyramid bridge *n.* Style of bridge appearing on and popularized by old Martin guitars. The pyramid bridge is a simple conventional fixed bridge with raised details at the ends of the bridge wings that are shaped like shallow pyramids. See also: belly bridge, bridge wing.

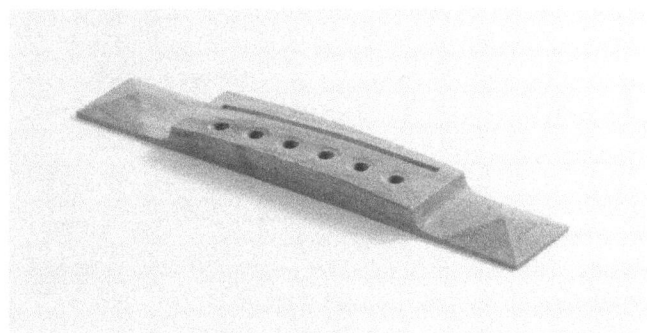

Custom CNC-machined pyramid guitar bridge by Andy Birko of Birkonium.

Pythagoras' law *n.* Research on the relationship between string length and fundamental pitch by Pythagoras yielded this law: Given constant string tension the frequency of vibration of a string is inversely proportional to its length. See also: Mersenne's laws.

Pythagorean scale *n.* The first mathematically based musical scale, based on experiments with string pitches made by Pythagoras ca. 500 BCE. The scale is based on integer ratios between notes.

PZT *abbr.* see lead zirconate titanate

Q

Q *n.* Parameter specifying the damping factor of an oscillating system and also its bandwidth. In lutherie this is most frequently encountered in descriptions of the peaks of frequency response curves (functions) of instruments. A high Q peak is tall and narrow (i.e., has high amplitude and a narrow bandwidth) and exhibits low damping. A low Q peak is short and wide and exhibits high damping. Very high Q peaks are generally considered to be detrimental to instrument tone, particularly when they fall on a note of the musical scale. These tend to indicate audible wolf notes. Very low Q peaks are also generally considered to be detrimental to instrument tone. The even response they provide to a wide range of frequencies results in a perceived lack of tonal character. The term is short for "quality factor", an unfortunate name for a strictly quantitative property. Syn.: Q factor, quality factor. See also: frequency response curve.

quarter sawn *adj.* This term refers to a method for cutting a log into boards and also to the resulting grain orientation of the boards. To saw quarter sawn lumber, a log is cut axially into quarters. Then for each quarter section, a slice is taken from one of the flat sides, then the quarter is rotated and a slice is taken from the other flat side. This process is repeated until the quarter section is all sawn into boards. When viewed from the end, each board will show grain lines (annular rings) oriented more or less perpendicular to the width of the board. There are other ways logs can be cut to yield boards that show this grain orientation, but for lutherie purposes we refer to the resulting boards as quarter sawn or simply quartered. Note that some wood merchants use a very liberal definition of quarter sawn lumber and may consider any board with grain oriented less than 45 degrees from vertical to be quarter sawn, but generally lutherie wood dealers consider boards with grain angle of less than 20 degrees to be quarter sawn, and generally are even more demanding where instrument top wood is concerned. Quarter sawn lumber is valued in lutherie as it is generally more dimensionally stable than flat sawn lumber, and generally easier to bend without distorting or breaking. See also: flat sawn, rift sawn.

End grain of quarter sawn Indian rosewood. On this sample the grain is not vertical, but the piece is still considered to be quarter sawn by the wood merchant.

quartered *n.* see quarter sawn

quartersawn *n.* see quarter sawn

R

R1E *adj*. see SLR1E

R2E *adj*. see SLR2E

rabab *n*. Middle eastern bowed instrument family.

rabbet *n*. Recessed edge or groove cut into the edge of a piece of wood. In guitar lutherie, the ledges cut into the edges of the body for the bindings are rabbets. Syn.: rebate.

Rabut, Guy USA violinmaker, author and educator. Rabut has produced a number of unconventional violins as well as more traditional instruments and has lectured on violin making and scroll carving.

radial sawn *adj*. Describing a radial method of sawing a log into boards. Radial sawing, like quarter sawing, produces boards with grain lines running more or less perpendicular to the wide surface of the board. It is a costly technique that produces a lot of waste. See also: quarter sawn.

radial surface *n*. A surface of a cut piece of wood that approximates a radial plane through the trunk of the tree from which it was cut. For a quarter sawn board the two wide surfaces of the board are radial surfaces. For a flat sawn board the two narrow sides are radial surfaces. See also: end grain surface, tangential surface.

radiation *n*. The process by which waves move through space. In lutherie we are primarily concerned with sound radiation, the process by which sound waves move through air and other materials.

radiation efficiency *n*. The efficiency with which an object radiates power. In lutherie we are primarily concerned with sound radiation. Radiation efficiency here means the difference between the power present at the object and the amount actually radiated. Radiation efficiency of 1 (100%) indicates that all power is radiated. Real objects (instruments or parts of instruments) always have radiation efficiencies lower than 1. Power not radiated is either dissipated in the object as heat or is reflected back into the object due to an impedance mismatch. See also: impedance.

Radif scale *n*. Scales used in classical Persian music.

radius *n*. see camber

radius *v*. To camber. See also: camber.

radius dish *n*. see dished workboard

radius gauge *n*. Measurement tool for measuring the radius of a curve. Most radius gauges are fixed radius templates and are used by matching a gauge to the curve you are attempting to measure.

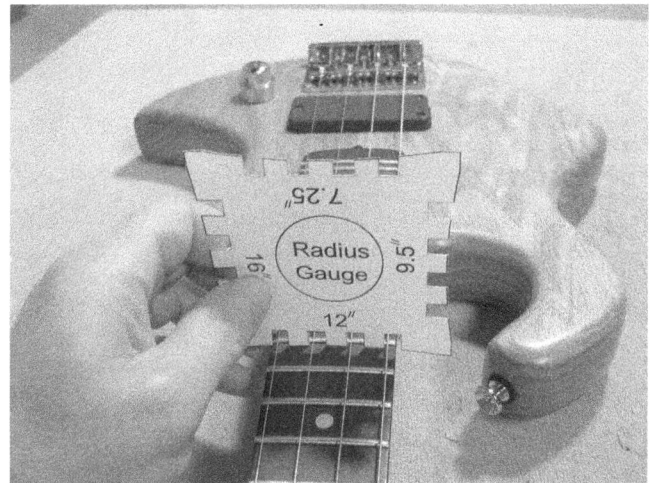

Radius gauge used to check the radius of the playing surface of the fretbaord of an electric bass. The gauge pictured has slots that allow the surface to be checked even if the strings are on the instrument.

radius sanding block *n*. A shaped sanding block with a concave sanding surface. Radius sanding blocks are available or can be made with different radius curves. They are used to produce a cambered surface. Self stick sandpaper is applied to the concave surface and the object is sanded with the block to produce or refine a cambered surface. See also: camber.

radiused sanding block *n*. see radius sanding block

raised fretboard *n*. A feature of some flattop (mostly classical) guitars. The fretboard extension is raised above the surface of the top. The fretboard usually does not float above the top: there is generally a neck extension that is attached to the top and to the underside of the fretboard. The raised fretboard was probably originally implemented to deal with bridge height and string breakover geometry. The feature appears in Stauffer Legnani guitars with floating fretboard extension of the early 1800's. See also: neck extension, floating fretboard.

Ramírez, José (1858-1923) Spanish luthier and founder of the eponymous guitar company. Ramírez built Torres inspired classical and flamenco guitars. The company is still in business and is run by his grandson, José Ramírez III. See also: Antonio de Torres Jurado.

Ramírez, Manuel (1864-1916) Spanish classical and flamenco guitar luthier, building in the style of Torres. A number of significant builders worked in his shop including Santos Hernandez, Domingo Esteso, Modesto Borreguero and Pascual Viudes. See also: Antonio de Torres Jurado.

ramp *n*. An incline or decline feature of a part. In lutherie ramps are often featured at the ends of braces and at the nut end of headstock slots. Syn.: bevel.

ramp *v*. To create a ramp or bevel on the end of a brace or other component.

rasgado *n*. (ras-GAH-doe) The strumming of the strings of the guitar to produce an arpeggio. From the Spanish verb rasgar, to rip or tear.

rasp *n*. File for shaping wood. A rasp is generally distinguished from a file by its cutting teeth but the term is often used to denote any file for use on wood. Rasps are generally machine-made. Rasps in which the teeth are raised by hand are called hand-stitched rasps. See also: hand-stitched rasp.

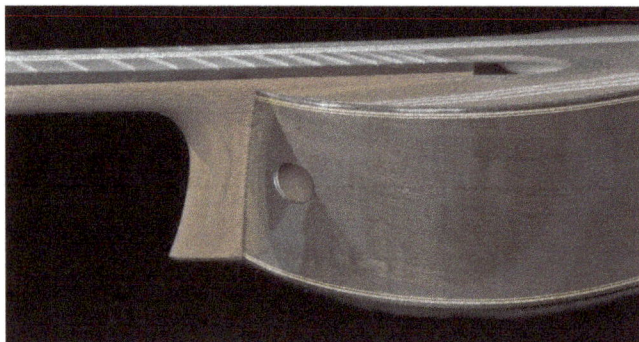

Raised fretboard on a classical guitar by Aaron Green.

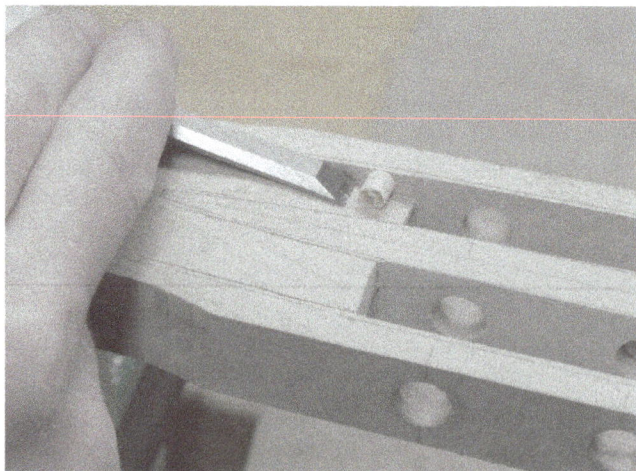

Carving the ramps on the headstock of a guitar.

Rawlings guitar *n.* One of the five guitars known to be built by Stradivari. Built in 1700, the instrument is currently in the collection of the National Music Museum in Vermillion SD, USA.

razor blade scraper *n.* A small temporary scraper made by turning the edge of a single edge razor blade, using a scraper burnisher. The scraper is used for fine scraping work, but the hook doesn't last long. See also: scraper burnisher.

reactive finish *n.* Wood finishes can be functionally classified by how they transform from liquid to solid form. The upper level of this classification breaks into two main types, evaporative finishes and reactive finishes. A reactive finish cures by reacting with air or a chemical added to the finish just prior to application. A reactive finish goes on in such a way that successive coats do not melt or burn into the coats already down. When fully cured a multiple coat reactive finish examined on edge can be seen to be composed of separate layers. Reactive finishes are more difficult to rub out than are evaporative finishes because cutting through the top layer results in an obvious witness line demarking the exposure of the next layer down. Oil varnish and polyester are examples of reactive finishes. See also: cutting through, evaporative finish, oil varnish, rub out, witness line.

reamer *n.* Tool used to shape a tapered hole. Various reamers are used in lutherie for reaming peg holes, end pin holes, and bridge pin holes.

rebate *n.* see rabbet

rebec *n.* Early European bowed instrument, European version of the rabab. See also: rabab

recap *v.* Wholesale replacement of capacitors in a tube amplifier, intended to improve its tone. Sometimes this involves replacing just the electrolytic capacitors in the amp power supply.

Using a bridge pin reamer to ream bridge pin holes.

rectified *adj.* Describing a nylon string that has been abrasively processed to improve the consistency of its diameter over its entire length. Nylon filament is generally not manufactured to tight diameter tolerances — the diameter of the material varies. When used as a string for a fretted instrument this variability can result in intonation variability. The process of rectification is intended to reduce intonation variability.

recurve *n.* The portion of an arched plate between the edge and the rest of the arch. The recurve or recurve area is generally lower in elevation than the edge of the plate.

red cedar *n.* see *Thuja plicata*

red maple *n.* see *Acer rubrum*

red spruce *n.* see *Picea rubens*

redwood *n.* see *Sequoia sempervirens*

reentrant tuning *n.* The tuning of a stringed instrument where the pitch of successive strings does not proceed from low to high. The higher pitched ukuleles make use of reentrant tuning. On those instruments the bottom string is pitched higher than the next one.

refret *n*. The state of having all new frets in a fretted instrument.

refret *v*. To install all new frets in an instrument.

refret saw *n*. Special back saw with short thin blades, used to clean out and/or deepen fret slots prior to refretting. The short blades can be used to saw inside a slot on a bound fretboard.

Regal Musical Instrument Co. Chicago IL, USA, instrument manufacturer. The roots of the company are from the Emil Wulschner & Son company in Indianapolis at the end of the 19th century, which used the Regal brand name. The company was renamed the Regal Musical Instrument Co. in the early 20th century. Lyon and Healy bought the rights to the Regal name and may have bought instruments from the company as well, starting in 1905. In addition to manufacturing traditional stringed instruments the company also manufactured resonator guitars. They were one of the largest instrument manufacturers by the 1930s. See also: Lyon and Healy, resonator guitar.

rehair *v*. To replace the hair on a bow.

Reig, Louis III Spanish guitarmaker (ca 1790-1860) from Valencia. His instruments were noted for an extreme level of decoration. Few instruments by this maker are known to exist.

reinforcing strip *n*. Any strip of material used to strengthen a seam or part.

relicing *v*. (REL-lick-ing) Treating an instrument or component to make it appear older and more thoroughly used than it actually is.

relief *n*. see neck relief

renaissance *adj*. Pertaining to the European Renaissance, the period between the 14th and 17th centuries.

requintilla *n*. (reh-keen-TEE-ya) High pitched string. The Spanish word usually describes a string in a course of strings that is tuned an octave higher than the primary string in the course.

resaw *v*. To cut thin panels from a thick board or billet. Resawing is done with a bandsaw with a wide blade. Guitar top and back halves, and both guitar and violin family rib sets are cut from thicker boards by this process.

resin impregnated wood *n*. Wood that has been impregnated with a hard resin, usually phenolic or polyester. This material is harder, denser, and more stable than plain wood. In lutherie it is used primarily as an ebony substitute because it is available in a completely black color. A popular brand name is Rocklite. Syn.: impreg.

resistance *n*. A fundamental electrical property, resistance is the measure of opposition to the passage of electrons. The ohm (Ω) is the unit of electrical resistance. In stringed musical instruments this is seen primarily as a property of magnetic pickups. Pickup resistance affects its resonant peak, which in turn affects overall tone of the pickup. See also: magnetic pickup, resonant peak.

resonance *n*. A large vibration caused by a periodic signal at or near a natural frequency of vibration in an object. All of the vibrating components of stringed musical instruments have resonances. The air inside the body of an instrument for example has a resonance at a frequency that is a function of the volume of air enclosed in the body and the size of the soundhole. Resonances with high Q (narrow bandwidth) are high in amplitude and can be excited only by signals at or very close to their center frequency. Those with low Q (wide bandwidth) are low amplitude and can be excited by a wider range of signal frequencies. See also: Q.

resonant peak *n.* Peak in the frequency response curve of an instrument or component. See also: frequency response curve.

resonator *n.* 1. Something that resonates. In lutherie the term is used to describe any physically vibrating system such as a mode of vibration of the top plate of an instrument. 2. The primary sound producing part of the resonator guitar, a large metal cone. 3. The back cover found on some banjos.

resonator guitar *n.* Wood or metal bodied guitar featuring a large metal cone as one of its principal sound producing components. Syn.: resophonic guitar.

responsiveness *n.* The quality of stringed instruments that describes either the level of playing force required to produce sound, or the quickness with which an instrument produces sound after being plucked or bowed. Both definitions are in common use, an indication that the term is ill-defined.

rest *n.* see brace end bracket

rest stroke *n.* Finger style plucking motion where the plucking finger ends up touching the adjacent string following the pluck. Generally produces a somewhat louder sound than that of the free stroke. Syn.: apoyando. See also: free stroke.

restoration *n.* In the context of lutherie, repair of an instrument to its original condition, generally minus wear and tear that would be normal for its age. Most luthiers' definition would include all necessary mechanical repairs and also the removal of any previous repair efforts that left the instrument in less than original condition.

resurrection *n.* This term was coined by luthier John Calkin to describe expedient work needed to get a modest or historically insignificant instrument into playable condition. See also: John Calkin.

retarder *n.* Substance added to finishing material to increase its drying time. Retarders are often added to hand applied finishing material to increase the amount of time the material can be worked.

retouching varnish *n.* Violin varnish intended specifically for repair work, not for varnishing an entire new instrument.

reverse gearing tuning machine *n.* see worm under tuning machine

reverse kerfed lining *n.* Kerfed lining that is applied with the kerfed side toward the ribs. Reverse kerfed lining makes the rib assembly stiffer, so it holds its shape better before the plates are attached. It also looks more like solid lining when viewed through the soundhole. See also: kerfed lining.

reverse scroll mandolin *n.* Regal mandolin introduced in 1914 that included an unusual body scroll that curled away from the neck. Syn.: Smurf head mandolin.

revoicing *n.* Modifications made to a finished instrument to alter its tonal qualities. This operation is considered by those that do it to be a repair procedure.

Reyes, Manuel *n.* Spanish luthier based in Córdoba, Reyes and his son Manuel Jr. build classical and flamenco guitars.

rib *n.* The side of a stringed musical instrument.

rib attachment wedge *n.* Wedge of wood used to hold the end of the instrument rib into the rib slot on the neck heel.

rib block *n.* A piece of wood from which the ribs for a violin family instrument can be cut.

rib jack *n.* Jacks (the opposite of clamps) used to hold the ribs of an instrument in position inside an outside mold. The jacks are used during the process of gluing on the top and/or back plate. Once the glue dries, the jacks are removed through the soundhole. See also: jack.

R

Rib attachment wedges ready to be pressed into place.

rib slot *n*. Slots cut into the neck heel for attachment of the ribs of the instrument. This construction style is used in Spanish guitars to attach the neck to the body. The ends of the ribs fit into these slots. The slots are in some cases thin enough to provide a dry press fit of the rib ends; in some cases the rib ends are glued in. Some instruments feature wide slots which are used with

Rib jacks are used to hold the rib and block assembly in position inside the outside mold.

Rib slot is chiseled into the side of the rough neck of a classical guitar. The end of the body rib will be inserted in this slot and held in place with a wedge.

wedges to hold the rib ends in place. See also: rib attachment wedge

Ribbecke, Tom California USA luthier, author and teacher. Specializes in archtop and semi-archtop guitars.

riccio *n*. (REECH-ee-oh) Scroll (Italian).

rift sawn *adj*. There are unfortunately three commonly used and contradictory definitions of this term. For this reason the term is obviously not definitive, and additional disambiguating information should be required. 1. Lumber cut so the grain is exactly 45 degrees from the wide surface of the board. This term is used almost exclusively to describe oak, which shows a unique grain pattern when cut this way. 2. Boards that are radially sawn out of a log so that the grain orientation of each board is perfectly perpendicular to the wide surface of the board. 3. Boards that have grain lines that run at an angle when viewed from the end. The exact angle that separates quarter sawn from rift sawn (and rift sawn from flat sawn) is not well established, but most lutherie wood suppliers consider a board to be rift sawn if grain lines appear from 20 to 70 degrees from perpendicular to the wide surface of the board. General lumber industry specifications are between 30 and 60 degrees. See also: quarter sawn, flat sawn, radially sawn, bastard grain.

riser block *n*. An optional piece for some models of band saw, the riser block extends the maximum cutting height of the saw. Use of a riser block requires the use of longer blades. Riser blocks are typically only an option on Delta 14″ band saws and knockoffs.

RMS *abbr*. see root mean square

Robb, Arthur North Wiltshire UK lute luthier and restorer of lutes and other instruments.

Roberto, Juan see John Roberts

Roberto-Venn school *n*. Lutherie school located in Phoenix AZ, USA.

Roberts, John Guitar luthier and cofounder of the Roberto-Venn School of Luthiery. Also known as Juan Roberto.

Robinia pseudoacacia *n*. Black locust. Species native to the USA, it has density and stiffness similar to Brazilian rosewood (*Dalbergia nigra*) and is considered by some to be a viable domestic alternative for guitar backs and sides.

rock maple *n*. see *Acer saccharum*

Rodríguez, Miguel Beneyto (1888-1875) Córdoba Spain guitar luthier. Also known as Miguel Sr.

Rodríguez Serrano, Rafael (1921-1965) Córdoba Spain guitar luthier, son of Miguel Beneyto Rodríguez and twin brother of Miguel Rodríguez Serrano.

Rodríguez Serrano, Miguel (1921-1998) Córdoba Spain guitar luthier, son of Miguel Beneyto Rodríguez and twin brother of Miguel Rodríguez Serrano. Also known as Miguel Jr.

roll *n*. In lutherie the terms yaw, pitch, and roll, used to describe rotation of an object in space, are most often used to describe adjustments necessary to fit an instrument's neck onto its body. When the instrument is viewed from the end, roll is rotation of the neck about an axis extending from your eye to the instrument. See also: pitch, yaw.

Roman arch *n*. Arching profile with a rounded apex. The tops of braces are often arched to this profile. See also: cathedral arch.

Romanillos, José Luis Spanish classical guitar luthier and author of the book *Antonio de Torres Guitar Maker - His Life and Work*.

romantic guitar *n*. Guitar made during the Romantic period, i.e. the late 18th to early 19th centuries.

room acoustics *n*. The study of the behavior of sound waves in an enclosed space.

root mean square *n*. Mathematically, the square root of the mean of squares of values. In lutherie this is encountered in descriptions of the electrical power output of amplifiers and also in descriptions of sound pressure. Syn.: RMS.

rope binding *n*. Instrument binding made in rope pattern. Syn.: barber pole binding. See also: rope pattern.

rope core *adj*. Describes wound violin family strings that have a twisted or braided core. Rope core strings have high internal damping.

rope pattern *n*. A marquetry pattern of alternating diagonally oriented pieces that give the impression of the twisting of rope. Rope pattern marquetry is used in guitar decoration for purflings, back strips and soundhole rosettes. See also: back strip, marquetry, purfling, rosette.

rose *n*. see rosette

rosette *n*. Decoration around or in a soundhole.

R

Rope binding and rope pattern marquetry soundhole rosette on a ukulele by Graham McDonald.

rosette channel *n*. Channel cut around the soundhole of guitars and other instruments. This channel is filled with decorative strips and tiles to form the rosette.

rosette log *n*. The center section of traditional classical guitar rosettes are composed of small wood mosaic tiles, generally fitted together to form a continuous pattern. These tiles are constructed by first gluing together a bundle of colored sticks to form a log. The log is then sliced into tiles.

rosette pocket *n*. see rosette channel

rosette tile *n*. The center section of traditional classical guitar rosettes are composed of small wood mosaic tiles,

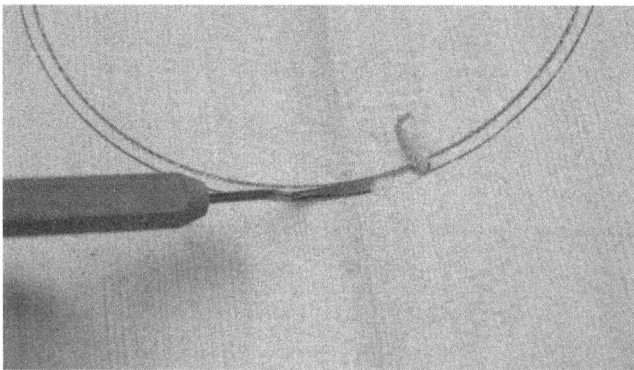

The side walls of this thin rosette channel have been cut using a compass gramil. The waste is being excavated using a small chisel.

generally fitted together to form a continuous pattern. The tiles are generally constructed as slices off a stick, which in turn is made of thin colored sticks cut from veneers and glued together.

rosewood *n*. Any tropical hardwood of the genus *Dalbergia*. Rosewood is used in guitar lutherie for backs and sides, fingerboards, bridges and headplates, and is also used for decorative bindings and purflings.

rosin *n*. Resin extracted from pine trees. Rosin is used as a hardening component of violin varnishes. Syn.: colophon, colophony.

Rossing, Tom Physics professor and author, with many publications on musical instrument acoustics.

rottenstone *n*. A fine dark volcanic abrasive powder used as the final step in traditional rubbing out of finishes. The abrasive is applied with a light oil such as paraffin oil. See also: paraffin oil, rubbing out.

Roudhloff, Dominique & Arnould Nineteenth century Mirecourt, France guitar luthiers. Their instruments are similar to others from that place and time such as Louis Panormo, but feature plain bridges with separate compensated saddles and x-braced tops. See also: Louis Panormo, X-bracing.

rough sawn *adj*. Lumber that is roughly sawn to dimension. The surfaces of rough sawn lumber are generally very rough, making it difficult to see what the wood will look like when smooth.

round wound string *n*. Steel string, typically for guitar or bass guitar, composed of a solid steel core wound with round wire.

router template *n*. see routing template See also: pocket, boss, pattern bit.

routing template *n*. A template used to cut a pocket or boss using a router and pattern bit. The template is typically a thin plate of wood or plastic with a hole cut in it that has the shape of the outline of the pocket or boss to be cut. The template is affixed to the wood and the wood inside the outline is routed out to the required depth. The bearing on the pattern bit rides on the inside edge of the template to exactly locate the walls of the pocket or boss. See also: pattern bit.

rubbed joint *n*. A glued joint that is held in place during gluing only by atmospheric pressure and gravity. The halves of blanks for arched plates are often glued using a rubbed joint. One half is held in a vise so its gluing surface is horizontal, glue is applied, the other half is positioned in contact with the first and rubbed around a bit to distribute the glue then positioned for drying. Since the wide surfaces of the glue joint are then not subject to atmospheric pressure, that pressure bearing on the opposite surfaces of pieces being glued supplies the clamping pressure. See also: atmospheric pressure clamping.

rubber *n*. see tampon

rubbing out *n*. Final step in most finishing schedules. Involves reducing micro surface irregularities (i.e., buffing, polishing) by application of abrasives. Rubbing out can be done using fine grit abrasive paper, solid or liquid polishing compounds, or loose abrasives like

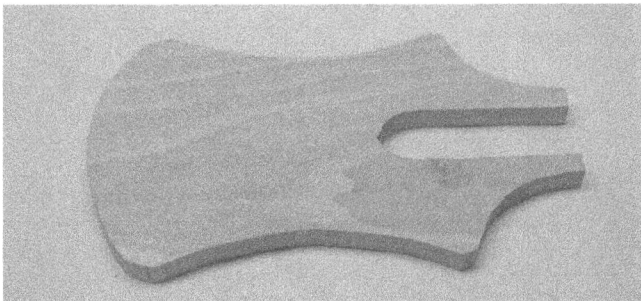

Routing template for a guitar headstock. This template is used to trim the outline of the headstock and also the pocket for the trussrod adjustment nut.

pumice mixed with oil. The term is generally used when this operation is done by hand.

rubbing pad *n*. see tampon

Ruck, Robert (1945-2018) Eugene OR, USA, classical and flamenco guitar luthier and one of the principals of the modern lutherie movement.

rule of 18 *n*. Historical technique used to calculate fret locations. The scale length was divided by 18, the result of which was the distance from nut to first fret. That distance was subtracted from the scale length and that value was divided by 18 to yield the distance from the first fret to the second fret. The process was repeated for all frets. The technique does not yield the same results as the modern 12th root of 2 method for performing these calculations, but the results may be within the range of human pitch differentiation for stringed musical instruments. See also: 12th root of 2, compensation, fret position constant.

run *n*. Defect in the application of a coat of finishing material. A run is an area where finishing material has pooled enough on a vertical or near vertical surface to run off that surface. See also: sag.

running mass *n*. see mass per unit length

runout *n*. Lack of parallelism between the grain lines and the long dimension of a board. Split boards generally do not exhibit runout, while most sawn boards have at least some. Severe runout can lead to structural weakness, but woodworkers need to be aware of even small amounts of runout because it affects the direction in which a board can be planed.

ryoba *n*. Japanese pull saw used for general cutting. This is a double edge saw, often with a cross cut edge and a ripping edge. See also: Japanese pull saw.

R

S

S2S *abbr*. Lumber finish specification abbreviation. It means "surfaced two sides" and means the board has been planed smooth on both broad surfaces only. Syn.: D2S (dimensioned two sides).

S4S *abbr*. Lumber finish specification abbreviation. It means "surfaced four sides" and means the board has been planed smooth on all four surfaces. Syn.: D4S (dimensioned four sides).

Sabionari guitar *n*. One of the five existing guitars known to be built by Stradivari. Built in 1679, it is currently in a private collection in Milan, Italy.

Sacconi, Simone Fernando (1895-1973) Italian violin luthier, repairman and author of the book *The Secrets of Stradivari*.

saddle *n*. Hard, protruding component over which the strings or other wire components run. The bridge saddle of guitar family instruments is the termination of the speaking length of the string. The saddle on violin family instruments is a piece of hard material inlaid into the edge of the top at the tail end, over which the tailgut runs. See also: speaking length, tailgut.

saddle slot *n*. Slot cut into the bridge of flattop acoustic guitar family instruments into which the saddle is mounted. See also: saddle.

safe edge *n*. An edge or side of a file or rasp that is smooth and devoid of cutting teeth. The safe edge of a file can be rubbed against a surface without cutting into that surface.

Safe-T-Planer *n*. Product name of a drill press mounted thickness planing device. Originally manufactured by

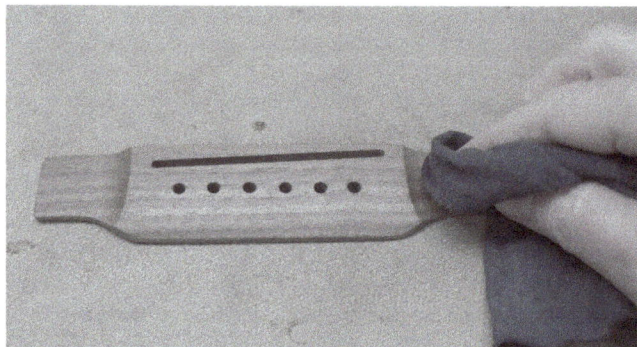

Guitar bridge under construction showing saddle slot and drilled pin holes.

Wagner, these inexpensive devices are used by many luthiers for small thicknessing jobs.

sag *n*. Defect in the application of a coat of finishing material. A sag is a bulge in the finishing material, caused by material building up in an area of a vertical or near vertical surface and beginning to run off the surface. See also: run.

Salò, Gasparo da (1540-1609) Italian violin luthier from Brescia, considered to be one of the first builders of violins.

same-note intonation variability *n*. Refers to the range of pitches obtained on repeatedly fretting the same string and fret of a fretted instrument. This is generally low for nylon string instruments but quite high for steel string

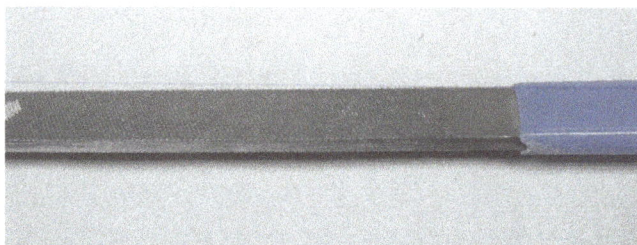

The edge of this file has been ground smooth and serves as a safe edge.

instruments, particularly on the upper frets, probably due to unintentional string bending. Appearance of high same-note intonation variability decreases the perceived effectiveness of intonation compensation efforts.

sami-sen *n.* see shamisen

sandarac *n.* Resin from the sandarac tree (*Tetraclinis articulata*) or from cypress pines (genus *Callitris*), used as a component of violin varnishes.

sanding block *n.* A block of hard or semi-hard material used to back up sandpaper for hand sanding. The block may be rectangular or shaped for sanding particular contours. See also: sandpaper.

sanding board *n.* Flat piece of wood covered with sandpaper. In use the sanding board can either be used as a large sanding block and moved to sand the work, or it can remain stationary while the work is moved over its surface. See also: sanding block, sandpaper.

sanding drum *n.* Cylinder covered with sandpaper or a fitted abrasive sanding sleeve, used in power sanding. The drum is rotated by a motor in use. See also: sanding sleeve, sandpaper.

Sanding drum mounted on a drill press.

sanding sleeve *n.* tube shaped sandpaper used as a covering for a sanding drum.

sandpaper *n.* Paper or other similar material onto which a coating of abrasive particles is glued. Used to smooth surfaces.

sandpaper grit *n.* Sandpaper comes is various grit grades. There are a number of standard grading systems for sandpaper grits. The most common grit grading convention for sandpaper used in woodworking in the USA is that of the Coated Abrasive Manufacturers Institute (CAMI). Woodworkers typically use grits that range from very coarse (40) to extra fine (320) when sanding wood. Sanding of finishes is usually done with much finer grades. Other sandpaper grit grading systems are common. The second most common is the Federation of European Producers of Abrasives (FEPA) system, also known as the "P" grading system. Grit size designations in this system are always proceeded by the letter "P". Luthiers should also be aware of the Japanese Industrial Standards Committee (JIS) system used by Japanese manufacturers; the Apex or Structured Abrasives system used by some manufacturers of automotive finishing papers; and the unique system used by the producers of Micro Mesh sandpaper. Syn.: grit.

sandpaper pull sanding *n.* A technique for fitting two flat parts together. The parts are roughly shaped to fit each other, then are held together with a piece of course grit sandpaper in between. The sandpaper is pulled one way and then the other while the pieces are held together. This sands the surface of one of the pieces to the contour of the other. A variation of the technique is used to angle the heel back in a neck reset for a guitar. Here the sandpaper is positioned between the heel and the instrument body and facing the heel. On each stroke the sandpaper is completely pulled out, which causes the heel to be sanded more deeply at the back end than at the top end. This angles the heel back. Syn.: floss sanding. See also: neck reset.

S

The contact surface of the heel of this guitar neck is being sanded by the sandpaper pull method.

Sanguino, Francisco Middle to late 18th century Spanish guitarmaker from Seville. His instruments are the earliest known to use fan bracing. See also: fan bracing.

santos rosewood *n*. see *Machaerium* spp.

sapwood *n*. Wood from the outer part of the log. In the live tree, this is where the sap flows. See also: heartwood.

Savart Journal *n*. An open access peer reviewed online research journal focusing on science and technology of stringed musical instruments. The journal's website is found at http://SavartJournal.org.

Savart, Felix (1791-1841) French physicist specializing in the study of magnetism and acoustics. He was interested in the physics of the violin and experimented extensively in this area. He is probably most famous for the construction of experimental violins with a trapezoidal body and plates lightly arched only on the outside.

saz *n*. see bağlama

scale *n*. see scale length

scale length *n*. The speaking length of the string of an instrument, minus any added compensation. For fretless instruments of the violin family the scale length is the actual distance between nut and bridge. For guitars and other fretted instruments that length also usually includes some added length for compensation for string stretching while fretting. A simple measure of the scale length of a fretted instrument can be had by measuring the distance from the nut to the twelfth fret and then multiplying that distance by two. Syn.: mensure. See also: compensation, nominal bridge position, speaking length.

scalloped brace *n*. Guitar top brace carved so that the horizontal profile includes peaks near the ends and a valley near the center, or a single peak somewhere near the middle. Scalloped braces are typical of pre-WWII Martin guitars and are a feature of many modern steel string guitars as well.

scalloped fretboard *n*. Fretboard that has had wood carved out of the playing surface, between the frets. The result is that a player playing on an instrument with such a fretboard rarely touches the fretboard surface while playing.

scarf joint *n*. A woodworking joint that joins two pieces with angled cut surfaces to increase gluing area of the joint. The headstock is often attached to the neck shaft of guitars with a scarf joint.

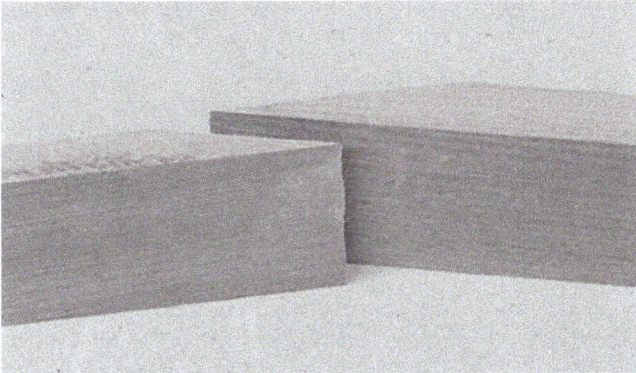

Headstock blank (left) ready to be scarfed to neck shaft blank (right).

scarf jointed headstock *n*. Headstock joined to the neck shaft using a scarf joint. There are two orientations of the scarf joint, one where the end grain of the headstock piece forms part of the neck shaft, and one where the neck shaft piece extends into the headstock. The former is generally referred to as a Spanish luthier's scarf joint and the latter has no separate proper name. See also: Spanish luthier's scarf joint.

Schmidt, Oscar Founded the Oscar Schmidt company in Jersey City NJ, USA, in 1879. The company produced various stringed instruments including guitars, ukuleles and autoharps. These were generally lower priced instruments. Instruments made under their own label often were labeled as Stella brand. They also produced house branded instruments for a number of music retailers.

Schneider, Richard (1936-1997) Washington state USA classical guitar luthier, author and educator. He is best known for his collaboration with Michael Kasha and the production of innovative modern classical guitars in what is now generally referred to as the Kasha style.

Schnitzer, Arnold New York USA double bass maker and author.

scientific pitch *n*. Archaic tuning system in which the frequency of middle C is 256Hz.

scientific pitch notation *n*. The most common alphabetic pitch notation. This system uses the upper case letters C - B, accidental marks, and a numeric subscript ranging from 0 to indicate octave. Octaves range from C to C. In this system C4 is middle C. Syn.: American Standard Pitch Notation, ASPN, International Pitch Notation, IPN. See also: Helmholtz pitch notation.

scoop cutaway *n*. A partial cutaway between the top of an acoustic guitar and the ribs near the neck. This type of cutaway provides better access to the upper frets while not diminishing the interior volume of the body too much.

scraper *n*. see card scraper

scraper burnisher *n*. A tool used to draw out an edge on a card scraper and then turn the edge so it can be used for scraping. The scraper burnisher is a hardened metal rod with a handle. See also: card scraper.

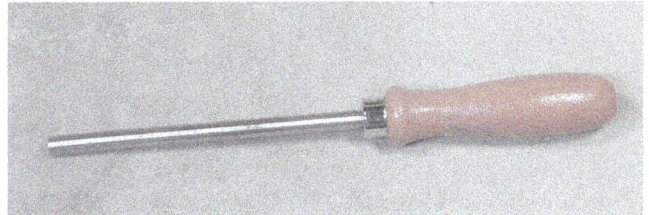

Scraper burnisher.

scraper plane *n*. Scraper mounted in a plane-like body. The tool is useful for scraping large flat areas and for planing highly figured wood. It is generally easier to use in this application than the card scraper because the blade does not have to be held and bent in the hands. See also: cabinet scraper.

screw *n*. Component of the violin bow used to adjust tension of the hair. See also: bow.

S

scribing *v.* A method for fitting two pieces together so they have continuous contact. The two pieces are oriented so that when the leg of a compass is slid across one of the surfaces the compass pencil (or scribing point) will mark a similar contour on the other piece. The marked piece is then sawed/planed/scraped to that line.

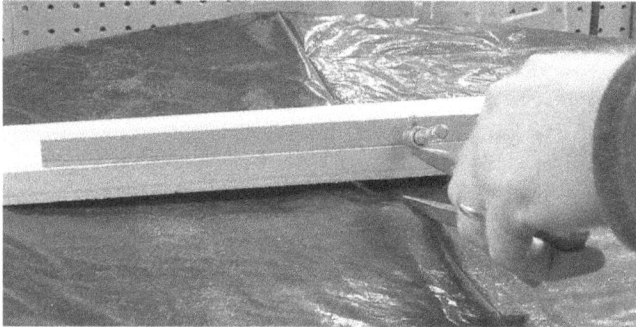

Scribing. A guitar brace is scribed to the contour of a dished workboard. The workboard is covered with plastic to prevent its sandpaper covering from sanding down the leg of the compass.

scroll *n.* Decorative design in the shaped of rolled up material. Scrolls are found on the pegbox end in violin family instruments and also on the bodies of F style mandolins.

scroll headstock *n.* Flat guitar headstock with a vertical shape that recalls a violin scroll. This type of headstock was used on guitars by Stauffer and Martin and also on electric guitars and basses by Fender.

scrub plane *n.* Hand plane used for the rapid removal of material. Planes used for this purpose tend to be relatively short (e.g., #4 or #5) and the edge of the blade is often ground into a slight convex arc.

SE *abbr.* see second epoch

seal coat *n.* see spit coat

sealer *n.* Finishing material used to prevent absorption of a subsequent finishing material into the wood. Sealer is generally used to prevent pigmented material from being absorbed into the wood. Sealers generally use alcohol as their solvent because alcohol is not readily absorbed by wood.

second epoch *n.* In his book *Antonio de Torres, Guitarmaker - His Life and Work*, José Romanillos cataloged the work of Torres divided into two epochs. The second epoch was from 1875 through 1892. Syn.: SE. See also: first epoch, José Romanillos.

second moment of area *n.* Property of the cross section of a beam that is used, along with material properties, to calculate bending and deflection in the beam. This property describes the stiffness of the beam that is relative to its cross sectional shape. This property is usually denoted by the letter *I* or *J*. Syn.: area moment of inertia.

second order beats *n.* Two tones close to an octave, fifth, or (possibly) fourth apart can yield audible beating. These beats are thought to be an artifact of auditory phase relationship processing in the ear. They are not a result of destructive interference as is the case with primary beats. See also: beats.

section modulus *n.* Property of the cross section of a beam that is used, along with material properties, to calculate bending and deflection in the beam. Denoted by the letter *s*, this property is calculated by dividing the second moment of area by the area of the cross section. Given a uniform material, this property describes stiffness per unit weight.

seedlac *n.* Unrefined shellac, shellac which still contains many impurities. Seedlac is generally darker in color than more refined grades of shellac.

segmented mirror *n.* A guitar repair tool consisting of strips of mirror taped together so that the mirror can be folded and inserted into the guitar body through the soundhole. Inside it is unfolded so the repair person can see the underside of the soundboard.

S

self-bound fretboard *n*. Fretboard fitted with blind fret slots, or bound with pieces cut off from the fretboard itself. The appearance of a self-bound fretboard is like that of a bound fretboard when viewed from the fret ends. The ends of the fret beads are visible but the fret tangs are not visible because the slots into which the tangs are inserted do not go all the way through the width of the fretboard. Syn.: faux bound fretboard.

Selmer Maccaferri guitar *n*. Guitar originally designed for Selmer company by Mario Maccaferri, or a guitar in that style. The instruments feature a Venetian cutaway, long narrow bridge and often some internal baffling. The original instruments had a large D-shaped soundhole and internal baffling. Later models from Selmer used a smaller oval soundhole and no internal baffling. These later models are referred to as "petite bouche" (small mouth) to distinguish them from the original instruments with larger soundholes. Syn.: Maccaferri guitar, Manouche guitar. See also: Venetian cutaway.

semi-hollow body *adj*. Describes an instrument, usually an electric guitar, with a hollow but not fully acoustic body. This construction is used to emulate the look of a hollow body instrument while providing the feedback resistance of a solid body instrument. Syn.: semi-solid

Fretboard blank milled for a self-bound fretboard. The fret slots do not go all the way across the board to the sides.

body. See also: feedback resistance, hollow body, solid body.

sensory integration *n*. Process by which the brain processes and combines input from multiple senses. Of interest to researchers performing listening experiments, which must be designed to eliminate or control for simultaneous input from senses other than hearing.

sequential refinement *n*. see successive approximation

Sequoia sempervirens *n*. California redwood, coastal redwood. This dark colored softwood is sometimes used for the tops of guitars and similar instruments. It is easy to work. The wood has a dry specific gravity of 0.4 and a MOE of 8.4 GPa.

set neck *n*. Term used to describe the method by which the neck of an instrument is attached to the body. An instrument with a set neck has its neck glued to the body. See also: bolt-on neck, neck through construction.

setback *n*. The distance an object's location is offset from its nominal position. Lutherie use of the term generally refers to the position of the bridge saddle or nut of a guitar, or the distance of one of the outer strings to the edge of the fingerboard.

setup *n*. Final adjustments to a finished stringed instrument for optimal playability. These usually include setting relief, action and intonation but may include other adjustments peculiar to the instrument. See also: action, intonation, relief.

shade *n*. In color mixing of pigments, the shade of a color is an indication of how much white or black pigment is mixed with a color. Darker shades contain more black, lighter shades contain more white. See also: tone.

shaft *n*. Any cylindrical component. In lutherie the term is used specifically to identify the shaft of the neck and to distinguish that part from the other parts of the neck: the heel and headstock.

S

shamisen *n*. Japanese plucked three string instrument with a skin top like a banjo.

sharpening stone *n*. An abrasive block used to sharpen edge tools.

sharping lever *n*. Pitch control device usually found on harps which provide for raising the pitch of a string by a fixed amount, usually a semitone or a whole tone.

Shaw, Tim Designer of the Sunrise pickup in the 1970s. Director of product development and guitar design at Fender Musical Instruments.

shelf life *n*. Amount of time a product may be stored in its original container and still perform to expectations. The term usually refers to finishing products and glue.

shellac *n*. Finishing product made from the secretions of an insect, *Coccus lacca*. Shellac is available in dry form, usually flakes, which must be dissolved in alcohol and possibly strained and dewaxed before use. It is also available in prepared form but this is seldom used in lutherie because it has such a short shelf life. Shellac is a component of some spirit varnishes and is used as a finishing product and sealer on its own. Shellac is used in

Dewaxed shellac flakes will be dissolved in alcohol and then strained to make shellac for finishing.

French polishing. See also: dewaxed shellac, French polish, shelf life, spirit varnish.

shellacquer *n*. Mixture of shellac and nitrocellulose lacquer and often a fast drying solvent like acetone. Used as a touch up spirit varnish or a fast building hand applied finish. See also: nitrocellulose lacquer, spirit varnish.

Sheppard, Frederick "Federico" Green Bay WI, USA, and Carrion de los Condes, Spain, classical guitar luthier, historian, teacher, and author. He is a subject matter expert on Paraguayan virtuoso classical guitarist and composer Agustín Barrios.

shielding *n*. Generally refers to electrical shielding of high impedance components and wiring to reduce electrically induced noise. Shielding may be added around wires, under pickguards and inside control cavities of electric guitars.

shielding tape *n*. Electrical shielding material in tape form. The tape usually consists of copper foil covered with a conductive adhesive. The copper can be soldered, and the conductive adhesive allows large or oddly shaped areas to be covered with overlapping pieces that will then be electrically connected. See also: shielding.

Shirazi, Nasser (1939-) Iranian born California USA based luthier of Middle Eastern instruments and author of books and articles about Middle Eastern instruments and their construction.

shoe shine sanding *v*. Sanding method to shape curved surfaces. A strip of sandpaper is held on each end and the sandpaper is moved back and forth over the surface, using the same motion used to shine shoes with a cloth. Instrument neck shafts are often smoothed using this method.

shoot *v*. 1. To apply a finishing material by spraying (e.g., to shoot lacquer). 2. To joint an edge, possibly

Shoe shine sanding the neck shaft of a guitar neck. The strip of sandpaper is pulled back and forth over the shaft while it is simultaneously moved along the length of the shaft.

using a shooting board (e.g., to shoot the edge). See also: joint, shooting board.

shooting board *n.* A board used as a platform for boards to be jointed using a hand plane. The boards to be jointed are placed on the shooting board with the edges to be jointed overhanging the edge of the shooting board a bit. Then the edge is planed with a plane resting on its side.

short oil varnish *n.* Oil varnish containing a relatively small quantity of non-drying oil. Short oil varnishes dry harder than long oil varnishes. Most varnishes used for

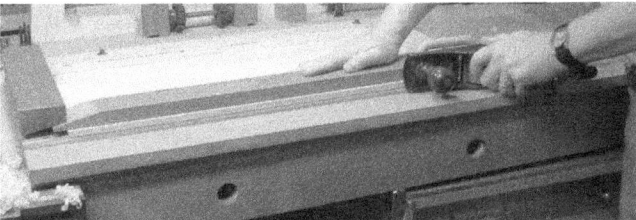

The center joint edges of a guitar top are jointed using a shooting board.

finishing stringed instruments are short oil varnishes. See also: long oil varnish, oil varnish.

shovel gouge *n.* An in-cannel gouge shaped like a shovel with a knob and a thin shaft connected to a rather short and wide blade. The tool is used for rough carving of arched plates. See also: in-cannel gouge.

SI units *n.* French. *Système international d'unités*, the international system of units of metric measurement. The common units of length used in lutherie are the millimeter (mm) and centimeter (cm). SI units are generally used in lutherie in countries that use them, but they are also often used in the USA for both violin family instruments and Spanish guitars. See also: USCS units.

siccative *n.* A drying agent, added to varnishes to make them dry or dry faster. See also: metallic dryer.

side bar prop *n.* see brace end bracket

side bender *n.* see side bending machine

side bending *v.* Hot bending the ribs of an instrument. This is generally performed using a bending iron or other hot pipe, or a specialized side bending machine. See also: bending iron, side bending machine.

side bending machine *n.* Machine to bend the ribs of an instrument. Such machines can usually bend one or both sides of the instrument at the same time. They consist of a heated form in the shape of the side and various cauls and clamps that bring the side material in full contact with the form.

side dot *n.* Position-indicating dot placed on the side of the fingerboard.

side lined fretless bass *n.* Fretless bass guitar with lines or other markers on the side of the fingerboard indicating fret positions. Side lines provide fret location indication to the player but can't be seen by the audience. See also: fretless bass, lined fretless bass.

side port *n.* see soundport

S

Side lined bass guitar. Fretting positions are indicated by lines inlaid into the side of the fretboard.

side purfling *n*. Purfling on the ribs of a guitar or similar instrument, between binding and the rest of the rib. See also: purfling.

side reinforcing strips *n*. Narrow strips of wood glued vertically cross grain to the inside of the ribs of a stringed instrument to reinforce the ribs and help prevent cracking of the ribs along the grain. These are found most often in guitar family instruments, particularly in dreadnought and archtop guitars.

side splints *n*. see side reinforcing strips

One line of maple side purfling between binding and ribs of this instrument.

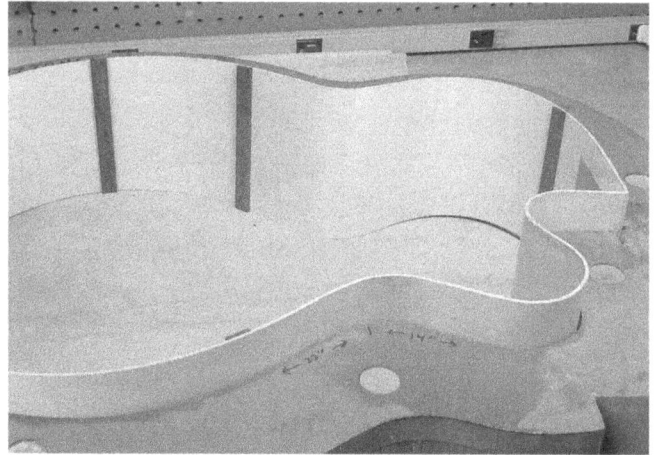

Rosewood side reinforcing strips attached to the maple ribs of an acoustic bass guitar under construction.

signal generator *n*. An electronic device, or a computer and software, for generating different waveforms at specified frequencies. Signal generators are often used in the evaluation of the vibration of an instrument at different pitches.

silicon carbide *n*. Sanding abrasive. Silicon carbide is black in color and is used primarily to sand metal and finishes. Sandpaper products coated with this are generally only available in fine grits.

silicone blanket *n*. see silicone heating blanket

silicone heating blanket Belt shaped length of silicone rubber into which are embedded heat-producing wires. These are used for side bending and are the source of heat for some side bending machines. See also: side bending, side bending machine.

silk *n*. Decorative fabric covering on the ends of cello and bass strings.

silking *n*. Visible medullary rays in well quartered softwood. See also: medullary ray.

S

silverface *adj*. Describes Fender tube guitar amplifiers built from the late 1960s through the early 1980s. These amps have a distinctive silver colored control panel. See also: blackface.

Siminoff, Roger USA guitar and mandolin luthier and author of lutherie books.

single acting trussrod *n*. Single acting rods, also sometimes called compression rods, can be tightened to provide more neck back bow only. A strategy for using this style of trussrod to provide limited front bow adjustment is to install the trussrod and then tighten it to slightly back bow the fingerboard. Then the fingerboard is planed flat. Syn.: compression trussrod. See also: back bow, front bow, single acting trussrod, trussrod.

single coil pickup *n*. Magnetic pickup with a single magnetic coil. Single coil pickups tend to have a brighter tone. They do not have inherent hum canceling characteristics. See also: humbucking pickup.

single cutaway *adj*. see cutaway

sinker wood *n*. Wood collected from logs that have been submerged in water for an extended length of time. The

Single coil neck pickup.

logs are generally not intentionally submerged but were sunk during the process of rafting logs down a river to a downstream saw mill. The logs are recovered, sawed and dried. Sinker wood is considered by some to offer superior tonal qualities but extensive studies and solid conclusions on this are lacking. See also: ponding.

siphon feed spray gun *n*. Spray gun in which the material to be sprayed flows into the gun via siphon. The material cup is mounted under the gun.

sitar *n*. Long neck Indian lute-like instrument with a hollow neck and movable frets. The instrument makes use of both fretted and sympathetic drone strings.

Sitka spruce *n*. see *Picea sitchensis*

six course guitar *n*. Guitar with six courses of strings. In the evolution of the instrument, the guitar went from a five course to a six course instrument beginning in Spain in the 1750's.

skew knife *n*. see violin maker's knife

skunk stripe *n*. Feature of necks of some guitars by Fender and other manufacturers. The back of the neck features a stripe of contrasting wood. This stripe is actually a filler piece, used to close up the channel used to insert the trussrod from the back of the neck.

slab sawn *n*. see flat sawn

slipper foot *n*. Protrusion of the neck shaft inside the guitar in Spanish style guitar construction. The slipper foot contacts the upper back of the instrument.

Sloane, Irving (1925-1998) Classical guitar luthier and author. Sloane wrote what is considered to be the first comprehensive modern book on guitar construction, *Classical Guitar Construction*.

slope shouldered *adj*. Describes an instrument body, usually that of an acoustic guitar, that maintains a very rounded profile from the neck to the upper bout.

S

slot head *n.* see slotted peghead

slotted peghead *n.* Guitar headstock which features two long slots which provide access to the string winding posts of the tuning machines. Typical of classical guitars.

Slotted peghead of a guitar under construction.

SLR1E *abbr.* Lumber finishing term: "straight line ripped one edge."

SLR2E *abbr.* Lumber finishing term: "straight line ripped two edges."

Smallman, Greg Australian classical guitar luthier, most famous for the introduction of the lattice braced top. See also: lattice bracing.

Smart, Lawrence Hailey ID, USA, mandolin luthier.

Smurf head mandolin *n.* see reverse scroll mandolin

soap bar pickup *n.* Form factor classification of a magnetic pickup for guitar or electric bass. Soap bar pickups have a rectangular profile, similar to that of a bar of soap. Different soap bar pickups have different dimensions.

socket chisel *n.* Chisel with a tang that ends in a conical socket into which the handle of the chisel is inserted.

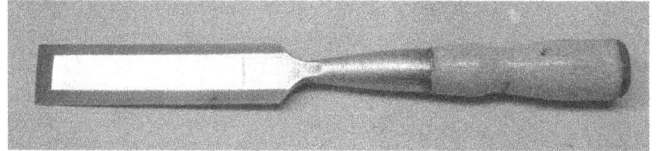

Socket chisel.

soft corner *n.* Describes the corners of instruments of the violin family, particularly the cello and the double bass. The plates of a bass with soft corners show no pronounced corners at all, with the upper and lower bouts smoothly transitioning into the center bout, as in guitar family instruments. See also: gamba corner, violin corner.

softwood *n.* Wood from coniferous trees; trees with needles. The term does not necessarily have anything to do with the hardness of the wood - there are hardwoods that are softer than some softwoods.

solder *n.* Metal alloy that melts at relatively low temperature, used to make metal-to-metal joints, usually to connect electronic components together.

solera *n.* (so-LAIR-ah) Workboard fixture used in the construction of Spanish guitars. The fixture includes an outline of the body and generally has provisions for some side supports to aid in the bending of the ribs of the instrument.

solid body *adj.* Electric guitars and similar instruments can be classified by general construction of the body. A solid body instrument has a body made from a solid

Roll of solder.

Solid body electric guitar.

piece (or pieces) of wood. See also: hollow body, semi-hollow body.

solid core *adj.* The core of a wound string consisting of a solid piece of material. Wound steel string guitar strings generally have solid cores. See also: floss core, rope core.

solid lining *n.* Lining made of solid wood, usually hot bent to shape before installation. See also: kerfed lining, laminated lining.

solvent *n.* Liquid that is used to dissolve solids or other liquids. In lutherie the term is most often used to describe substances that are components of evaporative finishes, or are thinners for finishing materials and glue, or are used as cleaning agents. See also: evaporative finishes.

solvent release finish *n.* see evaporative finish

S

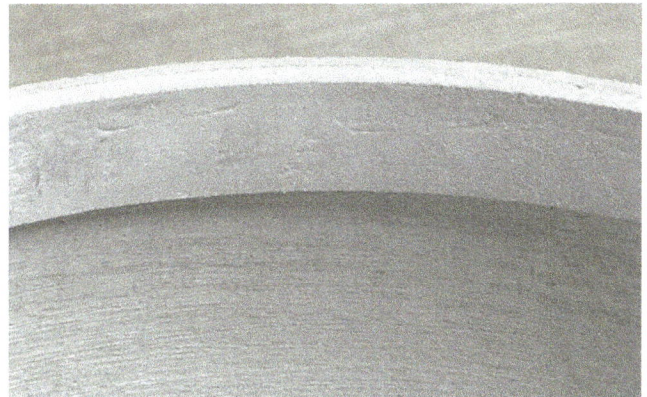

Solera with rib supports for a Romantic guitar.

Solid linings on a classical guitar.

Somogyi, Ervin California USA luthier, educator and author, Somogyi builds classical and steel string guitars and is the author of the books *The Responsive Guitar* and *Making the Responsive Guitar.*

soprano ukulele *n.* Smallest and highest pitched ukulele, it is generally tuned GCEA and has an overall length of approx. 21″ (533.4mm). Typical scale length is 13″ (330mm). Typical body dimensions are 9 ¹/₂″ (241.3mm) long and 6 ¹/₂″ (165.1mm) wide at the lower bout. Syn.: standard ukulele.

Sor, Fernando (1778-1839) Spanish composer and guitar virtuoso generally considered to be one of the primary popularizers of the classical guitar.

sorption hysteresis *n.* Referring to dimensional changes in wood due to moisture content, the fact that as moisture content changes over time the resulting dimensional changes are not consistently related. If moisture content is reduced, wood will shrink in size. But if moisture content is increased to the original value the wood will expand but not quite to its original dimensions.

sound generator *n.* see signal generator

S

sound pressure *n.* The force of sound on an area of surface perpendicular to the sound source, measured in proportion to mean atmospheric pressure. Sound pressure is measured in units of pascals (Pa) in the SI system. Sound pressure is related to perceived loudness.

sound pressure level *n.* Expression of sound pressure relative to a reference standard, which is the nominal lowest possible human perceivable sound pressure. Sound pressure level is expressed on a logarithmic decibel scale. The lowest value on this scale is 0 dB, equivalent to 20 micro pascal. Syn.: SPL. See also: decibel, pascal, sound pressure.

soundboard *n.* see top

soundhole *n.* Hole in a stringed instrument, usually in the top, from which sound radiates.

soundhole clamp *n.* see bridge clamp

soundhole reinforcing patch *n.* Thin wood patch(es) to support the grain of the top around the soundhole of a flattop guitar or similar instrument and prevent splitting. The most common styles include a short patch on either side of the soundhole, and a donut-shaped patch that is positioned around the soundhole. See also: patch.

soundport *n.* Hole in the ribs of a stringed instrument, intended to direct additional sound toward the player. Syn.: side port.

soundpost *n.* Structural component of violin family instruments. The soundpost is a wood post wedged between top and back plate near the location of the treble side foot of the bridge.

soundpost gauge *n.* Measuring device used to measure the distance between the underside of the top and top side of the back in an assembled instrument of the violin family in the area of the soundpost. This measurement is then used to rough cut a new soundpost to length. See also: soundpost.

Soundhole reinforcing patch inside a guitar top under construction.

soundpost patch *n*. A cross grain patch placed on the inside of the top of a violin family instrument at the soundpost position. The purpose of the patch is to prevent the soundpost from splitting the top. The patch is often added as a repair, but some builders include it in new instruments. See also: cross-grain, patch.

soundpost setter *n*. Tool used to move or remove a soundpost. See also: soundpost.

Southwell, Gary English guitar luthier specializing in classical and 19th century guitars.

spalted wood *n*. Wood containing colored streaking patterns which are the result of rotting due to fungal action. Spalted wood is used for decorative applications in lutherie such as for headplates and soundhole rosettes. It is often structurally unsound and if so needs to be stabilized and filled before used.

Spanish cedar *n*. see *Cedrela* spp.

Spanish guitar *n*. A guitar made in the Torres and post Torres Spanish style. Spanish guitars are usually classified as either classical guitars or flamenco guitars. See also: classical guitar, flamenco guitar, Antonio de Torres Jurado.

Spanish heel *n*. Refers to the method by which the body and neck of a guitar are joined. In this construction the heel of the neck is slotted on both sides to receive the ends of the ribs of the body. These slots may be just thick enough to accept the rib material, or they may be wide enough so that the ribs are secured in the slots using wedges. See also: heel cap.

Spanish luthier's scarf joint *n*. Scarf joint connecting neck shaft and head stock. When viewed from the side, the line of the underside of the headstock continues into the neck shaft for this style of joint. See also: scarf joint.

Spann, Joseph Guitar historian and author, known for his book *Spann's Guide to Gibson 1902-1941*.

speaking length *n*. The portion of the string of a musical instrument that vibrates. For an unstopped string, the speaking length is the portion between nut and bridge; for a stopped string, the speaking length is the portion between the stopping finger/fret and the bridge. The term is generally used to differentiate the active portion of the string from the "inactive" portions located above the nut and below the bridge, generally referred to as the after length. Syn.: vibrating string length. See also: after length, stopped string.

Spear, Robert Ithaca NY, USA, luthier best known for the violin octet designed by Carleen Hutchins.

specific gravity *n*. Unitless measure of density. The ratio of the mass of a substance to that of water. The density of wood is traditionally presented using specific gravity. The larger the number, the denser the wood.

spectrogram *n*. A three dimensional visual representation of sound. The horizontal dimension of the spectrogram is time. The vertical dimension is frequency. Relative intensity of the sound is generally indicated by color. Spectrograms are useful in the analysis of sound produced by musical instruments.

spectrograph *n*. Instrument or computer software that displays a frequency/amplitude graph of sound.

spectrographic analysis *n*. see audio spectroscopy

spiral down router bit *n*. see down spiral router bit

S

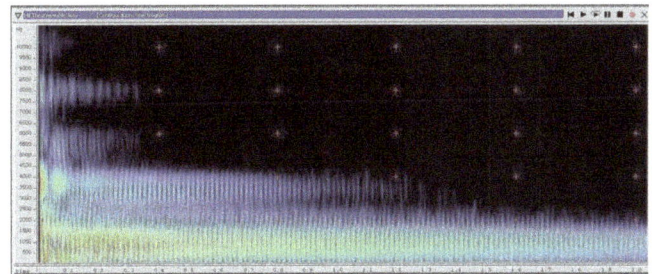

Spectrogram of a plucked note on an electric bass.

spiral up router bit *n*. see up spiral router bit

spirit varnish *n*. Varnish using alcohol as the solvent. Spirit varnishes are generally quick drying. Subsequent coats burn in to previous coats, forming a continuous mass. Spirit varnishes are often used for violins. See also: oil varnish, varnish.

spiriting off *v*. A step in French polishing following a bodying session. The surface is wiped down with straight stokes of a tampon just lightly moistened with alcohol. The purpose of spiriting off is to remove surface oil so it doesn't get trapped under the shellac during bodying. See also: bodying, bodying session, French polish.

spit coat *n*. The first application step in French polishing. Shellac is wiped on to the surface using a pad. This step seals the surface and provides some mass of shellac as a base for subsequent grain filling and bodying. Syn.: seal coat, wash coat. See also: bodying, French polish.

SPL *abbr*. see sound pressure level

splice joint *n*. Joint used to join two pieces end to end.

spline *n*. Thin piece of wood used to implement a splined joint. A thin slot (mortise) is cut into each of the surfaces to be mated and a tight fitting spline is glued into them.

spline curve *n*. Curve drawn by bending a thin flexible strip of material into the desired shape and then tracing it. CAD and other drawing software provide spline drawing facilities, based on some mathematical model of smooth curves. See also: Bézier curve, non-uniform rational b-spline.

splined neck joint *n*. Neck to body joint that makes use of a spline glued into a slot cut into the neck block and one cut into the heel.

spoilboard *n*. Sacrificial board used under work that will be cut all the way through, usually using a router or CNC machine. The depth of cut is adjusted for slightly deeper than the thickness of the work to be cut through,

so the cutter mars the surface of the spoilboard while making the cut. Spoilboards are usually either resurfaced for reuse or discarded.

spokeshave *n*. Small plane used for planing curved surfaces. In lutherie it is often used for shaping the neck shaft.

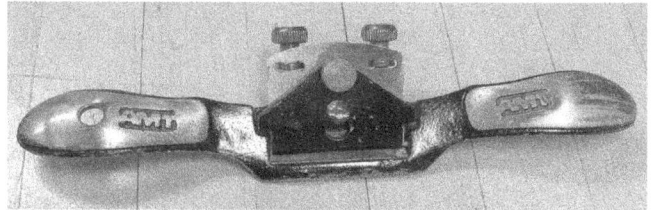

Spokeshave.

spool clamp *n*. A simple clamp consisting of a bolt with wing nut through two short round padded blocks of wood. Spool clamps are used for clamping the plates to the ribs and are the traditional tool for this purpose for violin family instruments.

spp. *abbr*. This abbreviation for the word "species" is used in the species part of a Latin binomial to indicate

Spool clamp.

two or more species of the same genus. For example the binomial for ebony is *Diospyros* spp. which indicates that two or more species of the genus *Diospyros* are included.

spray booth *n*. Small room used for spray finishing. A spray booth is usually equipped with explosion proof lighting and filtered ventilation.

spray finishing *v*. Application of finishing material with a spray gun. Generally only fast drying finishes such as solvent finishes are applied by spraying.

spreader adjustment valve *n*. The part of a spray gun which regulates the width of the spray pattern.

springback *n*. The tendency of bent wood to partially return to its unbent shape. Wood sides and bindings are often slightly over bent on a bending iron and then allowed to relax and cool into a mold. Wood bent in a bending machine is generally left to cool and dry in the machine to help eliminate springback.

spring clamp *n*. A small fast setting clamp capable of exerting modest clamping pressure.

spruce *n*. Any species of the genus *Picea*. Spruce is often used for the tops of stringed instruments and for braces due to its high stiffness to mass ratio. Commonly used species include Engelmann (*Picea engelmannii*), European (*Picea abies*), red (*Picea rubens*) and Sitka (*Picea sitchensis*).

squeeze out *n*. Glue that squeezes out of a joint when it is clamped. It is generally accepted that some amount of squeeze out is a good thing, as it indicates that the joint is completely covered in glue right to the edges, but that too much squeeze out indicates that too much glue was applied. Syn.: glue squeeze out.

stacked heel *n*. Neck heel that is made up of a number of pieces of wood stacked together. Stacked heels make efficient use of wood, as a single board can be cut to length for headstock, neck shaft, and a number of pieces that can be stacked and laminated together for the heel.

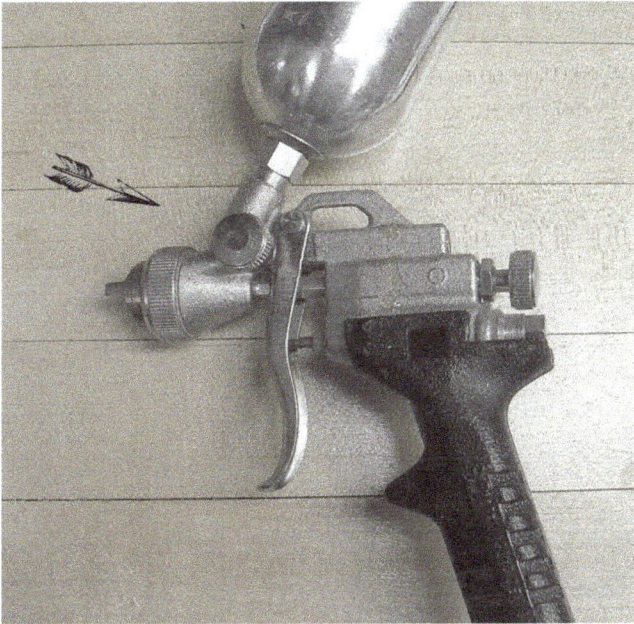

Spreader adjustment valve on a gravity feed spray gun.

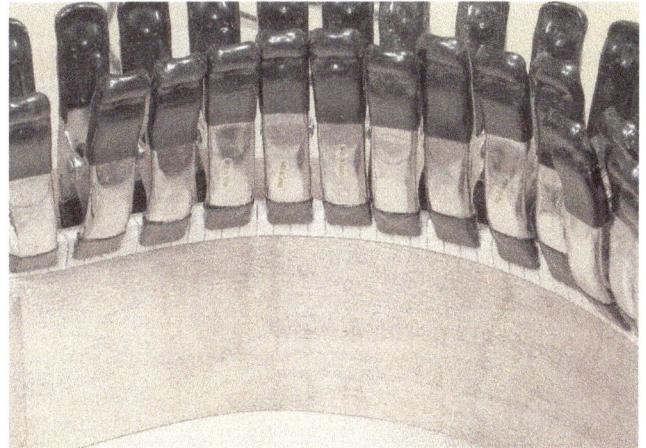

Spring clamps used to attach kerfed linings.

S

stacked humbucker *n*. Thin humbucking magnetic pickup in which the two coils are stacked one on top of the other. Stacked humbuckers have the thin aperture of single coil pickups. See also: aperture, humbucking pickup, single coil pickup.

stage acoustic guitar *n*. A guitar that is essentially a solid body electric but that has the look of an acoustic instrument, often with a round soundhole and spruce top.

standard ukulele *n*. see soprano ukulele

standing wave *n*. Characteristic pattern of vibration of strings, enclosed air and other vibrating parts of stringed instruments. As waves in these materials move to a boundary they are reflected back out of phase. The reflection reinforces the previous waves, causing a pattern which appears to be stationary or "standing."

Stahl, William C. Early 20th century music publisher, teacher and instrument retailer from Milwaukee WI, USA. Stahl retailed house brand banjos, guitars and mandolins built by other manufacturers.

Stauffer, Johann (1778-1853) Viennese luthier specializing in guitars and bowed instruments. His guitars featured narrow (by today's standards) bodies with ladder bracing and six-on-a-side tuning machines which were completely enclosed in the headstock. Some of his instruments featured bolt-on adjustable necks with floating fingerboards. Stauffer taught guitar making to C.F. Martin. See also: floating fingerboard, ladder bracing, C.F. Martin, Johann Scherzer

stearated sandpaper *n*. Sandpaper to which a metallic soap has been added to the abrasive to act as a lubricant. Stearated sandpaper is generally used for power sanding finishes, because heat buildup tends to melt the finish and corn it onto unlubricated paper. Use of stearated paper reduces this corning. Stearated sandpaper is generally not used on bare wood as the lubricant inhibits adhesion of some finishing materials. It is generally used when dry sanding finish. Stearated paper has a characteristic pale color resulting from a combination of the color of the abrasive and the white color of the soap. See also: corning, dry sanding.

steel string acoustic guitar *n*. Flattop acoustic guitar with steel strings. See also: archtop guitar.

steel string guitar *n*. see steel string acoustic guitar

Steinberger, Ned USA luthier originally specializing in carbon fiber body and neck electric guitars and basses, now specializing in solid body electric instruments of the violin family.

Stellac *n*. A brand of heat treated wood. See also: heat treatment (wood).

stepped rabbet *n*. Multilevel rabbet. In lutherie this is most often used to form the binding and purfling channel at the edge of an instrument body. The deeper outer rabbet will contain the deeper binding and the shallower inner rabbet will contain the plate purfling. This is used in preference to a simple rabbet because it allows for a purfling design that would otherwise require a rabbet so wide that cutting it would separate the plate from the ribs.

sticker *n*. A length of wood of small rectangular cross section used as a spacer between boards of air drying

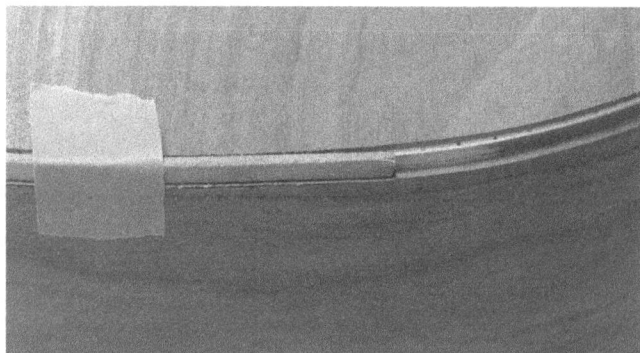

Stepped rabbet routed into the edge of a guitar body to accept bindings and purflings.

wood. Stickers provide air circulation between the boards for uniform air drying.

sticker stain *n*. Staining of air dried wood from contact with stickers. See also: sticker.

stickering *v*. Placing stickers between boards when air drying lumber.

stiff *v*. The final process in a French polish bodying session. Stiffing involves making strong, long strokes with the tampon, wet with a little alcohol and a tiny amount of shellac. The purpose is to remove some of the oil and to level some of the ridges left by bodying. See also: bodying, French polish.

stiffness *n*. Property of resisting bending. Rigidity. This property of an object is dependent on the material it is made of and on its shape. See also: strength.

stomp box *n*. General name for any electric guitar effects device that is packaged as a small box intended to be placed on the floor so the guitarist can activate it by pressing a switch on the top of the box with his or her foot.

stop *v*. To shorten the speaking length of a string by pressing the string to the fingerboard at some point along its length. This is the method by which strings of some stringed instruments can yield more than one pitch. See also: speaking length.

stop tailpiece *n*. String anchor for some Gibson style electric guitars. The tailpiece is a simple metal bar suspended by posts screwed into the top of the guitar.

stopped string *n*. A string that has had its speaking length shortened by being pressed to the fingerboard. See also: speaking length.

Strad *abbr*. see Stradivarius

Stradivari, Antonio (1644-1737) Cremonese (Italian) luthier of violin family instruments and guitars.

Considered by many to be the foremost violin maker of the Cremonese golden age of violin making.

Stradivarius *n*. 1. The Latinized form of the name Stradivari. 2. An instrument made by Stradivari. See also: Antonio Stradivari.

strap button *n*. Button-shaped object generally attached with a screw, used to attach a strap to an instrument.

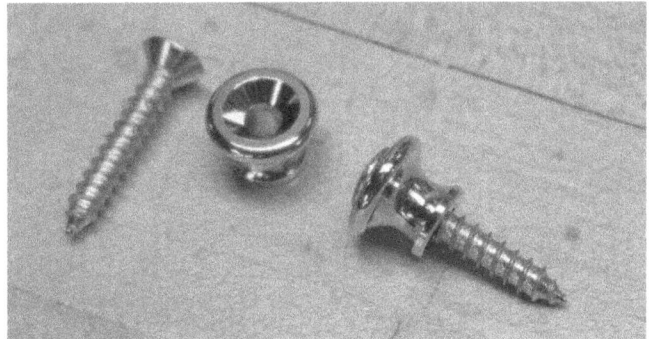

Strap buttons for an electric guitar.

Strat *abbr*. Abbreviation for (Fender) Stratocaster, a solid body electric guitar.

strength *n*. Mechanical property of material indicating its ability to withstand stress, i.e., how much force is required to break an object made of the material. This term is often used colloquially and incorrectly to mean stiffness.

string anchor *n*. Any device or structure used to anchor a string at the end opposite that connected to the tuning post. The term is also used as an adjective, as in string anchor hole, string anchor bushing, etc.

string capture *n*. The tendency of magnetic guitar pickups to distort and dampen string vibrations if the pickups or their pole pieces are placed too close to the strings.

string divergence *n*. 1. The change in string spacing from the nut to bridge of an instrument. 2. The amount string spacing increases over a specified distance. Strings diverge in most stringed instruments due to differing ergonomic requirements of the fretting and picking (or bowing) hands.

string ferrule *n*. Ferrule used as a string anchor in solid body electric guitars. One ferrule for each string is inset into the back of the body under the bridge. Each string is routed through a ferrule, through the body and bridge, and then passes over a saddle. The ferrules prevent the ball ends of the strings from pulling through the wood of the body.

string post *n*. The part of a steel string guitar tuning machine or similar machine around which the string is wound. See also: tuning machine.

string post ferrule *n*. Ferrule (bushing) used to prevent rotation of the string post of a tuning machine from enlarging its mounting hole.

string roller *n*. The part of a classical guitar tuning machine onto which the string is attached. See also: tuning machine.

string spacing *n*. Space between adjacent strings.

string tension *n*. Tension of strings when tuned to pitch.

String post.

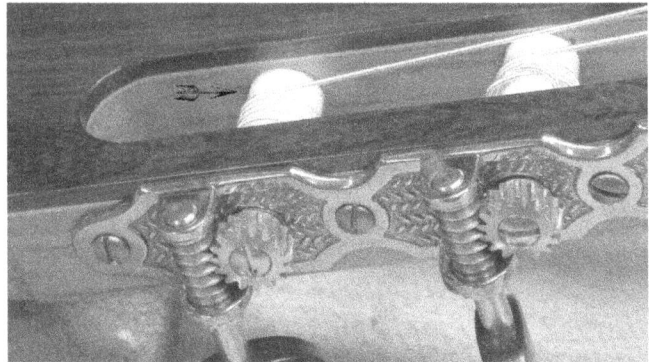

String roller.

Strobel, Henry Salem OR, USA, violin luthier, author, and publisher.

Stromberg Voisinet Chicago IL, USA, manufacturer of guitars. The company was founded in 1890 as the Groeschel Mandolin Company and renamed Stromberg Voisinet in 1921. The product line included inexpensive instruments, many elaborately decorated with decals. The company was sold in 1928 and became the Kay Musical Instrument company in 1931.

strop *v*. A final step in the sharpening of edge tools, usually involving rubbing the edge across leather charged with a fine abrasive compound.

Structured Abrasives *n*. A grading system for sandpaper grits used by some suppliers of automotive finishing sandpaper. All grades in this system begin with the prefix "A-" followed by a number. The numbers get smaller as the grit particle size gets smaller. Syn.: Apex. See also: sandpaper grit.

strut *n*. 1. A strut is a structural member that resists longitudinal compression. There are some bracing patterns that make use of struts. The most common of these run from the sides of the neck block to blocks on the waist near the back. 2. The term is also sometimes used in lutherie as a general term for longitudinal braces. Syn.: 1. flying brace. 2. bar, brace. See also: brace.

strutting *n.* see bracing

successive approximation *n.* The process of transformation to a final value by making progressively finer changes. The term is used in woodworking to describe the usual method by which raw materials are fashioned into finished and often complex shapes. For example an instrument neck shaft starts out as rectangular stock sawn to the rough dimensions of the finished neck. The vertical and horizontal profiles are then cut, bringing the piece a bit closer to the final shape. Facets cut on the shaft roughly approximate the final curved profile, and secondary facets approximate that profile even more accurately. Final scraping and sanding bring the piece to finished dimensions. Syn.: sequential refinement.

sugar maple *n.* see *Acer saccharum*

sunburst finish *n.* A multi-color finish that generally blends from a dark color at the edges of the instrument to a lighter color at the center, but can blend from a darker shade to lighter shade of the same color. Electric guitar sunbursts are generally either two color (brown to yellow) or three color (brown to red to yellow). Sunbursts are generally sprayed on with lacquer, using a light misting spray to effect the color transition. Sunburst finishes did appear on instruments that predate the use of spray equipment. These sunbursts were applied by hand using either water based dyes or alcohol based dyes to directly stain the bare wood. The technique for applying a water based dye sunburst is similar to the technique used to bleed colors together in watercolor painting called wet on wet. The surface is flooded with the ground (center) color and then the darker color is flooded around the edges. Because the surface is so wet, the two colors bleed together so that a soft boundary occurs between them. The technique for applying an alcohol based dye sunburst is to wipe on the separate colors of dye and then blend them together with the rag, using more dye and alcohol to bleed the colors together to create a soft boundary. Hand applied sunburst finishes of this type were often used on early Gibson guitars and mandolins. Sunburst finishes are also found on many violins. This effect is implemented by the use of many thin coats of colored oil varnish, applied using a technique called pushing back, which leaves higher concentration of color near the edges. See also: push back.

sunken top *n.* The long term effect of string tension on the flattop guitar tends to both bend the neck up toward the fingerboard and to torque the bridge, rotating its top toward the neck end of the body. These changes tend to push the portion of the top in front of the bridge down into the instrument, forming a concavity there. This condition is called a sunken top. although there is generally no repair for the deformation of the top, a neck reset can often restore the instrument to playable condition. See also: neck reset.

super glue *n.* see cyanoacrylate glue

super jumbo *adj.* General guitar size and shape designation of instruments substantially modeled after the Gibson SJ series of guitars.

S

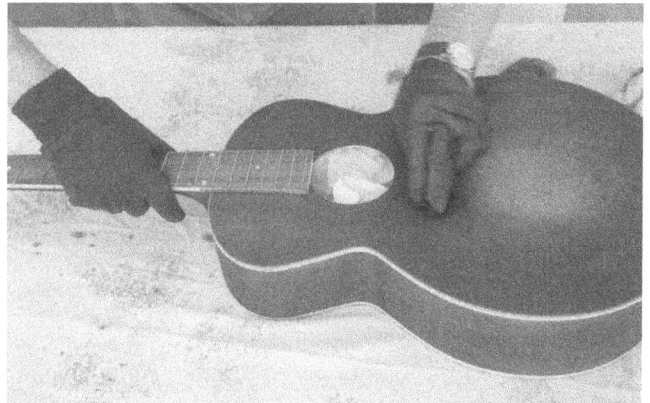

Applying a hand-applied sunburst finish to a guitar using alcohol based dyes.

Super Soft veneer softener Product name of diethylene glycol monoethyl ether, used as a liquid veneer softener, made by Spectrum Adhesives, Inc. Veneer softeners are used in lutherie as an aid in bending instrument sides made of difficult to bend woods.

surgical tubing *n*. Latex or silicone rubber tubing. Common lutherie uses of this tubing include as an elastic wrap to hold bindings in place during gluing, and as a holder for control pots or jacks that can be used to snake those components into place in a finished guitar.

Sustain Magazine of the Fellowship of European Luthiers (defunct). See also: Fellowship of European Luthiers.

sustain *n*. The quality of (plucked) stringed instruments which describes how long a note will sound after plucking.

swamp maple *n*. see *Acer rubrum*

Swartzia cubensis *n*. Katalox, (royal) Mexican ebony. A dark, high density tropical hardwood. Used in lutherie for fretboards and fittings, as a general substitute for ebony. It is hard and stiff and is generally difficult to work. The wood is native to Central America. It has a typical specific gravity of 0.95 when dry, and a modulus

of elasticity of 25 GPa. Radial shrinkage is 3.8%; tangential shrinkage is 7.7%.

sweep *n*. Numerical indication of how flat or curved a gouge is. Sweep values go from #1 to #11, with #1 being perfectly flat (the cutting edge is straight) and #11 being tightly curved.

Swietenia macrophylla *n*. Honduras mahogany. A medium dark, medium density tropical hardwood. Honduras (sometimes called true or genuine) mahogany is used in lutherie for guitar and mandolin backs and sides and necks, and also for blocks and linings. The wood is extremely stable due to its low shrinkage (radial: 2.9%, tangential: 4.3%), low shrinkage ratio, and interlocking grain structure. It is very easy to carve. It has pronounced pores, which are generally filled when the wood is finished. The wood is native to northern South America. It has a typical specific gravity of 0.59 in dry wood, and a modulus of elasticity of 10 GPa.

switchcaster *n*. A tongue-in-cheek term for any electric guitar that has been built or modified to have considerably more than the usual number of pickups, switches, knobs, or other electronic controls.

sycamore, European *n*. see *Acer pseudoplatanus*

sympathetic string *n*. A string which is not forced into vibration directly by plucking or bowing, but which vibrates as a result of vibration of the rest of the instrument. Some instruments which make use of sympathetic strings are the sitar and the hardanger fiddle. See also: hardanger fiddle, sitar.

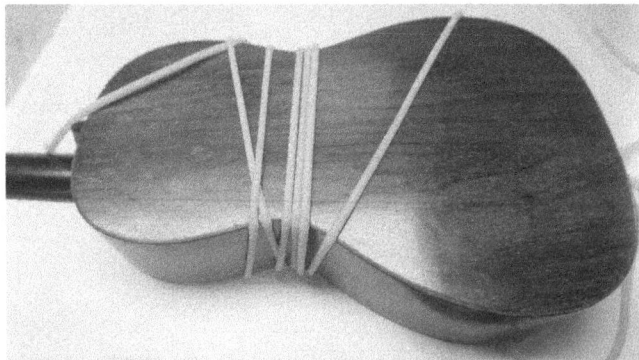

Surgical tubing is used to press re-glued binding into the waist of this guitar.

T

T fret *n.* Fret that has a thin tang that is inserted into a slot in the fretboard. The tang is thinner than the bead or exposed part of the fret. Syn.: tanged fret. See also: bar fret, fret, tied fret.

table *n.* see top

table d'harmonie *n.* (tabl dar-mo-NEE) Table or top (French).

table vernie *n.* (tabl vair-NEE) Cranked top (French).

tail block *n.* Structural component of stringed instruments. The tail block is a block of wood located at the tail end of the body. Its function is to serve as a gluing surface for the ends of the ribs and to support the end pin or strap button. Syn.: butt block. See also: end pin, strap button.

tail graft *n.* see end graft

tail strip *n.* see end graft

tailgut *n.* Wire, cable or rope used to attach the tailpiece to the end pin in violin family instruments. Tailguts are also used in some archtop guitars.

tailpiece *n.* Component of violin family instruments, archtop guitars, mandolins and other instruments. It serves as the string anchor after the bridge and is attached to the tail end of the body. See also: string anchor.

talon *n.* see frog

tampon *n.* Cloth applicator pad used in French polishing. The tampon is made by making a ball of crumpled cloth and covering it with a sheet of smooth cloth. There are many names for this type of applicator. Syn.: fad, muñeca, rubber, rubbing pad. See also: French polishing.

tanbor *n.* Middle Eastern and Central Asian family of instruments.

tanged fret *n.* see T fret

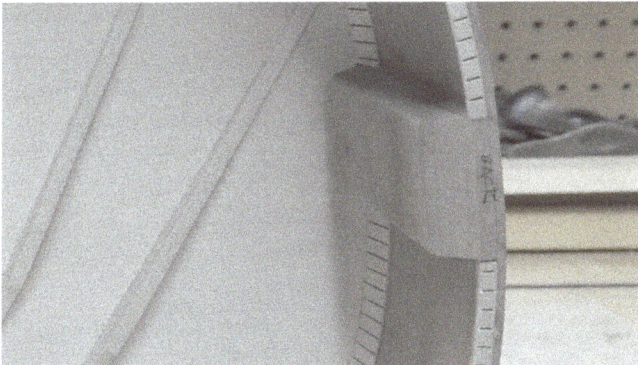

Tail block of a guitar under construction.

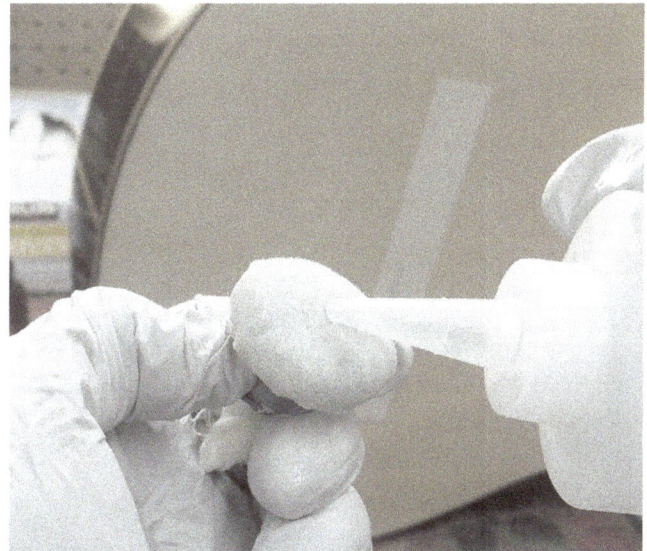

Shellac is applied to the tampon for French polishing.

tangential surface *n*. A surface of a cut piece of wood that approximates a plane tangential to the growth rings of the trunk of the tree from which it was cut. For a quarter sawn board the two narrow sides of the board are tangential surfaces. For a flat sawn board the two wide sides are tangential surfaces. See also: end grain surface, radial surface

Tao, Fan-Chia Principal engineer at musical instrument string maker D'Addario, researcher and educator, with expertise in the physics of vibrating strings and musical instrument acoustics.

tap plate *n*. see golpeador

tap tone *n*. The tone produced by tap tuning. See also: tap tuning.

tap tuning *n*. General class of techniques used to evaluate and possibly optimize the quality of tone of an instrument by tapping on the top plate before it is attached to the body and listening to the sound produced. See also: free plate tuning.

tapa *n*. Plate (Spanish).

tapa armónica n. (TA-pa ar-MOHN-ee-ka) Top plate (Spanish).

tapa junta *n*. (TA-pa HOON- ta) Back strip (Spanish).

taper jig *n*. see taper sled

taper sled *n*. Tool used to cut the tapered sides of instrument fingerboards. This is usually a shop-built jig which consists of a board with a runner on the bottom that fits into the miter slot of a table saw, and clamps on top to hold the fingerboard blank. The blank is positioned on the board, clamped down and the whole sled is run through the table saw.

tapered fingerboard *n*. Fingerboard, usually of a guitar, that tapers in thickness from the nut end to the body end. Classical guitars often use tapered fingerboards to enable the use of a low bridge and still maintain proper string

action. Syn.: longitudinally tapered fingerboard. See also: laterally tapered fingerboard.

tar *n*. 1. Middle Eastern to Central Asian plucked instrument. There are two common versions of the instrument, the Persian tar and the Caucasian tar. The instrument has a hollowed out body covered with skin. 2. Persian (Farsi) word for "string." This is a commonly found ending on names of stringed instruments (guitar, sitar, etc.).

taracea *n*. (tar-ah-SEY-ah) Spanish wood mosaic, used in the traditional decoration of Spanish guitars.

Tárrega, Francisco (1852-1909) Spanish composer and guitarist. Considered to be the progenitor of classical guitar.

tasseau arrière n. (ta-SO ah-ree-AIR) Neck block (French).

tasseau avant *n*. (ta-SO ah-VON) Tail block (French).

tastiera *n*. (tas-tee-YAIR-ah) Fretboard (Italian).

taquet *n*. (ta-KAY) Cleat (French).

tavola armonica *n*. (TA-vole-la are-MOAN-ee-ca) Top plate (Italian).

Taylor, Robert California USA guitar luthier, known for a high degree of automation in manufacturing.

tearout *n*. The process by which large chunks are inadvertently removed from the surface of wood during shaping and cutting operations. Highly figured wood is particularly prone to tearout. Planing or other use of edge tools into the grain may also result in tearout. Tearout can be reduced in planers and jointers with the use of helical cutter heads. It can be reduced in hand planing operations with the use of high angle planes.

Tele *abbr*. Abbreviation for (Fender) Telecaster, a solid body electric guitar.

temperament *n*. A system of tuning which departs from just intonation, for the purpose of providing better intonation under some set of circumstances. The most common system used by stringed instruments is equal temperament. See also: equal temperament.

tenon *n*. The male part of a mortise and tenon joint, a projection on a piece of wood that mates with a similarly shaped cavity on another piece of wood. Various types of mortise and tenon joints are used in lutherie. The most common are dovetail joints used to attach neck to body. See also: dovetail joint, mortise.

tenor ukulele *n*. Slightly bigger than the concert ukulele. The instrument is generally tuned GCEA and has an overall length of approx. 26″ (660.4mm). Typical scale length is 17″ (430mm). Typical body dimensions include a length of 12″ (304.8mm) and a width of 9″ (228.6mm) at the lower bout.

tenor violin *n*. Any violin family instrument falling in size between the viola and cello.

tension *n*. Pulling force on a string or structural part of an instrument. Tension is measured in newtons (SI units) or pounds force (USCS units). See also: SI units, USCS units.

tentellón *n*. (ten-tey-YOWN) Plural: tentellones. Small block of wood used as the gluing surface (lining) between the plate of an instrument and the ribs. Tentellones are typically used only as linings for the top plate, and are found most often in Spanish style guitars. The word is probably a transcription error from the Spanish word dentellón, the English equivalent of which is dentil, used to describe architectural features that have the look of teeth. Most Spanish makers would use the word peón to identify this part. Syn.: dentellone, glue block, peón, tentellone, tentiloni See also: lining.

tentiloni *n*. see tentellón

Tentellones..

terz guitar *n*. A small guitar that is tuned a minor third above standard guitar tuning. Syn.: chitarrino, terzina, tierce guitar.

tessera *n*. One of the small squares of wood that make up the mosaic pattern of the rosette of the Spanish guitar.

tessitura *n*. That part of the total range of notes that can be produced by an instrument (its compass) that is most readily available or useable.

JAMES BUCKLAND

Terz guitar by luthier James Buckland.

tête n. (tet) Head, headstock (French).

theorbo n. Lute family instrument of the 16th century. Like the harp guitar, the theorbo features both short, fretable strings and longer harp-like bass strings. See also: harp guitar.

theorboed adj. Describing a lute family instrument to which additional bass harp strings have been added.

Thermowood n. A brand of heat treated wood. See also: heat treatment (wood).

thickness gauge n. see caliper

thickness sander n. Sanding machine used to sand wood parts to thickness. Thickness sanders usually use one or more sandpaper covered drums. Syn.: drum sander.

thixotropic adj. The property of some gels to become liquid when stirred or otherwise physically moved around. Thixotropic substances are added to gel varnishes. See also: gel varnish.

Thuja plicata n. Western red cedar. Softwood, not of the cedar genus (cedrus), used for guitar tops. It is light in weight, moderately stiff, and soft. Dry wood has a specific gravity of 0.37 and a modulus of elasticity of 7.7 GPa. Syn.: western red cedar, red cedar.

thumbwheel n. Metal disk with knurled edge, used to make a mechanical adjustment by hand. Thumbwheels are used on the bridges of some archtop and some electric guitars to adjust action. See also: action.

tie block n. The back part of a classical guitar bridge (or other tie bridge) onto which the string ends are tied.

tie bridge n. A bridge that is constructed with string anchoring holes, into which the string ends are tied. Classical guitars traditionally have tie bridges.

tied fret n. Fret composed of a length of gut tied around the neck and fingerboard. Early fretted instruments such as lutes featured tied frets. See also: bar fret, T fret.

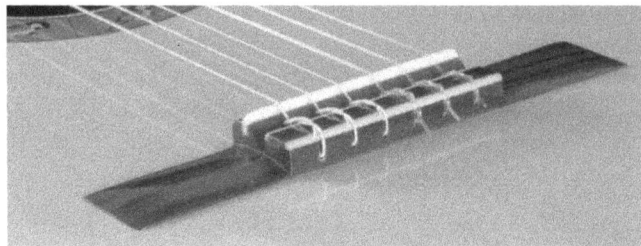

The tie block of this classical guitar bridge is the part onto which the strings are tied.

tiger maple n. see curly maple

Tilia americana n. Basswood. Fine grained hardwood native to the eastern United States. Used for painted electric guitar bodies and blocks for acoustic instruments. Plain white in color. Carves easily. Specific gravity of dry wood is 0.42. Modulus of elasticity is 10.1 GPa. Syn.: basswood, lime, linden.

Tilton, William Mid 19th century USA guitar luthier, most famous for his patented "improvements", consisting of neck and tail blocks of reduced size connected by a stiff dowel, and the use of a floating bridge and tailpiece string anchor. These features were intended to increase loudness and improve tone. Tilton built his own instruments and also retrofitted instruments built by others. Other manufacturing firms including the firm of Ferdinand Zogbaum and Rufus Fairchild, and the John C. Haynes Company made instruments using his patented features.

timbre n. A general term used to describe tone color or any quality other than loudness and the pitch of the fundamental. When used to describe relatively simple continuous tones, the term usually describes the perceptual effect of any partials present along with the fundamental, and their amplitudes. Syn.: tone color. See also: fundamental, harmonic, partial.

tiple n. see Colombian tiple

tipping off *v.* A final smoothing step when varnish is applied by brush. After the varnish is applied to the surface, the entire surface is lightly brushed using long strokes with just the tip of the brush and the brush held vertically in relation to the surface. Tipping off helps to distribute the varnish evenly and break up trapped air bubbles.

tiracantino *n.* (teer-a-can-TEEN-oh) Fine tuner (Italian).

tirando *n.* (teer-ON-doe) see free stroke

Titebond *n.* Brand name of a yellow woodworking glue commonly used in guitar lutherie. It is made by Franklin International.

toggle clamp *n.* Work holding clamp used for jigs and fixtures. The clamp is screwed to the fixture and provides a means to hold work to the fixture.

tololoche *n.* (tow-low-LOW-chey) Folk instrument from northern Mexico. It looks very much like a double bass but somewhat smaller. It is usually strung with nylon strings tuned ADGC.

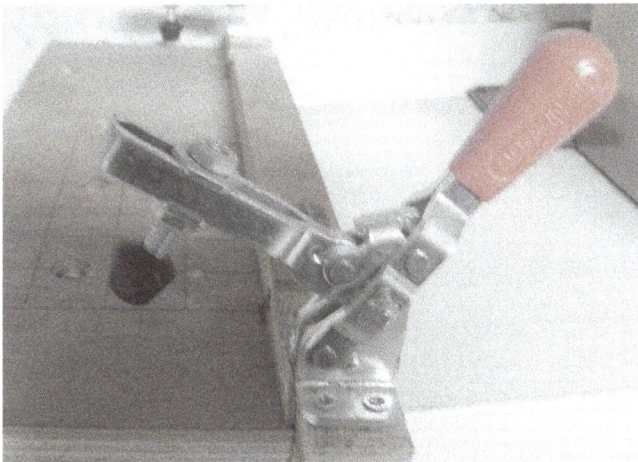

Toggle clamp.

tone *n.* In pigment or dye color mixing, the tone of a color is an indication of the mix of different pigments or dyes. See also: shade.

tone color *n.* see timbre

tonewood *n.* Wood that is used to make stringed musical instruments. The term is often used to indicate wood species that are suitable for stringed musical instruments and, by exclusion, those that are not. But the list of species generally considered to be tonewoods changes constantly and has changed constantly throughout history.

tongue depressor brace *n.* see popsicle stick brace

tool steel *n.* Steel that is hardened for use in making tool blades, such as knives, chisels, plane blades, etc.

toothed plane *n.* Plane with a blade that has a number of small V-shaped or square notches filed into the edge. Planing with such a plane leaves a ridged surface on the material planed. Toothed planes are often used when rough thicknessing a plate. The ridges on the surface indicate those areas that have been planed. They are also useful for thicknessing plates of figured wood, which tend to get gouged up when a plain blade is used. They are used also to prepare the surface of a backer board for veneering. See also: tearout.

T

JAMES BUCKLAND

Toothed plane blades.

top *n*. The bodies of stringed musical instruments have two large plates. The one that supports the bridge and has the soundhole(s) in it is called the top or belly or front. Of these three terms, the one most used to describe this plate for guitar family instruments is top. See also: belly, front.

top brace *n*. A brace on the top plate of an instrument.

top deflection *n*. Bending of the top plate. Top plate deflection is often measured in an attempt to optimize motion and radiation efficiency of the top. See also: radiation efficiency.

top plate *n*. see top

top-loaded (pinless) bridge *n*. Guitar bridge that anchors string ends in the bridge itself. A Fender style electric guitar top loaded bridge has the string anchors at the back of the bridge, instead of having string anchors in the guitar body. A top loaded bridge for an acoustic steel string guitar, also called a pinless bridge, has string anchors at the back of the bridge itself, instead of having strings anchor in holes through the bridge and into the body. Syn.: pinless bridge.

topo map *n*. see topographical map

topographic carving method *n*. Process for carving arched plates that begins with a topographic map of the finished plate. The plate blank is rough carved to topographic terraces and then refined to its ultimate shape.

topographical map *n*. A map that indicates altitude at any point on the map. The map consists of any number of closed curved lines called contour lines, each of which indicates a specific altitude. A topographical map is a convenient way to represent plate arching for archtop instruments.

tornovoz *n*. (TOR-no-VOHS) A metal tube often of conical shape that is attached to the underside of the soundhole. The tornovoz was used on some classical

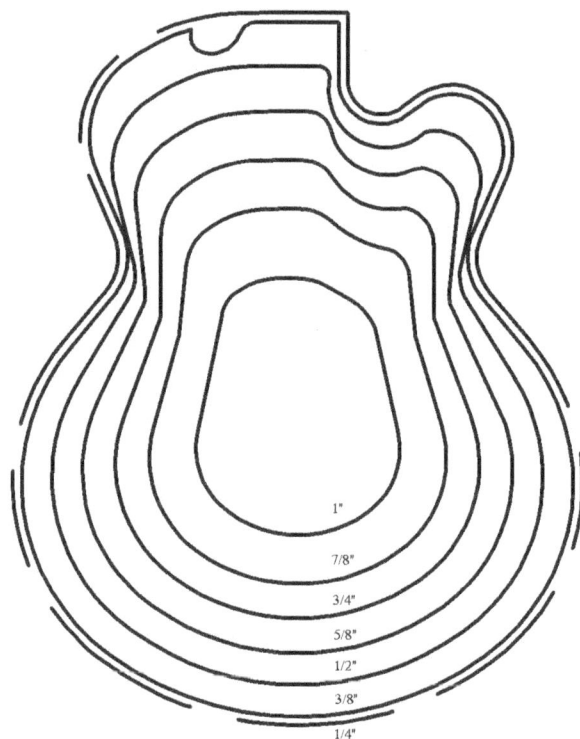

Arching profile of the top plate of an archtop guitar represented as a topographical map.

guitars during the nineteenth century and on some modern reproductions. Plural: tornovoces.

Torrefaction *n*. see heat treatment (wood)

torrefication *n*. see heat treatment (wood)

torrefied *adj*. see heat treatment (wood)

Torres *n*. see Antonio de Torres Jurado

Torres Jurado, Antonio de (1817-1892) Spanish guitarmaker and guitar player. Torres is considered to be the father of the modern classical guitar. His instruments used relatively thin tops with fan bracing and the

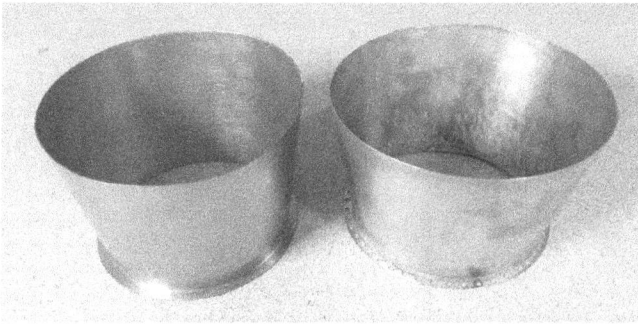

One brass tornovoz and one tin tornovoz. The two tornovoces are made for replica Torres guitars built by Federico Sheppard.

FEDERICO SHEPPARD

instruments were quite simple in decoration. Although Torres was not the first to employ any of these features the design of the modern classical guitar coalesced in his work. See also: classical guitar, fan bracing.

torsion bar *n*. Brace which carries its load by resisting twisting along its long axis. A torsion brace appears in the bracing design of Michael Kasha and in the bracing of most ladder braced guitars. This is a transverse brace mounted directly under the bridge. String tension tends to lever the bridge forward, twisting the top. This brace adds torsional stiffness, resisting twisting. See also: ladder bracing, Michael Kasha.

torsion box *n*. Box construction used for bench tops and other large flat work surfaces. The interior of the box contains a lattice, the edges of the slats of which contact the top and the bottom of the completed box. It is fairly easy to accurately cut these slats to width using a table saw. This type of construction makes it simple and inexpensive to construct a relatively lightweight and flat construction surface.

torsional vibration *n*. Strings vibrate in three distinct modes: transverse, longitudinal and torsional. Transverse vibration produces most and sometimes all of the sound produced by an instrument. Torsional vibration manifests as the twisting and untwisting of the string and is the result of twisting of the string by the action of the bow, pick or picking finger. See also: longitudinal vibration, transverse vibration.

tracking lines *n*. Visible lines left on the surface of wood when planing with a hand plane that is narrower than the piece planed. The lines are the result of the corners of the plane iron digging into the surface. Appearance of tracking lines is reduced by sharpening the iron to a slight convex edge.

trampoline mode *n*. A mode of vibration of the body of an instrument. The characteristic motion of these modes is that the top and back of the instrument move in the same direction at the same time, that is, when the top is moving down into the body the back is moving down out of the body, and vice versa.

transducer *n*. In general, a device which converts from one form of energy to another form. In lutherie the term usually refers to a device which converts vibrational energy to an electrical signal. The word pickup is a synonym, but this often is used to denote magnetic pickups only. Syn.: pickup.

transient *n*. Sound which rapidly changes in characteristic. This term is often used to describe the initial attack (pluck, bow movement) of a musical tone, and also its abrupt termination (usually by damping).

transfer function *n*. Property of an electronic device such as a pickup or amplifier. The transfer function is the ratio of input to output of the device, expressed in the frequency domain. It is an indication of what frequency based distortion or coloring is imparted by the device. The transfer function is generally presented as a curve. Syn.: frequency response function.

transfer pipette *n*. Plastic eyedropper used in lutherie as an applicator for glue. Transfer pipettes come with various tip sizes. For thin cyanoacrylate glue, a pipette

T

with a micro tip is used. Syn.: pipette. See also: cyanoacrylate glue, glue syringe.

Transfer pipette.

transverse *adj*. Set crosswise, at right angles to. In lutherie this modifier is often used to denote a brace or other part that is positioned from side to side, perpendicular to the instrument centerline.

transverse bar *n*. see transverse brace

transverse brace *n*. Any brace located perpendicular to the centerline of the instrument. These are sometimes referred to as harmonic bars, mostly if they refer to braces of the top, and mostly when referring to classical guitars.

transverse vibration *n*. Strings vibrate in three distinct modes: transverse, longitudinal and torsional. Transverse vibration produces most and sometimes all of the sound produced by an instrument. It is vibration of the string

Transverse brace on the top of a steel string guitar.

from side to side. See also: longitudinal vibration, torsional vibration.

trapeze tailpiece *n*. Tailpiece that resembles a trapeze, with parallel or near parallel bars or rods from the place where the tailpiece is mounted to the body to a bar-like string anchor assembly. Trapeze tailpieces are found on some archtop guitars.

traste *n*. (TRAS-tey) Fret (Spanish).

travel guitar *n*. Small body acoustic guitar intended for use while traveling. Some such instruments retain the scale length of a full-size instrument. Most can be stowed in an airline overhead compartment.

treble bleed circuit *n*. Typical passive tone control circuit for electric guitar magnetic pickups. The circuit consists of a potentiometer in series with a capacitor.

Tru-oil *n*. Product name of an oil varnish intended for application by padding. See also: gunstock oil.

truss rod *n*. A rod or system of rods used to reinforce the neck of a stringed instrument. There are three general types of truss rods. Non-adjustable truss rods provide stiffening only. Steel rods, bars or channels are often used in this application, as are rods and bars made of carbon fiber composite material. Adjustable truss rods include single acting and double acting types. Single acting rods, also sometimes called compression rods, can be adjusted to provide more neck back bow only. Double acting rods can be adjusted to provide more back bow or more front bow. See also: back bow, front bow.

tube *abbr*. see vacuum tube

tube amplifier *n*. An amplifier that makes use of vacuum tubes. Tube amps are considered by some to offer superior tone for guitar amplification due to their characteristic distortion of high level signals. See also: vacuum tube.

tulip poplar *n*. see *Liriodendron tulipifera*

Double acting truss rod sitting on top of the guitar neck blank into which it will be installed.

Tune-O-Matic *n*. Brand name of bridge for Gibson and Gibson-style electric guitars. The bridge is mounted on two posts and contains individually adjustable saddles.

tuner *n*. see tuning machine

tung oil *n*. Oil of the nut of the tung tree (*Vernicia fordii*). It is a drying oil, used as a finish for solid body electric guitars and basses. It is also used as a component of oil varnishes. The term is also used as an adjective to describe any finish that is applied with a pad.

tuning button *n*. The part of the tuning machine that is grasped and turned to tune the string. See also: tuning machine.

tuning fork rest *n*. A type of brace end bracket in which the end that contacts the brace is wider than the brace and is notched so that it extends past the top of the brace end. The notched ends look something like a tuning fork. Such brackets are often found on guitars by Louis Panormo. See also: brace end bracket, Louis Panormo.

tuning machine *n*. Geared mechanical device used to anchor one end of the string and provide accurate tension changes and thus accurate tuning of the string. Modern guitars, mandolins and acoustic basses generally use tuning machines. Antique guitars and earlier instruments and members of the violin family generally use tuning pegs. Syn.: tuner, machine head See also: tuning peg.

Tuning machines being installed on a steel string guitar.

tuning peg *n*. A tapered tuning shaft used in early instruments, violin family instruments and some flamenco guitars. A tuning peg has a drilled hole through which the end of the string is threaded. The peg is turned to tension the string. The large amount of surface area between the tapered shaft of the peg and the tapered walls of the hole it fits into provides enough friction to keep the peg from unwinding under string tension.

turtleoid *n*. Plastic binding and pickguard material that has the look of tortoise shell.

TWA *abbr*. see 8 hour time weighted average

twelfth root of 2 *n*. see 12th root of 2

twisted neck *n*. 1. An age-related flaw in a stringed instrument where the neck shaft twists over time. This defect is generally not repairable. 2. A neck design that deliberately twists the neck and fingerboard. The intention of this design is to improve ergonomics.

T

U

U-Bass *n.* Ukulele bass made by Kala featuring 21″ scale length and piezo pickup.

uke *abbr.* see ukulele

ukulele *n.* (YOO-coo-LAY-ley (conventional), OO-coo-LAY-ley (Hawaiian pronunciation)) Small Hawaiian guitar-like instrument with four single strings. Sizes in the ukulele family include soprano, tenor, concert and baritone. The instrument is probably derived from the Portuguese cavaquinho/machete. This instrument is known to have been introduced to Hawaii in the 1870s. The word ukulele in Hawaiian means "the gift that came from here." It is also sometimes translated as "jumping flea." Syn.: uke. See also: machete.

umber earth *n.* Brown pigment used in violin varnishes. It is a combination of iron oxide and manganese oxide.

under-saddle transducer *n.* Guitar transducer that mounts in the saddle slot of the bridge, under the saddle. Under-saddle transducers are usually made of piezo material. See also: saddle slot, piezo pickup.

unit density *n.* see mass per unit length

up spiral router bit *n.* Router bit which spirals up in operation, which helps to clear chips out of the routed pocket but can fuzz the upper edge of the pocket. Syn.: spiral up router bit. See also: down spiral router bit.

upper bout *n.* An area of widening near the top of the outline of a stringed instrument body. The bouts of a guitar are typically labeled upper bouts, waist, and lower bouts. The bouts of violin family instruments are typically labeled upper bouts, c bouts, and lower bouts. See also: bout, c bout, lower bout, waist.

upper transverse brace *n.* Transverse brace of the top of the acoustic flattop guitar, located near the soundhole and between the soundhole and the neck block. This brace supports the top in the area of the soundhole and also the end of the fretboard. See also: transverse brace.

Upper transverse brace.

urea formaldehyde glue *n.* Wood glue sometimes used in lutherie for gluing large surfaces, such as laminated plates. It is inexpensive. The glue generally comes as a powder which must be mixed with water prior to use, or as a powder and liquid hardener. It has a reasonably long open time.

USCS units *n.* United States Customary System of measurement units. The system of units of measurement used in the USA. The common unit of length used in lutherie is the inch. See also: SI units.

UV cured finish *n.* Finishing material that cures with exposure to ultraviolet light.

V

V bracing *n*. Guitar top bracing style introduced by Taylor. The bracing pattern is similar to that of A bracing, but the longitudinal braces converge from neck block to tail block. This style of bracing can be used with conventionally located soundholes. See also: A bracing, fan bracing, ladder bracing, X bracing.

V joint *n*. Neck shaft to headstock joint used on a number of guitars and guitar-like instruments. The neck shaft and headstock are separate pieces, glued together. The neck shaft terminates in a sharp, acute V, which fits into a V-shaped slot on the headstock. There are a number of construction variations of this joint. Blind V joints found on most 19th century instruments have a blind mortise chiseled into the back of the solid headstock. Later instruments often make use of an easier to implement joint where the mortise is sawn into the headstock and then covered over by the headplate. Another variant is related to the shape of the V: a shoulderless joint features a pure V shape; joints with shoulders are shaped with small straight ends perpendicular to the sides of the neck. Another variation is whether the tenon is raised above the surface of the back of the headstock or not.

V neck *adj*. see boat neck

vacuum clamping *n*. Clamping using vacuum. This generally involves a fixture which includes a thick plastic bag to contain the assembly to be clamped. When air is evacuated from the bag the parts are clamped together by atmospheric pressure. See also: atmospheric pressure clamping.

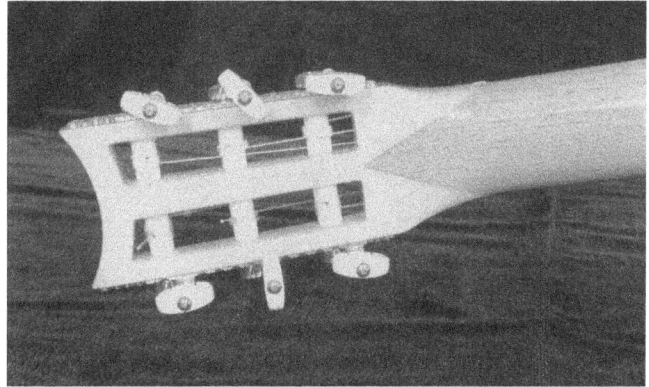

Headstock is joined to the neck shaft of this guitar with a V joint. The joint pictured is blind, shoulderless, and flush with the back of the headstock.

vacuum press *n*. Fixture for clamping a large surface using vacuum. Used in lutherie in veneering and in assembly of the plates of guitars. The parts to be assembled are glued, then placed on a backing board, and then fitted into a thick plastic bag. A vacuum is applied to the bag using a vacuum pump, pressing the components together while the glue cures.

vacuum tube *n*. Active electronic component used in some amplifier circuits. Although supplanted by transistors and other solid state components in most modern applications, vacuum tubes are still used in some electric guitar amplifiers. See also: tube amplifier.

Valco Chicago USA manufacturer of guitar and amplifiers. Reorganized from the National-Dobro Company in 1942, Valco produced instruments under brand names including National and Supro. They built amplifiers for Vega, Gretch and Martin. The company merged with Kay in 1967 and was defunct a year later.

valve *n*. Vacuum tube (British).

vapor trail *n*. Characteristic surface effect during French polishing. As the tampon is moved across the surface of the instrument during polishing, the oil floating up through the shellac leaves a cloudy trail behind the moving pad. This cloudy trail dissipates almost immediately, but remains long enough to be visible. French polishers use this as an indication that there is enough oil on the tampon. See also: French polish.

varnish *n*. General term used to describe finishing material, usually applied with a brush. The two major classes of varnish used in lutherie are oil varnish and spirit varnish. See also: oil varnish, spirit varnish.

vaulted *adj*. Domed or arched.

vehicle *n*. Basic liquid component of finishing materials. Water, alcohol, and mineral spirits are common vehicles. In use, the vehicle typically evaporates during curing of the finish. See also: binder, dye, pigment.

Velazquez, Alfredo Orlando FL, USA, classical and flamenco guitar luthier. Son of Manuel Valazquez.

Velazquez, Manuel (1917–2014) Puerto Rico born luthier based in Orlando FL, USA, Velazquez built classical and flamenco guitars.

veneer *n*. Thin slices of wood used as a covering over other wood, or any thin slices of wood. Wood veneer is used for the laminates of laminated back and sides and for laminated guitar headstocks.

veneer hammering *v*. A traditional method of gluing veneer to a backer, using atmospheric pressure and a veneer hammer, a hammer-shaped tool with a broad rounded edge used as a squeegee. Glue is applied to the veneer and it is positioned on the backer board, then the veneer hammer is pressed down into the veneer and pulled along the surface to pull the glue toward the edges. This evacuates all the air from between veneer and backer, and when this is complete the wide surfaces of the joint are no longer subject to atmospheric pressure. This means that atmospheric pressure acting on the opposite surfaces of the veneer and backer clamp the

Black-dyed and plain maple veneer sheets.

pieces together. See also: atmospheric pressure clamping.

Venetian cutaway *n*. Style of cutaway in the body of a guitar or similar instrument. The Venetian cutaway features a rounded point. See also: cutaway, Florentine cutaway.

Venetian cutaway on an archtop jazz guitar.

Venetian inch *n.* Unit of measurement used by lute makers. According to Robert Lundberg it is 27.4mm in length. See also: Robert Lundberg.

Venetian turpentine *n.* Pine rosin, used as a resin in violin varnishes.

Venn, Robert USA electric guitar luthier and one of the founders of the Roberto-Venn lutherie school. See also: Roberto-Venn school.

vermilion *n.* see cinnabar

vertical belt sander *n.* Motorized belt sander in which the belt and platen are maintained in a vertical position. The belt moves down, into the work holding table. Vertical belt sanders are useful for sanding and shaping when it is desired to maintain right angles between surfaces of the work piece.

vertical grain *adj.* This term almost always is used to describe softwoods only and describes lumber cut so the orientation of the grain is nearly perpendicular to the wide surface of the board. The equivalent term for hardwood is quarter sawn. See also: quarter sawn.

vesica piscis *n.* (ves-SIKE-uh PAI-sis) Latin, literally "fish bladder." It is a geometric construction used in the drawing of instruments and their component parts. A circle is drawn and then another circle of the same diameter is drawn so that the center point of the first circle falls on the circumference of the second. The (American) football shaped area at the intersection of the two circles is the *vesica piscis*.

vibrating string length *n.* see speaking length

vibrato tailpiece *n.* Device for anchoring the strings at the body end of an instrument that enables the player to raise or lower the pitch of all strings simultaneously by pulling or pushing on a handle. The device can be used to implement vibrato or other pitch changes.

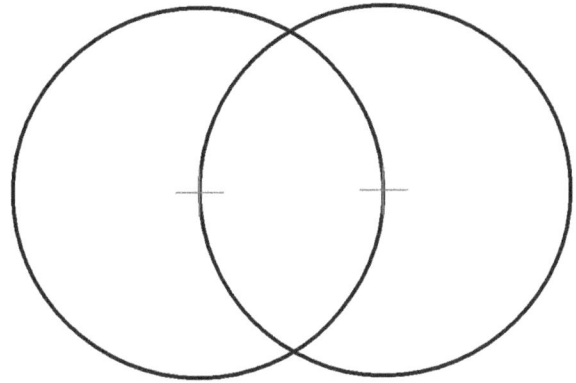

Vesica piscis.

vihuela *n.* (vi-WELL-la) 1. 15th-16th century string instrument with flat plates and five or six string courses. Variations of the instrument (or of playing style) include vihuela de mano (played with the fingers), vihuela de penola (played with a plectrum) and vihuela de arco (played with a bow). 2. Modern Mexican folk instrument with five strings and reentrant tuning.

vihuela de mano *n.* 15th-16th century plucked string instrument with flat plates and five or six string courses. Played with the fingers. The term is Spanish. The same instrument in Italy and Portugal was referred to as the viola de mano. Syn.: viola de mano. See also: vihuela.

VIOCADEAS research project *n.* Project directed by George Bissinger aimed at reverse engineering the violin. Vibration and acoustic information are collected in an attempt to characterize material properties, and CT scans are collected to obtain accurate dimensional data. See also: George Bissinger.

viol *n.* Bowed 16th-17th century string instrument with frets, flat back and sloped shoulders. Viols usually have six strings and are played in an upright position, in the style of the cello. See also: baryton, double bass viol, division viol, lyra viol, viola da gamba, viola d'amore.

V

viol corner *n*. see gamba corner

viola *n*. 1. Instrument of the violin family, tuned a fifth lower than the violin. 2. Italian name for all bowed instruments. The term was used in the Renaissance and later. The two main classes of these instruments were the viole da braccio and viole da gamba, the former held on the arm in the current conventional manner for violins, and the latter held on the leg and played upright.

viola d'amore *n*. Unfretted treble bowed instrument with sympathetic strings.

viola da gamba *n*. Bass viol, held between the legs in the manner of the modern cello. See also: viol.

viola da spalla *n*. Eighteenth century instrument like a cello but played across the chest in the orientation of a guitar.

viola de mano *n*. see vihuela de mano

viola pomposa *n*. Violin family instrument of unknown origin, featured in two works by Telemann.

violetta *n*. 1. Three string violin family instrument. 2. German 18th century name for the viola.

violin *n*. Four string unfretted bowed instrument.

violin bridge tuning *n*. Carving of the bridge of violin family instruments aimed at producing better tone. Some builders will tune the bridge to a specific primary frequency. The paring usually involves opening up the eyes and spaces between the bridge wings and thinning of the legs.

violin corner *n*. Describes the corners of the double bass. Violin corners are similar to those found on violins, sharp and pointy transitions between the curves of the upper and lower bouts and that of the center bout. See also: soft corner, gamba corner.

violin maker's knife *n*. Skew knife with a simple wood handle, often shop made.

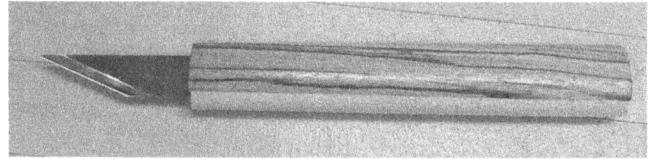
Violin maker's knife.

violin octet *n*. A family of scaled violin instruments originally developed by Carleen Hutchins. Instruments in the family are based on scaling the violin, with the intent of providing a close tonal relationship among the instruments. The family includes treble violin, soprano violin, mezzo violin, alto violin, tenor violin, baritone, small bass and contrabass. See also: Carleen Hutchins.

Violin Society of America *n*. Founded in 1973, the Violin Society of America is a nonprofit organization created for the purpose of promoting the art and science of making, repairing and preserving stringed musical instruments and their bows. The society publishes the *Journal of the Violin Society of America*, and hosts a yearly convention. The society also holds annual workshops with Oberlin College.

violin varnish *n*. General class of finishing materials usually used on violin family instruments. Violin varnishes tend to retain some elasticity when cured. The two basic types of violin varnish are spirit varnish, which uses alcohol as a solvent, and oil varnish. See also: oil varnish, spirit varnish.

violincello *n*. see cello

violino piccolo *n*. Violin family instrument tuned a fourth above the violin.

Virzi Tone Producer *n*. Acoustic enhancement device used by Lloyd Loar in instruments made by Gibson. The device is a disk made of spruce that is suspended from the soundboard on the inside of the instrument. Syn.: Virzi disk. See also: Lloyd Loar.

V

vise *n*. General purpose stationary clamp/holding device.

Voboam family *n*. 17th–18th century lute and baroque guitar luthiers from Paris, France. The family includes René (<1606–<1671) and his sons Alexandre (?–c.1679), Nicolas Alexandre (1633/1646–1692/1704), and Jean (1633/1646–c.1692).

VOC *abbr*. see volatile organic compounds

voicing *v*. Modifications made to the assembled instrument or to one of its major components (usually the top plate) intended to modify the instrument's tonal qualities.

volatile organic compounds *n*. A general term used to describe components of finishing materials and their solvents that readily evaporate. Some of these compounds have adverse health effects. Syn.: VOC.

volute *n*. (voh-LOOT) 1. Scroll (French). 2. Generally ornamentation in the shape of a spiral or scroll. In lutherie the term often refers to a discontinuation of the line from the neck shaft to the headstock or pegbox. The volute is standard on violin family instruments where it

Bench vise used to hold fretboard while cambering its playing surface.

serves to make a smooth transition between neck shaft and pegbox. On guitars and similar instruments it is considered to be used simply for ornamentation, although some builders and musicians maintain that it provides tactile feedback to the player, indicating first position.

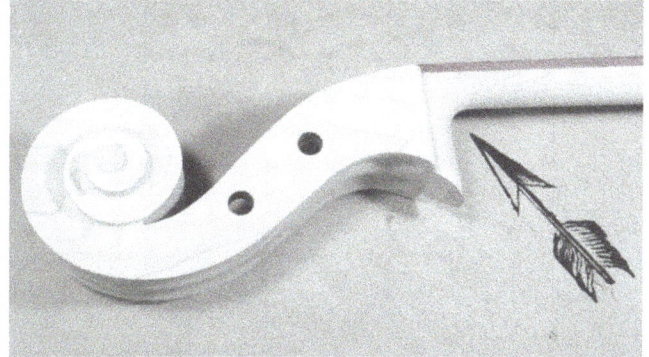

Volute of an electric upright bass under construction.

VSA *abbr*. see Violin Society of America

Vuillaume, Jean Baptiste (1798–1875) French violin luthier working in Mirecourt and Paris. A prolific builder of over 3000 instruments, he is known as a master copier of the instruments of Stradivari. He developed two violin variants, the contralto violin and the octobasse. He worked with Felix Savart on musical instrument acoustics. See also: contralto violin , Felix Savart, octobasse, Antonio Stradivari.

Vuillaume guitar *n*. One of the five guitars known to be made by Stradivari. Thought to be built in 1711, the instrument is currently in the collection of the Cité de la Musique in Paris, France.

W

waist *n*. An area of indentation near the middle of the outline of a stringed instrument body. The bouts of a guitar are typically labeled upper bouts, waist, and lower bouts. See also: bout, upper bout, lower bout.

waist bar *n*. Transverse brace on the top plate of flattop guitars. This brace is located beneath the soundhole, at or near the waist of the instrument. Syn.: lower transverse brace. See also: transverse brace.

Wake, Harry Sebastian (1900-1998) Violinmaker and author. Wake is the author of a series of books and videos on the construction of the violin family instruments. Syn.: H. S. Wake.

Waldo Company Late 19th to early 20th century USA manufacturer of bowl-back f-hole mandolin family instruments.

Waldron, Kevin Bell Buckle TN, USA, luthier and supplier of parts, materials, tools, and templates for stringed instrument construction.

Wallo, Joseph (1921-2009) Maryland USA guitar luthier, repairman, author and vendor of lutherie supplies. He built both classical and steel string guitars. Author of the book *How to Make a Classic Guitar*.

walnut oil *n*. A drying oil used alone as a finish, as the oil for French polishing, or as a component of varnish. Walnut oil comes from walnuts. See also: drying oil.

wane *n*. Bark or missing wood on an edge of a board.

WAS *abbr*. see wood acquisition syndrome

Boards exhibiting wane.

wash coat *n*. An application of any thinned finishing material, generally for the purpose of sealing. See also: spit coat.

Washburn Brand of musical instruments originally offered by Lyon and Healy. See also: Lyon and Healy.

watchkey tuning machines *n*. see Preston tuning machines

water stone *n*. A type of sharpening stone that is soaked in water prior to use.

waterbase lacquer *n*. see waterborne finish

waterborne finish A coalescing finish that offers water clean up, waterborne finishing products are used as finishes for acoustic and electric guitars. The finish is sprayed or brushed on. Additional coats burn in completely if the finish is not allowed to fully cure. The material is generally milky in appearance but cures to a clear finish. Some products have a more traditional amber tint. See also: coalescing finish.

waterglass *n*. Sodium silicate, sodium metasilicate. This substance has been used experimentally in lutherie as a treatment for top wood.

waterproof sandpaper *n*. Sandpaper composed of paper and adhesive that does not dissolve in water. Used in wet sanding. Syn.: wet-or-dry. See also: wet sanding.

waveform *n*. The shape of a continuous wave plotted as a graph of amplitude over time. See also: amplitude.

wavelength *n*. The length of one cycle of a repeating waveform.

waxed pickup *n*. Magnetic pickup to which melted wax has been added to dampen mechanical vibration of its component parts. Syn.: potted pickup. See also: microphonic.

web strip *n*. Any cross grain strip of wood used over a seam to help reinforce it. See also: back reinforcing strip.

wedding cake rosette *n*. see parchment rosette

wedge bridge *n*. Unique archtop guitar bridge built by James D'Acquisto. The saddle height of the bridge is adjustable via a sliding wedge. See also: James D'Acquisto.

Weissenborn guitar *n*. Acoustic slide guitar with a hollow "neck", played on the lap. The instrument was developed in the 1920s by Hermann Weissenborn and was designed for playing Hawaiian music.

Wells, Sylvan USA guitar luthier and founder of the modern incarnation of Bay State Guitars.

wenge *n*. (WEN-gay) see *Millettia laurentii*

Westbrook, James English guitar historian, collector and author. Westbrook specializes in instruments of the 19th century. His PhD dissertation is considered to be the definitive work on English instruments of that period. He operates the Guitar Museum and is also the author of the books *The Century that Shaped the Guitar* and *Guitars Through the Ages*.

western red cedar *n*. see *Thuja plicata*

wet or dry sandpaper *n*. see waterproof sandpaper

wet inlay *n*. A decorative inlay technique that makes use of a liquid mastic scraped into shallow routed channels or pockets. The mastic hardens and provides a line or pattern contrasting with the base material.

wet sanding *v*. Sanding with the aid of a liquid lubricant. Water, sometimes with a bit of detergent added, thin oil or mineral spirits are typical lubricants. Wet sanding can be done using waterproof sandpaper, often referred to as wet-or-dry sandpaper. The technique is usually used to level the surface of a finish. Wet sanding prevents heat buildup, which prevents corning. See also: corning, dry sanding, waterproof sandpaper.

whammy bar *n*. The actuator bar or rod of a vibrato tailpiece. See also: vibrato tailpiece.

wheat pattern *n*. Marquetry pattern that resembles the seed head of wheat. See also: marquetry.

white *adj*. Unfinished, that is, no finish has been applied to the instrument yet. Syn.: in the white.

white glue *n*. see polyvinyl acetate glue

white spruce *n*. see *Picea glauca*

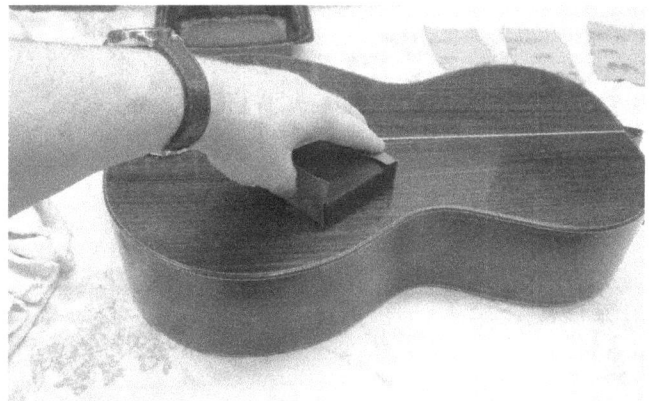

Wet sanding the finish of a guitar. Waterproof sandpaper is used on a foam rubber block and water with some detergent added is used as a sanding lubricant.

W

White (unfinished) steel string guitar.

White, Woodley Hawaii USA guitar and ukulele luthier.

winding *n.* 1. The outer part of wound strings. Such strings consist of a central core and a wound covering made of wire or tape. 2. Magnetic pickups contain a coil of wire around ferrous cores and/or magnets. The coil of wire is referred to as the pickup's windings. See also: core, magnetic pickup.

winding sticks *n.* Simple indicators used to identify longitudinal twist in a structure that is intended to be flat. The sticks are generally in the shape of either flat sticks or right angles and are longer than the width of the surface under examination. They are positioned at the ends of the nominally flat surface and then a sighting is taken across the sticks. Even small amounts of twist in the surface are indicated if the top surfaces of the sticks near their ends do not line up.

wing *n.* see bridge wing

wiping varnish *n.* Oil based varnish thin enough to be applied with a pad. These are true varnishes, containing a resin and oil, but they are often marketed as "oil" finishes.

wire channel *n.* A drilled hole or routed channel in the body of a solid body electric guitar through which wires are routed. Syn.: wiring channel.

wire wool *n.* Steel wool (British).

wiring diagram *n.* Diagram showing the circuitry for an electric instrument such as an electric guitar.

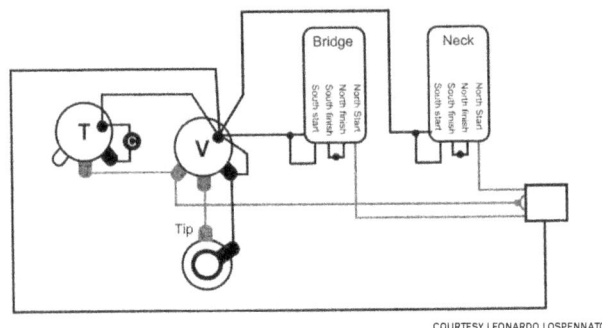

COURTESY LEONARDO LOSPENNATO

Wiring diagram.

witness line *n.* A defect in the application of varnish finishes or other finishes that are applied in layers that remain distinct rather than burning in to form a single continuous layer. When such a finish is leveled using abrasives, it is possible to cut through, that is, to completely abrade the top layer in places, exposing an underlying layer. The visible boundary line between the layers is called a witness line. The fix for witness lines is to apply additional layers of finish and to level so as not to cut through the top layer. See also: burn in, cut through.

wolf note *n.* see wolf tone

wolf tone *n.* An exceptionally loud or howling tone of a stringed (usually bowed) instrument. Wolf tones are the result of the pitch of the note played being close to the natural frequency of a strong resonance of the structure of the instrument.

wood acquisition syndrome *n.* "Disease" afflicting many luthiers. Symptoms include buying substantially more wood than can be used in a lifetime, and rationalization of the behavior. Syn.: WAS.

wood grading "system" *n*. Lutherie wood is often graded using elastic and loosely defined grades. Grading is specific to each wood supplier, so grades from different suppliers are not necessarily consistent. Grades range from A (or 1A) up to AAAAA (or 5A). Some wood dealers use only the range A through AAA. Some use that smaller range and add an additional "master grade". Grading is by appearance only. Softwoods are generally graded by uniformity of color, straightness of grain, closeness of grain lines, and absence of runout. Hardwood grading is much more ill-defined, but for figured woods depth and evenness of figure are graded highly. See also: runout.

workboard *n*. A flat board, possibly including clamping and positioning devices used to hold or mold an instrument or component during assembly. See also: fixture, jig, mold.

worm gear *n*. A gear shaped like a cylinder into which a continuous spiral set of teeth is cut. Worm gears are used in tuning machines. They are attached to the shaft that is turned by the tuning button and drive a small gear attached to the tuning post. See also: tuning machine.

worm under tuning machine *n*. Tuning machines make use of a worm gear attached to the button shaft which drives a pinion gear attached to the string post or roller.

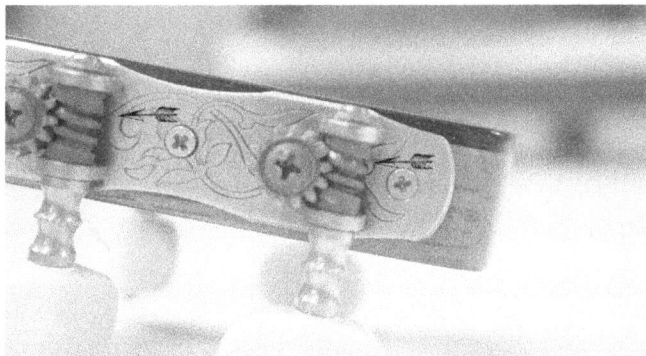

Worm gears.

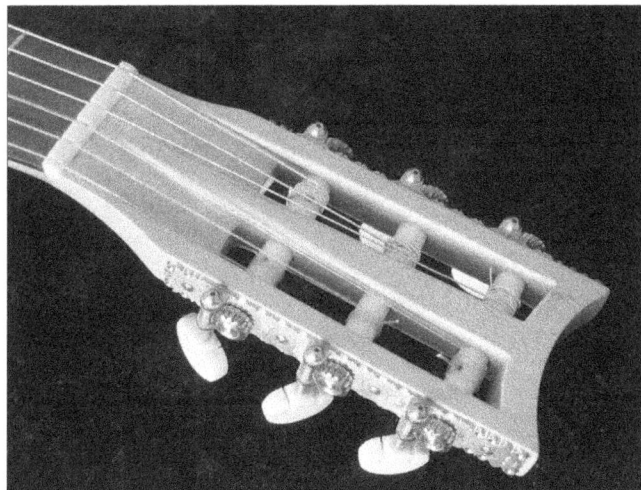

Panormo replica guitar featuring worm under tuning machines.

Modern machines position the worm gear above the pinion gear and have left hand threads, pitched like this: //////. Many old (19th and early 20th century) machines used a right hand threaded (\\\\\\) worm gear positioned under the pinion gear. These original older style machines are referred to as worm under, reverse gearing (or reverse geared or reverse gear) tuning machines.

wound string *n*. Strings can be classified by their general construction. A wound string contains a central core over which is wound one or more layers of windings. See also: core, plain string, windings.

wraparound bridge *n*. A post style bridge for electric guitar that combines the function of bridge and stop tailpiece in the same unit. The strings load into the bridge from the front, then wrap around over the top of the bridge and saddles. Syn.: Les Paul Jr. bridge. See also: post style bridge, stop tailpiece.

W

X

X brace *n*. One of the two main braces of the top plate of a flattop guitar that uses X bracing. See also: X bracing.

X bracing *n*. A bracing strategy for the top of flattop guitars that features two main braces configured in an X pattern, the center point of which is positioned on the centerline of the plate just above the bridge position. X bracing is used primarily on modern steel string guitars. See also: A bracing, fan bracing, ladder bracing, V bracing.

The underside of the top of a steel string acoustic guitar using X bracing.

Y

yaw *n*. In lutherie the terms yaw, pitch, and roll, used to describe rotation of an object in space, are most often used to describe adjustments necessary to fit an instrument's neck onto its body. When the instrument is viewed looking at its top, yaw is rotation of the neck from side to side about an axis extending from your eye to the centerline of the instrument at the neck/body join. See also: pitch, roll.

yellow glue *n*. see aliphatic resin glue

yellow poplar *n*. see *Liriodendron tulipifera*

yield stress *n*. The stress at which a material ceases to deform elastically. For practical purposes this is the amount of stress that a part can withstand. More than that and the part either breaks or stretches in a manner which is not reversible when the stress is removed.

Yong, Chin Hoe (Jeffrey) Malaysian guitar luthier known for his use of southeast Asian hardwoods in instrument construction.

Young's modulus n. see modulus of elasticity

yuehchyn *n*. Chinese guitar-like instrument.

Z

zanfoña n. see hurdy gurdy

Zhevlakov, Dmitry Russian maker of classical guitar mosaic rosettes.

zero fret n. The speaking length of strings in most fretted instruments is terminated at the headstock end at the nut. Some instruments provide this termination with a fret at the nominal nut position. The string path to the tuning machines puts this fret in contact with the strings at all times. The effect is that an open string is also terminated at a fret. See also: speaking length.

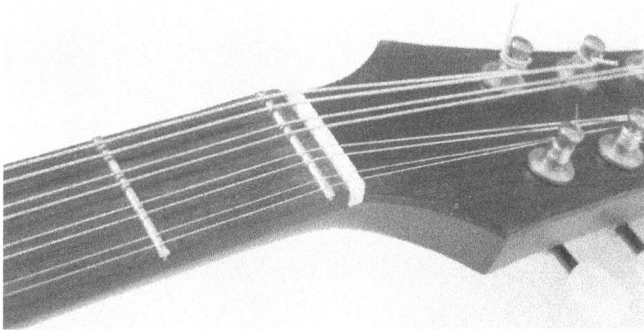

Zero fret on a mandolin by Graham McDonald. The nut slots are cut deep enough so the strings are in contact with the zero fret.

zirconia n. Sanding abrasive. It is blue in color and extremely tough. Available only in course grits, sandpaper coated with this abrasive is suitable for carving and abrasive planing.

zither n. Any of a class of instruments featuring a rectangular soundbox across which are stretched a number of harp-like strings. Zithers are generally played horizontally.

Concert zither.